MPI: The Complete Reference

D1489368

Scientific and Engineering Computation
Janusz Kowalik, Editor

Data-Parallel Programming on MIMD Computers
by Philip J. Hatcher and Michael J. Quinn, 1991

Unstructured Scientific Computation on Scalable Multiprocessors
edited by Piyush Mehrotra, Joel Saltz, and Robert Voigt, 1991

Parallel Computational Fluid Dynamics: Implementations and Results
edited by Horst D. Simon, 1992

Enterprise Integration Modeling: Proceedings of the First International Conference
edited by Charles J. Petrie, Jr., 1992

The High Performance Fortran Handbook
by Charles H. Koelbel, David B. Loveman, Robert S. Schreiber, Guy L. Steele Jr.
and Mary E. Zosel, 1993

Using MPI: Portable Parallel Programming with the Message-Passing Interface
by William Gropp, Ewing Lusk, and Anthony Skjellum, 1994

PVM: Parallel Virtual Machine–A User's Guide and Tutorial for Network Parallel Computing
by Al Geist, Adam Beguelin, Jack Dongarra, Weicheng Jiang, Bob Manchek, and Vaidy Sunderam, 1994

Enabling Technologies for Petaflops Computing
by Thomas Sterling, Paul Messina, and Paul H. Smith

An Introduction to High-Performance Scientific Computing
by Lloyd D. Fosdick, Elizabeth R. Jessup, Carolyn J.C. Schauble, and Gitta Domik

Practical Parallel Programming
by Gregory V. Wilson

MPI: The Complete Reference
by Marc Snir, Steve Otto, Steven Huss-Lederman, David Walker, and Jack Dongarra

MPI: The Complete Reference

Marc Snir
Steve Otto
Steven Huss-Lederman
David Walker
Jack Dongarra

The MIT Press
Cambridge, Massachusetts
London, England

Parts of this book came from, "MPI: A Message-Passing Interface Standard" by the Message Passing Interface Forum. That document is © the University of Tennessee. These sections were copied by permission of the University of Tennessee.

This book was set in LaTeX by the authors and was printed and bound in the United States of America.

Library of Congress Catalog Card Number: 95-80471

ISBN 0-262-69184-1

Contents

Series Foreword

The world of modern computing potentially offers many helpful methods and tools to scientists and engineers, but the fast pace of change in computer hardware, software, and algorithms often makes practical use of the newest computing technology difficult. The Scientific and Engineering Computation series focuses on rapid advances in computing technologies and attempts to facilitate transferring these technologies to applications in science and engineering. It will include books on theories, methods, and original applications in such areas as parallelism, large-scale simulations, time-critical computing, computer-aided design and engineering, use of computers in manufacturing, visualization of scientific data, and human-machine interface technology.

The series will help scientists and engineers to understand the current world of advanced computation and to anticipate future developments that will impact their computing environments and open up new capabilities and modes of computation.

This book is about the Message Passing Interface (MPI), an important and increasingly popular standarized and portable message passing system that brings us closer to the potential development of practical and cost-effective large-scale parallel applications. It gives a complete specification of the MPI standard and provides illustrative programming examples. This advanced level book supplements the companion, introductory volume in the Series by William Gropp, Ewing Lusk and Anthony Skjellum, *Using MPI: Portable Parallel Programming with the Message-Passing Interface.*

Janusz S. Kowalik

Preface

MPI, the Message Passing Interface, is a standardized and portable message-passing system designed by a group of researchers from academia and industry to function on a wide variety of parallel computers. The standard defines the syntax and semantics of a core of library routines useful to a wide range of users writing portable message-passing programs in Fortran 77 or C. Several well-tested and efficient implementations of MPI already exist, including some that are free and in the public domain. These are beginning to foster the development of a parallel software industry, and there is excitement among computing researchers and vendors that the development of portable and scalable, large-scale parallel applications is now feasible.

The MPI standardization effort involved over 80 people from 40 organizations, mainly from the United States and Europe. Most of the major vendors of concurrent computers at the time were involved in MPI, along with researchers from universities, government laboratories, and industry. The standardization process began with the Workshop on Standards for Message Passing in a Distributed Memory Environment, sponsored by the Center for Research on Parallel Computing, held April 29-30, 1992, in Williamsburg, Virginia [29]. A preliminary draft proposal, known as MPI1, was put forward by Dongarra, Hempel, Hey, and Walker in November 1992, and a revised version was completed in February 1993 [11].

In November 1992, a meeting of the MPI working group was held in Minneapolis, at which it was decided to place the standardization process on a more formal footing. The MPI working group met every 6 weeks throughout the first 9 months of 1993. The draft MPI standard was presented at the Supercomputing '93 conference in November 1993. After a period of public comments, which resulted in some changes in MPI, version 1.0 of MPI was released in June 1994.

These meetings and the email discussion together constituted the MPI Forum, membership of which has been open to all members of the high performance computing community.

This book serves as an annotated reference manual for MPI, and a complete specification of the standard is presented. We repeat the material already published in the MPI specification document [15], though an attempt to clarify has been made. The annotations mainly take the form of explaining why certain design choices were made, how users are meant to use the interface, and how MPI implementors should construct a version of MPI. Many detailed, illustrative programming examples are also given, with an eye toward illuminating the more advanced or subtle features of MPI.

The complete interface is presented in this book, and we are not hesitant to explain even the most esoteric features or consequences of the standard. As such, this volume does not work as a gentle introduction to MPI, nor as a tutorial. For such purposes, we recommend the companion volume in this series by William Gropp, Ewing Lusk, and Anthony Skjellum, *Using MPI: Portable Parallel Programming with the Message-Passing Interface.* The parallel application developer will want to have copies of both books handy.

For a first reading, and as a good introduction to MPI, the reader should first read: Chapter 1, through Section 1.7.1; the material on point to point communications covered in Sections 2.1 through 2.5 and Section 2.8; the simpler forms of collective communications explained in Sections 4.1 through 4.7; and the basic introduction to communicators given in Sections 5.1 through 5.2. This will give a fair understanding of MPI, and will allow the construction of parallel applications of moderate complexity.

This book is based on the hard work of many people in the MPI Forum. The authors gratefully recognize the members of the forum, especially the contributions made by members who served in positions of responsibility: Lyndon Clarke, James Cownie, Al Geist, William Gropp, Rolf Hempel, Robert Knighten, Richard Littlefield, Ewing Lusk, Paul Pierce, and Anthony Skjellum. Other contributors were: Ed Anderson, Robert Babb, Joe Baron, Eric Barszcz, Scott Berryman, Rob Bjornson, Nathan Doss, Anne Elster, Jim Feeney, Vince Fernando, Sam Fineberg, Jon Flower, Daniel Frye, Ian Glendinning, Adam Greenberg, Robert Harrison, Leslie Hart, Tom Haupt, Don Heller, Tom Henderson, Anthony Hey, Alex Ho, C.T. Howard Ho, Gary Howell, John Kapenga, James Kohl, Susan Krauss, Bob Leary, Arthur Maccabe, Peter Madams, Alan Mainwaring, Oliver McBryan, Phil McKinley, Charles Mosher, Dan Nessett, Peter Pacheco, Howard Palmer, Sanjay Ranka, Peter Rigsbee, Arch Robison, Erich Schikuta, Mark Sears, Ambuj Singh, Alan Sussman, Robert Tomlinson, Robert G. Voigt, Dennis Weeks, Stephen Wheat, and Steven Zenith. We especially thank William Gropp and Ewing Lusk for help in formatting this volume.

Support for MPI meetings came in part from ARPA and NSF under grant ASC-9310330, NSF Science and Technology Center Cooperative agreement No. CCR-8809615, and the Commission of the European Community through Esprit Project P6643. The University of Tennessee also made financial contributions to the MPI Forum.

MPI: The Complete Reference

1 Introduction

Message passing is a programming paradigm used widely on parallel computers, especially Scalable Parallel Computers (SPCs) with distributed memory, and on Networks of Workstations (NOWs). Although there are many variations, the basic concept of processes communicating through messages is well understood. Over the last ten years, substantial progress has been made in casting significant applications into this paradigm. Each vendor has implemented its own variant. More recently, several public-domain systems have demonstrated that a message-passing system can be efficiently and portably implemented. It is thus an appropriate time to define both the syntax and semantics of a standard core of library routines that will be useful to a wide range of users and efficiently implementable on a wide range of computers. This effort has been undertaken over the last three years by the Message Passing Interface (MPI) Forum, a group of more than 80 people from 40 organizations, representing vendors of parallel systems, industrial users, industrial and national research laboratories, and universities.

The designers of MPI sought to make use of the most attractive features of a number of existing message-passing systems, rather than selecting one of them and adopting it as the standard. Thus, MPI has been strongly influenced by work at the IBM T. J. Watson Research Center [1, 2], Intel's NX/2 [24], Express [23], nCUBE's Vertex [22], p4 [6, 5], and PARMACS [3, 7]. Other important contributions have come from Zipcode [25, 26], Chimp [13, 14], PVM [17, 27], Chameleon [19], and PICL [18]. The MPI Forum identified some critical shortcomings of existing message-passing systems, in areas such as complex data layouts or support for modularity and safe communication. This led to the introduction of new features in MPI.

The MPI standard defines the user interface and functionality for a wide range of message-passing capabilities. Since its completion in June of 1994, MPI has become widely accepted and used. Implementations are available on a range of machines from SPCs to NOWs. A growing number of SPCs have an MPI supplied and supported by the vendor. Because of this, MPI has achieved one of its goals — adding credibility to parallel computing. Third party vendors, researchers, and others now have a reliable and portable way to express message-passing, parallel programs.

The major goal of MPI, as with most standards, is a degree of portability across different machines. The expectation is for a degree of portability comparable to that given by programming languages such as Fortran. This means that the same message-passing source code can be executed on a variety of machines as long as the MPI library is available, while some tuning might be needed to take best advantage of the features of each system. Though message passing is often thought of in the context of distributed-memory parallel computers, the same code can run well on a shared-memory parallel computer. It can run on a network of workstations, or, indeed, as a set of processes running on a single workstation. Knowing that efficient MPI implementations exist across a wide variety of computers gives a high degree of flexibility in code development, debugging, and in choosing a platform for production runs.

Another type of compatibility offered by MPI is the ability to run transparently on heterogeneous systems, that is, collections of processors with distinct architectures. It is possible for an MPI implementation to span such a heterogeneous collection, yet provide a virtual computing model that hides many architectural differences. The user need not worry whether the code is sending messages between processors of like or unlike architecture. The MPI implementation will automatically do any necessary data conversion and utilize the correct communications protocol. However, MPI does not prohibit implementations that are targeted to a single, homogeneous system, and does not mandate that distinct implementations be interoperable. Users that wish to run on an heterogeneous system must use an MPI implementation designed to support heterogeneity.

Portability is central but the standard will not gain wide usage if this was achieved at the expense of performance. For example, Fortran is commonly used over assembly languages because compilers are almost always available that yield acceptable performance compared to the non-portable alternative of assembly languages. A crucial point is that MPI was carefully designed so as to allow efficient implementations. The design choices seem to have been made correctly, since MPI implementations over a wide range of platforms are achieving high performance, comparable to that of less portable, vendor-specific systems.

An important design goal of MPI was to allow efficient implementations across machines of differing characteristics. For example, MPI carefully avoids specifying how operations will take place. It only specifies what an operation does logically. As a result, MPI can be easily implemented on systems that buffer messages at the sender, receiver, or do no buffering at all. Implementations can take advantage of specific features of the communication subsystem of various machines. On machines with intelligent communication coprocessors, much of the message passing protocol can be offloaded to this coprocessor. On other systems, most of the communication code is executed by the main processor. Another example is the use of opaque objects in MPI. By hiding the details of how MPI-specific objects are represented, each implementation is free to do whatever is best under the circumstances.

Another design choice leading to efficiency is the avoidance of unnecessary work.

MPI was carefully designed so as to avoid a requirement for large amounts of extra information with each message, or the need for complex encoding or decoding of message headers. MPI also avoids extra computation or tests in critical routines since this can degrade performance. Another way of minimizing work is to encourage the reuse of previous computations. MPI provides this capability through constructs such as persistent communication requests and caching of attributes on communicators. The design of MPI avoids the need for extra copying and buffering of data: in many cases, data can be moved from the user memory directly to the wire, and be received directly from the wire to the receiver memory.

MPI was designed to encourage overlap of communication and computation, so as to take advantage of intelligent communication agents, and to hide communication latencies. This is achieved by the use of nonblocking communication calls, which separate the initiation of a communication from its completion.

Scalability is an important goal of parallel processing. MPI allows or supports scalability through several of its design features. For example, an application can create subgroups of processes that, in turn, allows collective communication operations to limit their scope to the processes involved. Another technique used is to provide functionality without a computation that scales as the number of processes. For example, a two-dimensional Cartesian topology can be subdivided into its one-dimensional rows or columns without explicitly enumerating the processes.

Finally, MPI, as all good standards, is valuable in that it defines a known, minimum behavior of message-passing implementations. This relieves the programmer from having to worry about certain problems that can arise. One example is that MPI guarantees that the underlying transmission of messages is reliable. The user need not check if a message is received correctly.

1.1   The Goals of MPI

The goal of the Message Passing Interface, simply stated, is to develop a widely used standard for writing message-passing programs. As such the interface should establish a practical, portable, efficient, and flexible standard for message passing.

A list of the goals of MPI appears below.

• Design an application programming interface. Although MPI is currently used as a run-time for parallel compilers and for various libraries, the design of MPI primarily reflects the perceived needs of application programmers.

• Allow efficient communication. Avoid memory-to-memory copying, allow overlap of computation and communication, and offload to a communication coprocessor-processor, where available.

- Allow for implementations that can be used in a heterogeneous environment.
- Allow convenient C and Fortran 77 bindings for the interface. Also, the semantics of the interface should be language independent.
- Provide a reliable communication interface. The user need not cope with communication failures.
- Define an interface not too different from current practice, such as PVM, NX, Express, p4, etc., and provides extensions that allow greater flexibility.
- Define an interface that can be implemented on many vendor's platforms, with no significant changes in the underlying communication and system software.
- The interface should be designed to allow for thread-safety.

1.2   Who Should Use This Standard?

The MPI standard is intended for use by all those who want to write portable message-passing programs in Fortran 77 and C. This includes individual application programmers, developers of software designed to run on parallel machines, and creators of environments and tools. In order to be attractive to this wide audience, the standard must provide a simple, easy-to-use interface for the basic user while not semantically precluding the high-performance message-passing operations available on advanced machines.

1.3   What Platforms are Targets for Implementation?

The attractiveness of the message-passing paradigm at least partially stems from its wide portability. Programs expressed this way may run on distributed-memory multicomputers, shared-memory multiprocessors, networks of workstations, and combinations of all of these. The paradigm will not be made obsolete by architectures combining the shared- and distributed-memory views, or by increases in network speeds. Thus, it should be both possible and useful to implement this standard on a great variety of machines, including those "machines" consisting of collections of other machines, parallel or not, connected by a communication network.

The interface is suitable for use by fully general Multiple Instruction, Multiple Data (MIMD) programs, or Multiple Program, Multiple Data (MPMD) programs, where each process follows a distinct execution path through the same code, or even executes a different code. It is also suitable for those written in the more restricted style of Single Program, Multiple Data (SPMD), where all processes follow the same execution path through the same program. Although no explicit support for threads is provided, the interface has been designed so as not to prejudice their use. With this version of MPI no support is provided for dynamic spawning of tasks; such support is expected in future versions of MPI; see Section 9.5.

MPI provides many features intended to improve performance on scalable parallel computers with specialized interprocessor communication hardware. Thus, we expect that native, high-performance implementations of MPI will be provided on such machines. At the same time, implementations of MPI on top of standard Unix interprocessor communication protocols will provide portability to workstation clusters and heterogeneous networks of workstations. Several proprietary, native implementations of MPI, and public domain, portable implementation of MPI are now available. See Section 9.4 for more information about MPI implementations.

1.4   What is Included in MPI?

The standard includes:

- Point-to-point communication
- Collective operations
- Process groups
- Communication domains
- Process topologies
- Environmental Management and inquiry
- Profiling interface
- Bindings for Fortran 77 and C

1.5   What is Not Included in MPI?

MPI does not specify:

- Explicit shared-memory operations
- Operations that require more operating system support than was standard during the adoption of MPI; for example, interrupt-driven receives, remote execution, or active messages
- Program construction tools
- Debugging facilities

- Explicit support for threads
- Support for task management
- I/O functions

There are many features that were considered and not included in MPI. This happened for a number of reasons: the time constraint that was self-imposed by the MPI Forum in finishing the standard; the feeling that not enough experience was available on some of these topics; and the concern that additional features would delay the appearance of implementations.

Features that are not included can always be offered as extensions by specific implementations. Future versions of MPI will address some of these issues (see Section 9.5).

1.6   Version of MPI

The original MPI standard was created by the Message Passing Interface Forum (MPIF). The public release of version 1.0 of MPI was made in June 1994. The MPIF began meeting again in March 1995. One of the first tasks undertaken was to make clarifications and corrections to the MPI standard. The changes from version 1.0 to version 1.1 of the MPI standard were limited to "corrections" that were deemed urgent and necessary. This work was completed in June 1995 and version 1.1 of the standard was released. This book reflects the updated version 1.1 of the MPI standard.

1.7   MPI Conventions and Design Choices

This section explains notational terms and conventions used throughout this book.

1.7.1   Document Notation

Rationale.   Throughout this document, the rationale for design choices made in the interface specification is set off in this format. Some readers may wish to skip these sections, while readers interested in interface design may want to read them carefully. (*End of rationale.*)

Advice to users.   Throughout this document, material that speaks to users and illustrates usage is set off in this format. Some readers may wish to skip these sections, while readers interested in programming in MPI may want to read them carefully. (*End of advice to users.*)

Advice to implementors. Throughout this document, material that is primarily commentary to implementors is set off in this format. Some readers may wish to skip these sections, while readers interested in MPI implementations may want to read them carefully. (*End of advice to implementors.*)

1.7.2 Procedure Specification

MPI procedures are specified using a language independent notation. The arguments of procedure calls are marked as IN, OUT or INOUT. The meanings of these are:

- the call uses but does not update an argument marked IN,
- the call may update an argument marked OUT,
- the call both uses and updates an argument marked INOUT.

There is one special case — if an argument is a handle to an opaque object (defined in Section 1.8.3), and the object is updated by the procedure call, then the argument is marked OUT. It is marked this way even though the handle itself is not modified — we use the OUT attribute to denote that what the handle *references* is updated.

The definition of MPI tries to avoid, to the largest possible extent, the use of INOUT arguments, because such use is error-prone, especially for scalar arguments.

A common occurrence for MPI functions is an argument that is used as IN by some processes and OUT by other processes. Such an argument is, syntactically, an INOUT argument and is marked as such, although, semantically, it is not used in one call both for input and for output.

Another frequent situation arises when an argument value is needed only by a subset of the processes. When an argument is not significant at a process then an arbitrary value can be passed as the argument.

Unless specified otherwise, an argument of type OUT or type INOUT cannot be aliased with any other argument passed to an MPI procedure. An example of argument aliasing in C appears below. If we define a C procedure like this,

```
void copyIntBuffer( int *pin, int *pout, int len )
{   int i;
    for (i=0; i<len; ++i) *pout++ = *pin++;
}
```

then a call to it in the following code fragment has aliased arguments.

```
int a[10];
```

```
copyIntBuffer( a, a+3, 7);
```

Although the C language allows this, such usage of MPI procedures is forbidden unless otherwise specified. Note that Fortran prohibits aliasing of arguments.

All MPI functions are first specified in the language-independent notation. Immediately below this, the ANSI C version of the function is shown, and below this, a version of the same function in Fortran 77.

1.8   Semantic Terms

This section describes semantic terms used in this book.

1.8.1   Processes

An MPI program consists of autonomous processes, executing their own (C or Fortran) code, in an MIMD style. The codes executed by each process need not be identical. The processes communicate via calls to MPI communication primitives. Typically, each process executes in its own address space, although shared-memory implementations of MPI are possible. This document specifies the behavior of a parallel program assuming that only MPI calls are used for communication. The interaction of an MPI program with other possible means of communication (e.g., shared memory) is not specified.

MPI does not specify the execution model for each process. A process can be sequential, or can be multi-threaded, with threads possibly executing concurrently. Care has been taken to make MPI "thread-safe," by avoiding the use of implicit state. The desired interaction of MPI with threads is that concurrent threads be all allowed to execute MPI calls, and calls be reentrant; a blocking MPI call blocks only the invoking thread, allowing the scheduling of another thread.

MPI does not provide mechanisms to specify the initial allocation of processes to an MPI computation and their binding to physical processors. It is expected that vendors will provide mechanisms to do so either at load time or at run time. Such mechanisms will allow the specification of the initial number of required processes, the code to be executed by each initial process, and the allocation of processes to processors. Also, the current standard does not provide for dynamic creation or deletion of processes during program execution (the total number of processes is fixed); however, MPI design is consistent with such extensions, which are now under consideration (see Section 9.5). Finally, MPI always identifies processes according to their relative rank in a group, that is, consecutive integers in the range `0..groupsize-1`.

1.8.2   Types of MPI Calls

When discussing MPI procedures the following terms are used.

local If the completion of the procedure depends only on the local executing process. Such an operation does not require an explicit communication with another user process. MPI calls that generate local objects or query the status of local objects are local.

non-local If completion of the procedure may require the execution of some MPI procedure on another process. Many MPI communication calls are non-local.

blocking If return from the procedure indicates the user is allowed to re-use resources specified in the call. Any visible change in the state of the calling process affected by a blocking call occurs before the call returns.

nonblocking If the procedure may return before the operation initiated by the call completes, and before the user is allowed to re-use resources (such as buffers) specified in the call. A nonblocking call may initiate changes in the state of the calling process that actually take place after the call returned: e.g. a nonblocking call can initiate a receive operation, but the message is actually received after the call returned.

collective If all processes in a process group need to invoke the procedure.

1.8.3   Opaque Objects

MPI manages system memory that is used for buffering messages and for storing internal representations of various MPI objects such as groups, communicators, datatypes, etc. This memory is not directly accessible to the user, and objects stored there are **opaque**: their size and shape is not visible to the user. Opaque objects are accessed via **handles**, which exist in user space. MPI procedures that operate on opaque objects are passed handle arguments to access these objects. In addition to their use by MPI calls for object access, handles can participate in assignments and comparisons.

In Fortran, all handles have type **INTEGER**. In C, a different handle type is defined for each category of objects. Implementations should use types that support assignment and equality operators.

In Fortran, the handle can be an index in a table of opaque objects, while in C it can be such an index or a pointer to the object. More bizarre possibilities exist.

Opaque objects are allocated and deallocated by calls that are specific to each object type. These are listed in the sections where the objects are described. The calls accept a handle argument of matching type. In an allocate call this is an OUT argument that returns a valid reference to the object. In a call to deallocate this is an INOUT argument which returns with a "null handle" value. MPI provides a "null handle" constant for each object type. Comparisons to this constant are used to test for validity of the handle. MPI calls do not change the value of handles, with the exception of calls that allocate and deallocate objects, and of the call MPI_TYPE_COMMIT, defined in Section 3.4.

A null handle argument is an erroneous IN argument in MPI calls, unless an exception is explicitly stated in the text that defines the function. Such exceptions are allowed for handles to request objects in Wait and Test calls (Section 2.9). Otherwise, a null handle can only be passed to a function that allocates a new object and returns a reference to it in the handle.

A call to deallocate invalidates the handle and marks the object for deallocation. The object is not accessible to the user after the call. However, MPI need not deallocate the object immediately. Any operation pending (at the time of the deallocate) that involves this object will complete normally; the object will be deallocated afterwards.

An opaque object and its handle are significant only at the process where the object was created, and cannot be transferred to another process.

MPI provides certain predefined opaque objects and predefined, static handles to these objects. Such objects may not be destroyed.

Rationale. This design hides the internal representation used for MPI data structures, thus allowing similar calls in C and Fortran. It also avoids conflicts with the typing rules in these languages, and easily allows future extensions of functionality. The mechanism for opaque objects used here loosely follows the POSIX Fortran binding standard.

The explicit separation of user space handles and "MPI space" objects allows deallocation calls to be made at appropriate points in the user program. If the opaque objects were in user space, one would have to be very careful not to go out of scope before any pending operation requiring that object completed. The specified design allows an object to be marked for deallocation, the user program can then go out of scope, and the object itself persists until any pending operations are complete.

The requirement that handles support assignment/comparison is made since such operations are common. This restricts the domain of possible implementations. The alternative would have been to allow handles to have been an arbitrary, opaque type. This would force the introduction of routines to do assignment and comparison, adding complexity, and was therefore ruled out. (*End of rationale.*)

Advice to users. A user may accidently create a dangling reference by assigning to a handle the value of another handle, and then deallocating the object associated with these handles. Conversely, if a handle variable is deallocated before the associated object is freed, then the object becomes inaccessible (this may occur, for example, if the handle is a local variable within a subroutine, and the subroutine is exited before the associated object is deallocated). It is the user's responsibility to manage correctly such references. (*End of advice to users.*)

Advice to implementors. The intended semantics of opaque objects is that each opaque object is separate from each other; each call to allocate such an object copies all the information required for the object. Implementations may avoid excessive copying by substituting referencing for copying. For example, a derived datatype may contain references to its components, rather then copies of its components; a call to MPI_COMM_GROUP may return a reference to the group associated with the communicator, rather than a copy of this group. In such cases, the implementation must maintain reference counts, and allocate and deallocate objects such that the visible effect is as if the objects were copied. (*End of advice to implementors.*)

1.8.4 Named Constants

MPI procedures sometimes assign a special meaning to a special value of an argument. For example, tag is an integer-valued argument of point-to-point communication operations, that can take a special wild-card value, MPI_ANY_TAG. Such arguments will have a range of regular values, which is a proper subrange of the range of values of the corresponding type of the variable. Special values (such as MPI_ANY_TAG) will be outside the regular range. The range of regular values can be queried using environmental inquiry functions (Chapter 7).

MPI also provides predefined named constant handles, such as MPI_COMM_WORLD, which is a handle to an object that represents all processes available at start-up time and allowed to communicate with any of them.

All named constants, with the exception of MPI_BOTTOM in Fortran, can be used in initialization expressions or assignments. These constants do not change values during execution. Opaque objects accessed by constant handles are defined and do not change value between MPI initialization (MPI_INIT() call) and MPI completion (MPI_FINALIZE() call).

1.8.5 Choice Arguments

MPI functions sometimes use arguments with a choice (or union) data type. Distinct calls to the same routine may pass by reference actual arguments of different types.

The mechanism for providing such arguments will differ from language to language. For Fortran, we use <type> to represent a choice variable, for C, we use (void *).

1.9 Language Binding

This section defines the rules for MPI language binding in Fortran 77 and ANSI C. Defined here are various object representations, as well as the naming conventions used for expressing this standard.

It is expected that any Fortran 90 and C++ implementations use the Fortran 77 and ANSI C bindings, respectively. Although we consider it premature to define other bindings to Fortran 90 and C++, the current bindings are designed to encourage, rather than discourage, experimentation with better bindings that might be adopted later.

Since the word PARAMETER is a keyword in the Fortran language, we use the word "argument" to denote the arguments to a subroutine. These are normally referred to as parameters in C, however, we expect that C programmers will understand the word "argument" (which has no specific meaning in C), thus allowing us to avoid unnecessary confusion for Fortran programmers.

There are several important language binding issues not addressed by this standard. This standard does not discuss the interoperability of message passing between languages. It is fully expected that good quality implementations will provide such interoperability.

1.9.1 Fortran 77 Binding Issues

All MPI names have an MPI_ prefix, and all characters are upper case. Programs should not declare variables or functions with names with the prefix, MPI_ or PMPI_, to avoid possible name collisions.

All MPI Fortran subroutines have a return code in the last argument. A few MPI operations are functions, which do not have the return code argument. The return code value for successful completion is MPI_SUCCESS. Other error codes are implementation dependent; see Chapter 7.

Handles are represented in Fortran as INTEGERs. Binary-valued variables are of type LOGICAL.

Array arguments are indexed from one.

Unless explicitly stated, the MPI F77 binding is consistent with ANSI standard Fortran 77. There are several points where the MPI standard diverges from the ANSI Fortran 77 standard. These exceptions are consistent with common practice

```
double precision a
integer b
...
call MPI_send(a,...)
call MPI_send(b,...)
```

Figure 1.1
An example of calling a routine with mismatched formal and actual arguments.

in the Fortran community. In particular:

- MPI identifiers are limited to thirty, not six, significant characters.
- MPI identifiers may contain underscores after the first character.
- An MPI subroutine with a choice argument may be called with different argument types. An example is shown in Figure 1.1. This violates the letter of the Fortran standard, but such a violation is common practice. An alternative would be to have a separate version of MPI_SEND for each data type.

Advice to implementors. Although not required, it is strongly suggested that named MPI constants (**PARAMETER**s) be provided in an include file, called mpif.h. On systems that do not support include files, the implementation should specify the values of named constants.

Vendors are encouraged to provide type declarations and interface blocks for MPI functions in the `mpif.h` file on Fortran systems that support those. Such declarations can be used to avoid some of the limitations of the Fortran 77 binding of MPI. For example, the C binding specifies that "addresses" are of type MPI_Aint; this type can be defined to be a 64 bit integer, on systems with 64 bit addresses. This feature is not available in the Fortran 77 binding, where "addresses" are of type **INTEGER**. By providing an interface block where "address" parameters are defined to be of type **INTEGER(8)**, the implementor can provide support for 64 bit addresses, while maintaining compatibility with the MPI standard. (*End of advice to implementors.*)

All MPI named constants can be used wherever an entity declared with the **PARAMETER** attribute can be used in Fortran. There is one exception to this rule: the MPI constant MPI_BOTTOM (section 3.7) can only be used as a buffer argument.

1.9.2   C Binding Issues

We use the ANSI C declaration format. All MPI names have an `MPI_` prefix, defined constants are in all capital letters, and defined types and functions have one capital letter after the prefix. Programs must not declare variables or functions with names beginning with the prefix `MPI_` or `PMPI_`. This is mandated to avoid possible name collisions.

The definition of named constants, function prototypes, and type definitions must be supplied in an include file mpi.h.

Almost all C functions return an error code. The successful return code will be `MPI_SUCCESS`, but failure return codes are implementation dependent. A few C functions do not return error codes, so that they can be implemented as macros.

Type declarations are provided for handles to each category of opaque objects. Either a pointer or an integer type is used.

Array arguments are indexed from zero.

Logical flags are integers with value 0 meaning "false" and a non-zero value meaning "true."

Choice arguments are pointers of type `void*`.

Address arguments are of MPI defined type MPI_Aint. This is defined to be an int of the size needed to hold any valid address on the target architecture.

All named MPI constants can be used in initialization expressions or assignments like C constants.

2 Point-to-Point Communication

2.1 Introduction and Overview

The basic communication mechanism of MPI is the transmittal of data between a pair of processes, one side sending, the other, receiving. We call this "point to point communication." Almost all the constructs of MPI are built around the point to point operations and so this chapter is fundamental. It is also quite a long chapter since: there are many variants to the point to point operations; there is much to say in terms of the semantics of the operations; and related topics, such as probing for messages, are explained here because they are used in conjunction with the point to point operations.

MPI provides a set of send and receive functions that allow the communication of **typed** data with an associated **tag**. Typing of the message contents is necessary for heterogeneous support — the type information is needed so that correct data representation conversions can be performed as data is sent from one architecture to another. The tag allows selectivity of messages at the receiving end: one can receive on a particular tag, or one can wild-card this quantity, allowing reception of messages with any tag. Message selectivity on the source process of the message is also provided.

A fragment of C code appears in Example 2.1 for the example of process 0 sending a message to process 1. The code executes on both process 0 and process 1. Process 0 sends a character string using `MPI_Send()`. The first three parameters of the send call specify the data to be sent: the outgoing data is to be taken from `msg`; it consists of `strlen(msg)+1` entries, each of type `MPI_CHAR` (The string `"Hello there"` contains `strlen(msg)=11` significant characters. In addition, we are also sending the `'\0'` string terminator character). The fourth parameter specifies the message destination, which is process 1. The fifth parameter specifies the message tag. Finally, the last parameter is a **communicator** that specifies a **communication domain** for this communication. Among other things, a communicator serves to define a set of processes that can be contacted. Each such process is labeled by a process **rank**. Process ranks are integers and are discovered by inquiry to a communicator (see the call to `MPI_Comm_rank()`). `MPI_COMM_WORLD` is a default communicator provided upon start-up that defines an initial communication domain for all the processes that participate in the computation. Much more will be said about communicators in Chapter 5.

The receiving process specified that the incoming data was to be placed in `msg` and that it had a maximum size of 20 entries, of type MPI_CHAR. The variable status, set by MPI_Recv(), gives information on the source and tag of the message and how many elements were actually received. For example, the receiver can examine this variable to find out the actual length of the character string received. Datatype matching (between sender and receiver) and data conversion on heterogeneous systems are discussed in more detail in Section 2.3.

Example 2.1 C code. Process 0 sends a message to process 1.

```
char msg[20];
int myrank, tag = 99;
MPI_Status status;
...
MPI_Comm_rank( MPI_COMM_WORLD, &myrank );  /* find my rank */
if (myrank == 0) {
   strcpy( msg, "Hello there");
   MPI_Send( msg, strlen(msg)+1, MPI_CHAR, 1, tag, MPI_COMM_WORLD);
} else if (myrank == 1) {
   MPI_Recv( msg, 20, MPI_CHAR, 0, tag, MPI_COMM_WORLD, &status);
}
```

The Fortran version of this code is shown in Example 2.2. In order to make our Fortran examples more readable, we use Fortran 90 syntax, here and in many other places in this book. The examples can be easily rewritten in standard Fortran 77. The Fortran code is essentially identical to the C code. All MPI calls are procedures, and an additional parameter is used to return the value returned by the corresponding C function. Note that Fortran strings have fixed size and are not null-terminated. The receive operation stores "Hello there" in the first 11 positions of msg.

Example 2.2 Fortran code.

```
CHARACTER*20 msg
INTEGER myrank, ierr, status(MPI_STATUS_SIZE)
INTEGER tag = 99
...
CALL MPI_COMM_RANK( MPI_COMM_WORLD, myrank, ierr)
IF (myrank .EQ. 0) THEN
    msg = "Hello there"
    CALL MPI_SEND( msg, 11, MPI_CHARACTER, 1,
                   tag, MPI_COMM_WORLD, ierr)
```

```
ELSE IF (myrank .EQ. 1) THEN
   CALL MPI_RECV( msg, 20, MPI_CHARACTER, 0,
                    tag, MPI_COMM_WORLD, status, ierr)
END IF
```

These examples employed *blocking* send and receive functions. The send call blocks until the send buffer can be reclaimed (i.e., after the send, process 0 can safely over-write the contents of msg). Similarly, the receive function blocks until the receive buffer actually contains the contents of the message. MPI also provides *nonblocking* send and receive functions that allow the possible overlap of message transmittal with computation, or the overlap of multiple message transmittals with one-another. Non-blocking functions always come in two parts: the posting functions, which begin the requested operation; and the test-for-completion functions, which allow the application program to discover whether the requested operation has completed. Our chapter begins by explaining blocking functions in detail, in Section 2.2–2.7, while nonblocking functions are covered later, in Sections 2.8–2.12.

We have already said rather a lot about a simple transmittal of data from one process to another, but there is even more. To understand why, we examine two aspects of the communication: the semantics of the communication primitives, and the underlying protocols that implement them. Consider the previous example, on process 0, after the blocking send has completed. The question arises: if the send has completed, does this tell us anything about the receiving process? Can we know that the receive has finished, or even, that it has begun?

Such questions of semantics are related to the nature of the underlying protocol implementing the operations. If one wishes to implement a protocol minimizing the copying and buffering of data, the most natural semantics might be the "rendezvous" version, where completion of the send implies the receive has been initiated (at least). On the other hand, a protocol that attempts to block processes for the minimal amount of time will necessarily end up doing more buffering and copying of data and will have "buffering" semantics.

The trouble is, one choice of semantics is not best for all applications, nor is it best for all architectures. Because the primary goal of MPI is to standardize the operations, yet not sacrifice performance, the decision was made to include all the major choices for point to point semantics in the standard.

The above complexities are manifested in MPI by the existence of **modes** for point to point communication. Both blocking and nonblocking communications have modes. The mode allows one to choose the semantics of the send operation and, in effect, to influence the underlying protocol of the transfer of data.

In **standard** mode the completion of the send does not necessarily mean that the matching receive has started, and no assumption should be made in the application program about whether the out-going data is buffered by MPI. In **buffered** mode the user can guarantee that a certain amount of buffering space is available. The catch is that the space must be explicitly provided by the application program. In **synchronous** mode a rendezvous semantics between sender and receiver is used. Finally, there is **ready** mode. This allows the user to exploit extra knowledge to simplify the protocol and potentially achieve higher performance. In a ready-mode send, the user asserts that the matching receive already has been posted. Modes are covered in Section 2.13.

2.2   Blocking Send and Receive Operations

This section describes standard-mode, blocking sends and receives.

2.2.1   Blocking Send

MPI_SEND(buf, count, datatype, dest, tag, comm)

IN	buf	initial address of send buffer
IN	count	number of entries to send
IN	datatype	datatype of each entry
IN	dest	rank of destination
IN	tag	message tag
IN	comm	communicator

```
int MPI_Send(void* buf, int count, MPI_Datatype datatype, int dest,
             int tag, MPI_Comm comm)
```

```
MPI_SEND(BUF, COUNT, DATATYPE, DEST, TAG, COMM, IERROR)
    <type> BUF(*)
    INTEGER COUNT, DATATYPE, DEST, TAG, COMM, IERROR
```

MPI_SEND performs a standard-mode, blocking send. The semantics of this function are described in Section 2.4. The arguments to MPI_SEND are described in the following subsections.

2.2.2   Send Buffer and Message Data

The send buffer specified by MPI_SEND consists of **count** successive entries of the type indicated by **datatype**, starting with the entry at address **buf**. Note that we specify the message length in terms of number of *entries*, not number of *bytes*. The former is machine independent and facilitates portable programming. The **count** may be zero, in which case the data part of the message is empty. The basic datatypes correspond to the basic datatypes of the host language. Possible values of this argument for Fortran and the corresponding Fortran types are listed below.

MPI datatype	Fortran datatype
MPI_INTEGER	INTEGER
MPI_REAL	REAL
MPI_DOUBLE_PRECISION	DOUBLE PRECISION
MPI_COMPLEX	COMPLEX
MPI_LOGICAL	LOGICAL
MPI_CHARACTER	CHARACTER(1)
MPI_BYTE	
MPI_PACKED	

Possible values for this argument for C and the corresponding C types are listed below.

MPI datatype	C datatype
MPI_CHAR	signed char
MPI_SHORT	signed short int
MPI_INT	signed int
MPI_LONG	signed long int
MPI_UNSIGNED_CHAR	unsigned char
MPI_UNSIGNED_SHORT	unsigned short int
MPI_UNSIGNED	unsigned int
MPI_UNSIGNED_LONG	unsigned long int
MPI_FLOAT	float
MPI_DOUBLE	double
MPI_LONG_DOUBLE	long double
MPI_BYTE	
MPI_PACKED	

The datatypes MPI_BYTE and MPI_PACKED do not correspond to a Fortran or C datatype. A value of type MPI_BYTE consists of a byte (8 binary digits). A byte is uninterpreted and is different from a character. Different machines may have different representations for characters, or may use more than one byte to represent characters. On the other hand, a byte has the same binary value on all machines. The use of MPI_PACKED is explained in Section 3.8.

MPI requires support of the datatypes listed above, which match the basic data-types of Fortran 77 and ANSI C. Additional MPI datatypes should be provided if the host language has additional data types. Some examples are: MPI_LONG_LONG, for C integers declared to be of type longlong; MPI_DOUBLE_COMPLEX for double precision complex in Fortran declared to be of type DOUBLE COMPLEX; MPI_REAL2, MPI_REAL4 and MPI_REAL8 for Fortran reals, declared to be of type REAL*2, REAL*4 and REAL*8, respectively; MPI_INTEGER1 MPI_INTEGER2 and MPI_INTEGER4 for Fortran integers, declared to be of type INTEGER*1, INTEGER*2 and INTEGER*4, respectively. In addition, MPI provides a mechanism for users to define new, derived, datatypes. This is explained in Chapter 3.

2.2.3   Message Envelope

In addition to data, messages carry information that is used to distinguish and selectively receive them. This information consists of a fixed number of fields, which we collectively call the **message envelope**. These fields are

source, **destination**, **tag**, and **communicator**.

The message source is implicitly determined by the identity of the message sender. The other fields are specified by arguments in the send operation.

The comm argument specifies the **communicator** used for the send operation. The communicator is a local object that represents a **communication domain**. A communication domain is a global, distributed structure that allows processes in a **group** to communicate with each other, or to communicate with processes in another group. A communication domain of the first type (communication within a group) is represented by an **intracommunicator**, whereas a communication domain of the second type (communication between groups) is represented by an **intercommunicator**. Processes in a group are ordered, and are identified by their integer **rank**. Processes may participate in several communication domains; distinct communication domains may have partially or even completely overlapping groups of processes. Each communication domain supports a disjoint stream of communications. Thus, a process may be able to communicate with another process via two distinct communication domains, using two distinct communicators. The same process may be identified by a different rank in the two domains; and communications in the two domains do not interfere. MPI applications begin with a default communication domain that includes all processes (of this parallel job); the default communicator MPI_COMM_WORLD represents this communication domain. Communicators are explained further in Chapter 5.

The message destination is specified by the dest argument. The range of valid values for dest is 0,...,n-1, where n is the number of processes in the group. This range includes the rank of the sender: if comm is an intracommunicator, then a process may send a message to itself. If the communicator is an intercommunicator, then destinations are identified by their rank in the remote group.

The integer-valued message tag is specified by the tag argument. This integer can be used by the application to distinguish messages. The range of valid tag values is 0,...,UB, where the value of UB is implementation dependent. It is found by querying the value of the attribute MPI_TAG_UB, as described in Chapter 7. MPI requires that UB be no less than 32767.

2.2.4 Comments on Send

Advice to users. Communicators provide an important encapsulation mechanism for libraries and modules. They allow modules to have their own communication space and their own process numbering scheme. Chapter 5 discusses functions for defining new communicators and use of communicators for library design.

Users that are comfortable with the notion of a flat name space for processes and a single communication domain, as offered by most existing communication libraries, need only use the predefined variable MPI_COMM_WORLD as the comm argument. This will allow communication with all the processes available at initialization time. (*End of advice to users.*)

Advice to implementors. The message envelope is often encoded by a fixed-length message header. This header carries a communication domain id (sometimes referred to as the **context id**. This id need not be system wide unique; nor does it need to be identical at all processes within a group. It is sufficient that each ordered pair of communicating processes agree to associate a particular id value with each communication domain they use. In addition, the header will usually carry message source and tag; source can be represented as rank within group or as an absolute task id.

The context id can be viewed as an additional tag field. It differs from the regular message tag in that wild card matching is not allowed on this field, and that value setting for this field is controlled by communicator manipulation functions. (*End of advice to implementors.*)

2.2.5   Blocking Receive

MPI_RECV (buf, count, datatype, source, tag, comm, status)

OUT	buf	initial address of receive buffer
IN	count	max number of entries to receive
IN	datatype	datatype of each entry
IN	source	rank of source
IN	tag	message tag
IN	comm	communicator
OUT	status	return status

```
int MPI_Recv(void* buf, int count, MPI_Datatype datatype, int source,
             int tag, MPI_Comm comm, MPI_Status *status)
```

```
MPI_RECV(BUF, COUNT, DATATYPE, SOURCE, TAG, COMM, STATUS, IERROR)
   <type> BUF(*)
   INTEGER COUNT, DATATYPE, SOURCE, TAG, COMM,
   STATUS(MPI_STATUS_SIZE), IERROR
```

MPI_RECV performs a standard-mode, blocking receive. The semantics of this function are described in Section 2.4. The arguments to MPI_RECV are described in the following subsections.

2.2.6   Receive Buffer

The receive buffer consists of storage sufficient to contain count consecutive entries of the type specified by datatype, starting at address buf. The length of the received message must be less than or equal to the length of the receive buffer. An overflow error occurs if all incoming data does not fit, without truncation, into the receive buffer. We explain in Chapter 7 how to check for errors. If a message that is shorter than the receive buffer arrives, then the incoming message is stored in the initial locations of the receive buffer, and the remaining locations are not modified.

2.2.7   Message Selection

The selection of a message by a receive operation is governed by the value of its message envelope. A message can be received if its envelope matches the source, tag and comm values specified by the receive operation. The receiver may specify a wildcard value for source (MPI_ANY_SOURCE), and/or a wildcard value for tag

(MPI_ANY_TAG), indicating that any source and/or tag are acceptable. One cannot specify a wildcard value for comm.

The argument source, if different from MPI_ANY_SOURCE, is specified as a rank within the process group associated with the communicator (remote process group, for intercommunicators). The range of valid values for the source argument is $\{0,...,n\text{-}1\}\cup\{MPI_ANY_SOURCE\}$, where n is the number of processes in this group. This range includes the receiver's rank: if comm is an intracommunicator, then a process may receive a message from itself. The range of valid values for the tag argument is $\{0,...,$UB$\}\cup\{$MPI_ANY_TAG$\}$.

2.2.8   Return Status

The receive call does not specify the size of an incoming message, but only an upper bound. The source or tag of a received message may not be known if wildcard values were used in a receive operation. Also, if multiple requests are completed by a single MPI function (see Section 2.9), a distinct error code may be returned for each request. (Usually, the error code is returned as the value of the function in C, and as the value of the IERROR argument in Fortran.)

This information is returned by the status argument of MPI_RECV. The type of status is defined by MPI. Status variables need to be explicitly allocated by the user, that is, they are not system objects.

In C, status is a structure of type MPI_Status that contains three fields named MPI_SOURCE, MPI_TAG, and MPI_ERROR; the structure may contain additional fields. Thus, status.MPI_SOURCE, status.MPI_TAG and status.MPI_ERROR contain the source, tag and error code, respectively, of the received message.

In Fortran, status is an array of INTEGERs of length MPI_STATUS_SIZE. The three constants MPI_SOURCE, MPI_TAG and MPI_ERROR are the indices of the entries that store the source, tag and error fields. Thus status(MPI_SOURCE), status(MPI_TAG) and status(MPI_ERROR) contain, respectively, the source, the tag and the error code of the received message.

The status argument also returns information on the length of the message received. However, this information is not directly available as a field of the status variable and a call to MPI_GET_COUNT is required to "decode" this information.

MPI_GET_COUNT(status, datatype, count)

IN	status	return status of receive operation
IN	datatype	datatype of each receive buffer entry
OUT	count	number of received entries

```
int MPI_Get_count(MPI_Status *status, MPI_Datatype datatype,
            int *count)
```

```
MPI_GET_COUNT(STATUS, DATATYPE, COUNT, IERROR)
    INTEGER STATUS(MPI_STATUS_SIZE), DATATYPE, COUNT, IERROR
```

MPI_GET_COUNT takes as input the status set by MPI_RECV and computes the number of entries received. The number of entries is returned in count. The datatype argument should match the argument provided to the receive call that set status. (Section 3.4 explains that MPI_GET_COUNT may return, in certain situations, the value MPI_UNDEFINED.)

2.2.9 Comments on Receive

Note the asymmetry between send and receive operations. A receive operation may accept messages from an arbitrary sender, but a send operation must specify a unique receiver. This matches a "push" communication mechanism, where data transfer is effected by the sender, rather than a "pull" mechanism, where data transfer is effected by the receiver.

Source equal to destination is allowed, that is, a process can send a message to itself. However, for such a communication to succeed, it is required that the message be buffered by the system between the completion of the send call and the start of the receive call. The amount of buffer space available and the buffer allocation policy are implementation dependent. Therefore, it is unsafe and non-portable to send self-messages with the standard-mode, blocking send and receive operations described so far, since this may lead to deadlock. More discussions of this appear in Section 2.4.

Advice to users. A receive operation must specify the type of the entries of the incoming message, and an upper bound on the number of entries. In some cases, a process may expect several messages of different lengths or types. The process will post a receive for each message it expects and use message tags to disambiguate incoming messages.

In other cases, a process may expect only one message, but this message is of unknown type or length. If there are only few possible kinds of incoming messages, then each such kind can be identified by a different tag value. The function MPI_PROBE described in Section 2.10 can be used to check for incoming messages without actually receiving them. The receiving process can first test the tag value of the incoming message and then receive it with an appropriate receive operation.

In the most general case, it may not be possible to represent each message kind by a different tag value. A two-phase protocol may be used: the sender first sends a message containing a description of the data, then the data itself. The two messages are guaranteed to arrive in the correct order at the destination, as discussed in Section 2.4. An alternative approach is to use the packing and unpacking functions described in Section 3.8. These allow the sender to pack in one message a description of the data, followed by the data itself, thus creating a "self-typed" message. The receiver can first extract the data description and next use it to extract the data itself.

Superficially, tags and communicators fulfill a similar function. Both allow one to partition communications into distinct classes, with sends matching only receives from the same class. Tags offer imperfect protection since wildcard receives circumvent the protection provided by tags, while communicators are allocated and managed using special, safer operations. It is preferable to use communicators to provide protected communication domains across modules or libraries. Tags are used to discriminate between different kinds of messages within one module or library.

MPI offers a variety of mechanisms for matching incoming messages to receive operations. Oftentimes, matching by sender or by tag will be sufficient to match sends and receives correctly. Nevertheless, it is preferable to avoid the use of wildcard receives whenever possible. Narrower matching criteria result in safer code, with less opportunities for message mismatch or nondeterministic behavior. Narrower matching criteria may also lead to improved performance. (*End of advice to users.*)

Rationale. Why is status information returned via a special **status** variable?

Some libraries return this information via INOUT **count**, **tag** and **source** arguments, thus using them both to specify the selection criteria for incoming messages and to return the actual envelope values of the received message. The use of a separate argument prevents errors associated with INOUT arguments (for example, using the MPI_ANY_TAG constant as the tag argument in a send). Another potential source of errors, for nonblocking communications, is that status information may be updated after the call that passed in **count**, **tag** and **source**. In "old-style" designs, an error could occur if the receiver accesses or deallocates these variables before the communication completed. Instead, in the MPI design for nonblocking communications, the status argument is passed to the call that completes the communication, and is updated by this call.

Other libraries return status by calls that refer implicitly to the "last message received." This is not thread safe.

Why isn't count a field of the status variable?

On some systems, it may be faster to receive data without counting the number of entries received. Incoming messages do not carry an entry count. Indeed, when user-defined datatypes are used (see Chapter 3), it may not be possible to compute such a count at the sender. Instead, incoming messages carry a byte count. The translation of a byte count into an entry count may be time consuming, especially for user-defined datatypes, and may not be needed by the receiver. The current design avoids the need for computing an entry count in those situations where the count is not needed.

Note that the current design allows implementations that compute a count during receives and store the count in a field of the status variable. (*End of rationale.*)

Advice to implementors. Even though no specific behavior is mandated by MPI for erroneous programs, the recommended handling of overflow situations is to return, in status, information about the source, tag and size of the incoming message. The receive operation will return an error code. A quality implementation will also ensure that memory that is outside the receive buffer will not be overwritten.

In the case of a message shorter than the receive buffer, MPI is quite strict in that it allows no modification of the other locations in the buffer. A more lenient statement would allow for some optimizations but this is not allowed. The implementation must be ready to end a copy into the receiver memory exactly at the end of the received data, even if it is at a non-word-aligned address. (*End of advice to implementors.*)

2.3   Datatype Matching and Data Conversion

2.3.1   Type Matching Rules

One can think of message transfer as consisting of the following three phases.

1. Data is copied out of the send buffer and a message is assembled.

2. A message is transferred from sender to receiver.

3. Data is copied from the incoming message and disassembled into the receive buffer.

Type matching must be observed at each of these phases. The type of each variable in the sender buffer must match the type specified for that entry by the send operation. The type specified by the send operation must match the type specified by the receive operation. Finally, the type of each variable in the receive buffer must match the type specified for that entry by the receive operation. A program that fails to observe these rules is erroneous.

To define type matching precisely, we need to deal with two issues: matching of types of variables of the host language with types specified in communication operations, and matching of types between sender and receiver.

The types between a send and receive match if both operations specify identical type names. That is, MPI_INTEGER matches MPI_INTEGER, MPI_REAL matches MPI_REAL, and so on. The one exception to this rule is that the type MPI_PACKED can match any other type (Section 3.8).

The type of a variable matches the type specified in the communication operation if the datatype name used by that operation corresponds to the basic type of the host program variable. For example, an entry with type name MPI_INTEGER matches a Fortran variable of type INTEGER. Tables showing this correspondence for Fortran and C appear in Section 2.2.2. There are two exceptions to this rule: an entry with type name MPI_BYTE or MPI_PACKED can be used to match any byte of storage (on a byte-addressable machine), irrespective of the datatype of the variable that contains this byte. The type MPI_BYTE allows one to transfer the binary value of a byte in memory unchanged. The type MPI_PACKED is used to send data that has been explicitly packed with calls to MPI_PACK, or receive data that will be explicitly unpacked with calls to MPI_UNPACK (Section 3.8).

The following examples illustrate type matching.

Example 2.3 Sender and receiver specify matching types.
```
CALL MPI_COMM_RANK(comm, rank, ierr)
IF (rank.EQ.0) THEN
    CALL MPI_SEND(a(1), 10, MPI_REAL, 1, tag, comm, ierr)
ELSE IF (rank.EQ.1) THEN
    CALL MPI_RECV(b(1), 15, MPI_REAL, 0, tag, comm, status, ierr)
END IF
```

This code is correct if both **a** and **b** are real arrays of size ≥ 10. (In Fortran, it might be correct to use this code even if **a** or **b** have size < 10, e.g., **a**(1) might be be equivalenced to an array with ten reals.)

Example 2.4 Sender and receiver do not specify matching types.

```
CALL MPI_COMM_RANK(comm, rank, ierr)
IF (rank.EQ.0) THEN
    CALL MPI_SEND(a(1), 10, MPI_REAL, 1, tag, comm, ierr)
ELSE IF (rank.EQ.1) THEN
    CALL MPI_RECV(b(1), 40, MPI_BYTE, 0, tag, comm, status, ierr)
END IF
```

This code is erroneous, since sender and receiver do not provide matching datatype arguments.

Example 2.5 Sender and receiver specify communication of untyped values.

```
CALL MPI_COMM_RANK(comm, rank, ierr)
IF (rank.EQ.0) THEN
    CALL MPI_SEND(a(1), 40, MPI_BYTE, 1, tag, comm, ierr)
ELSE IF (rank.EQ.1) THEN
    CALL MPI_RECV(b(1), 60, MPI_BYTE, 0, tag, comm, status, ierr)
END IF
```

This code is correct, irrespective of the type and size of **a** and **b** (unless this results in an out of bound memory access).

Type MPI_CHARACTER The type MPI_CHARACTER matches one character of a Fortran variable of type **CHARACTER**, rather then the entire character string stored in the variable. Fortran variables of type **CHARACTER** or substrings are transferred as if they were arrays of characters. This is illustrated in the example below.

Example 2.6 Transfer of Fortran **CHARACTER**s.

```
CHARACTER*10 a
CHARACTER*10 b

CALL MPI_COMM_RANK(comm, rank, ierr)
IF (rank.EQ.0) THEN
    CALL MPI_SEND(a, 5, MPI_CHARACTER, 1, tag, comm, ierr)
ELSE IF (rank.EQ.1) THEN
```

```
    CALL MPI_RECV(b(6:10),5,MPI_CHARACTER,0,tag,comm,status,ierr)
END IF
```

The last five characters of string b at process 1 are replaced by the first five characters of string a at process 0.

Advice to users. If a buffer of type MPI_BYTE is passed as an argument to MPI_SEND, then MPI will send the data stored at contiguous locations, starting from the address indicated by the buf argument. This may have unexpected results when the data layout is not as a casual user would expect it to be. For example, some Fortran compilers implement variables of type CHARACTER as a structure that contains the character length and a pointer to the actual string. In such an environment, sending and receiving a Fortran CHARACTER variable using the MPI_BYTE type will not have the anticipated result of transferring the character string. For this reason, the user is advised to use typed communications whenever possible. (*End of advice to users.*)

Rationale. Why does MPI force the user to specify datatypes? After all, type information is available in the source program.

MPI is meant to be implemented as a library, with no need for additional preprocessing or compilation. Thus, one cannot assume that a communication call has information on the datatype of variables in the communication buffer. This information must be supplied at calling time, either by calling a different function for each datatype, or by passing the datatype information as an explicit parameter. Datatype information is needed for heterogeneous support and is further discussed in Section 2.3.2.

Futures extensions of MPI might take advantage of polymorphism in C++ or Fortran 90 in order to pass the datatype information implicitly. (*End of rationale.*)

Advice to implementors. Some compilers pass Fortran CHARACTER arguments as a structure with a length and a pointer to the actual string. In such an environment, MPI send or receive calls need to dereference the pointer in order to reach the string. (*End of advice to implementors.*)

2.3.2 Data Conversion

One of the goals of MPI is to support parallel computations across heterogeneous environments. Communication in a heterogeneous environment may require data conversions. We use the following terminology.

Type conversion changes the datatype of a value, for example, by rounding a REAL to an INTEGER.

Representation conversion changes the binary representation of a value, for example, changing byte ordering, or changing 32-bit floating point to 64-bit floating point.

The type matching rules imply that MPI communications never do type conversion. On the other hand, MPI requires that a representation conversion be performed when a typed value is transferred across environments that use different representations for such a value. MPI does not specify the detailed rules for representation conversion. Such a conversion is expected to preserve integer, logical or character values, and to convert a floating point value to the nearest value that can be represented on the target system.

Overflow and underflow exceptions may occur during floating point conversions. Conversion of integers or characters may also lead to exceptions when a value that can be represented in one system cannot be represented in the other system. An exception occurring during representation conversion results in a failure of the communication. An error occurs either in the send operation, or the receive operation, or both.

If a value sent in a message is untyped (i.e., of type MPI_BYTE), then the binary representation of the byte stored at the receiver is identical to the binary representation of the byte loaded at the sender. This holds true, whether sender and receiver run in the same or in distinct environments. No representation conversion is done. Note that representation conversion may occur when values of type MPI_CHARACTER or MPI_CHAR are transferred, for example, from an EBCDIC encoding to an ASCII encoding.

No representation conversion need occur when an MPI program executes in a homogeneous system, where all processes run in the same environment.

Consider the three examples, 2.3–2.5. The first program is correct, assuming that a and b are REAL arrays of size ≥ 10. If the sender and receiver execute in different environments, then the ten real values that are fetched from the send buffer will be converted to the representation for reals on the receiver site before they are stored in the receive buffer. While the number of real elements fetched from the send buffer equal the number of real elements stored in the receive buffer, the number of bytes stored need not equal the number of bytes loaded. For example, the sender may use a four byte representation and the receiver an eight byte representation for reals.

The second program is erroneous, and its behavior is undefined.

The third program is correct. The exact same sequence of forty bytes that were loaded from the send buffer will be stored in the receive buffer, even if sender and receiver run in a different environment. The message sent has exactly the same length (in bytes) and the same binary representation as the message received. If a and b are of different types, or if they are of the same type but different data representations are used, then the bits stored in the receive buffer may encode values that are different from the values they encoded in the send buffer.

Representation conversion also applies to the envelope of a message. The source, destination and tag are all integers that may need to be converted.

MPI does not require support for inter-language communication. The behavior of a program is undefined if messages are sent by a C process and received by a Fortran process, or vice-versa.

2.3.3   Comments on Data Conversion

Rationale.   MPI does not handle inter-language communication because there are no agreed-upon standards for the correspondence between C types and Fortran types. Therefore, MPI applications that mix languages would not be portable. Vendors are expected to provide inter-language communication consistent with their support for inter-language procedure invocation. (*End of rationale.*)

Advice to implementors.   The datatype matching rules do not require messages to carry data type information. Both sender and receiver provide complete data type information. In a heterogeneous environment, one can either use a machine independent encoding such as XDR, or have the receiver convert from the sender representation to its own, or even have the sender do the conversion.

Additional type information might be added to messages in order to allow the system to detect mismatches between datatype at sender and receiver. This might be particularly useful in a slower but safer debug mode for MPI.

Although MPI does not specify interfaces between C and Fortran, vendors are expected to provide such interfaces, so as to allow Fortran programs to invoke parallel libraries written in C, or communicate with servers running C codes (and vice-versa). Initialization for Fortran and C should be compatible, mechanisms should be provided for passing MPI objects as parameters in interlanguage procedural invocations, and inter-language communication should be supported. For example, consider a system where a Fortran caller can pass an INTEGER actual parameter to a C routine with an int formal parameter. In such a system a Fortran routine should be able to send a message with datatype MPI_INTEGER to be received by a

C routine with datatype MPI_INT. (*End of advice to implementors.*)

2.4 Semantics of Blocking Point-to-point

This section describes the main properties of the send and receive calls introduced in Section 2.2. Interested readers can find a more formal treatment of the issues in this section in [10].

2.4.1 Buffering and Safety

The receive described in Section 2.2.5 can be started whether or not a matching send has been posted. That version of receive is **blocking**. It returns only after the receive buffer contains the newly received message. A receive could complete before the matching send has completed (of course, it can complete only after the matching send has started).

The send operation described in Section 2.2.1 can be started whether or not a matching receive has been posted. That version of send is **blocking**. It does not return until the message data and envelope have been safely stored away so that the sender is free to access and overwrite the send buffer. The send call is also potentially **non-local**. The message might be copied directly into the matching receive buffer, or it might be copied into a temporary system buffer. In the first case, the send call will not complete until a matching receive call occurs, and so, if the sending process is single-threaded, then it will be blocked until this time. In the second case, the send call may return ahead of the matching receive call, allowing a single-threaded process to continue with its computation. The MPI implementation may make either of these choices. It might block the sender or it might buffer the data.

Message buffering decouples the send and receive operations. A blocking send might complete as soon as the message was buffered, even if no matching receive has been executed by the receiver. On the other hand, message buffering can be expensive, as it entails additional memory-to-memory copying, and it requires the allocation of memory for buffering. The choice of the right amount of buffer space to allocate for communication and of the buffering policy to use is application and implementation dependent. Therefore, MPI offers the choice of several communication modes that allow one to control the choice of the communication protocol. Modes are described in Section 2.13. The choice of a buffering policy for the standard mode send described in Section 2.2.1 is left to the implementation. In any case, lack of buffer space will not cause a standard send call to fail, but will merely cause it to block. In well-constructed programs, this results in a useful throttle effect. Consider a situation where a producer repeatedly produces new values and sends them to a consumer. Assume that the producer produces new values faster than the consumer can consume them. If standard sends are used, then the producer will be automatically throttled, as its send operations will block when buffer space is unavailable.

In ill-constructed programs, blocking may lead to a **deadlock** situation, where all processes are blocked, and no progress occurs. Such programs may complete when sufficient buffer space is available, but will fail on systems that do less buffering, or when data sets (and message sizes) are increased. Since any system will run out of buffer resources as message sizes are increased, and some implementations may want to provide little buffering, MPI takes the position that **safe** programs do not rely on system buffering, and will complete correctly irrespective of the buffer allocation policy used by MPI. Buffering may change the performance of a safe program, but it doesn't affect the result of the program.

MPI does not enforce a safe programming style. Users are free to take advantage of knowledge of the buffering policy of an implementation in order to relax the safety requirements, though doing so will lessen the portability of the program.

The following examples illustrate safe programming issues.

Example 2.7 An exchange of messages.
```
CALL MPI_COMM_RANK(comm, rank, ierr)
IF (rank.EQ.0) THEN
    CALL MPI_SEND(sendbuf, count, MPI_REAL, 1, tag, comm, ierr)
    CALL MPI_RECV(recvbuf, count, MPI_REAL, 1, tag, comm, status, ierr)
ELSE IF (rank.EQ.1) THEN
    CALL MPI_RECV(recvbuf, count, MPI_REAL, 0, tag, comm, status, ierr)
    CALL MPI_SEND(sendbuf, count, MPI_REAL, 0, tag, comm, ierr)
END IF
```

This program succeeds even if no buffer space for data is available. The program is safe and will always complete correctly.

Example 2.8 An attempt to exchange messages.
```
CALL MPI_COMM_RANK(comm, rank, ierr)
IF (rank.EQ.0) THEN
    CALL MPI_RECV(recvbuf, count, MPI_REAL, 1, tag, comm, status, ierr)
    CALL MPI_SEND(sendbuf, count, MPI_REAL, 1, tag, comm, ierr)
```

```
ELSE IF (rank.EQ.1) THEN
    CALL MPI_RECV(recvbuf, count, MPI_REAL, 0, tag, comm, status, ierr)
    CALL MPI_SEND(sendbuf, count, MPI_REAL, 0, tag, comm, ierr)
END IF
```

The receive operation of the first process must complete before its send, and can complete only if the matching send of the second processor is executed. The receive operation of the second process must complete before its send and can complete only if the matching send of the first process is executed. This program will always deadlock.

Example 2.9 An exchange that relies on buffering.
```
CALL MPI_COMM_RANK(comm, rank, ierr)
IF (rank.EQ.0) THEN
    CALL MPI_SEND(sendbuf, count, MPI_REAL, 1, tag, comm, ierr)
    CALL MPI_RECV(recvbuf, count, MPI_REAL, 1, tag, comm, status, ierr)
ELSE IF (rank.EQ.1) THEN
    CALL MPI_SEND(sendbuf, count, MPI_REAL, 0, tag, comm, ierr)
    CALL MPI_RECV(recvbuf, count, MPI_REAL, 0, tag, comm, status, ierr)
END IF
```

The message sent by each process must be copied somewhere before the send operation returns and the receive operation starts. For the program to complete, it is necessary that at least one of the two messages be buffered. Thus, this program will succeed only if the communication system will buffer at least count words of data. Otherwise, the program will deadlock. The success of this program will depend on the amount of buffer space available in a particular implementation, on the buffer allocation policy used, and on other concurrent communication occurring in the system. This program is unsafe.

Advice to users. Safety is a very important issue in the design of message passing programs. MPI offers many features that help in writing safe programs, in addition to the techniques that were outlined above. Nonblocking message passing operations, as described in Section 2.8, can be used to avoid the need for buffering outgoing messages. This eliminates deadlocks due to lack of buffer space, and potentially improves performance, by avoiding the overheads of allocating buffers and copying messages into buffers. Use of other communication modes, described in Section 2.13, can also avoid deadlock situations due to lack of buffer space.

Quality MPI implementations attempt to be lenient to the user, by providing buffering for standard blocking sends whenever feasible. Programs that require buffering in order to progress will not typically break, unless they move large amounts of data. The caveat, of course, is that "large" is a relative term.

Safety is further discussed in Section 9.2. (*End of advice to users.*)

Advice to implementors.   The challenge facing implementors is to be as lenient as possible to applications that require buffering, without hampering performance of applications that do not require buffering. Applications should not deadlock if memory is available to allow progress in the communication. But copying should be avoided when it is not necessary. (*End of advice to implementors.*)

2.4.2   Multithreading

MPI does not specify the interaction of blocking communication calls with the thread scheduler in a multi-threaded implementation of MPI. The desired behavior is that a blocking communication call blocks only the issuing thread, allowing another thread to be scheduled. The blocked thread will be rescheduled when the blocked call is satisfied. That is, when data has been copied out of the send buffer, for a send operation, or copied into the receive buffer, for a receive operation. When a thread executes concurrently with a blocked communication operation, it is the user's responsibility not to access or modify a communication buffer until the communication completes. Otherwise, the outcome of the computation is undefined.

2.4.3   Order

Messages are *non-overtaking*. Conceptually, one may think of successive messages sent by a process to another process as ordered in a sequence. Receive operations posted by a process are also ordered in a sequence. Each incoming message matches the first matching receive in the sequence. This is illustrated in Figure 2.1. Process zero sends two messages to process one and process two sends three messages to process one. Process one posts five receives. All communications occur in the same communication domain. The first message sent by process zero and the first message sent by process two can be received in either order, since the first two posted receives match either. The second message of process two will be received before the third message, even though the third and fourth receives match either.

Thus, if a sender sends two messages in succession to the same destination, and both match the same receive, then the receive cannot get the second message if the first message is still pending. If a receiver posts two receives in succession, and both

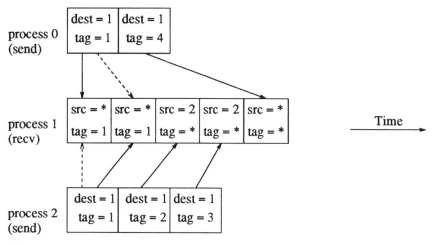

Figure 2.1
Messages are matched in order.

match the same message, then the second receive operation cannot be satisfied by
this message, if the first receive is still pending.

These requirements further define message matching. They guarantee that
message-passing code is deterministic, if processes are single-threaded and the wildcard MPI_ANY_SOURCE is not used in receives. Some other MPI functions, such as
MPI_CANCEL or MPI_WAITANY, are additional sources of nondeterminism.

In a single-threaded process all communication operations are ordered according to program execution order. The situation is different when processes are
multi-threaded. The semantics of thread execution may not define a relative order
between two communication operations executed by two distinct threads. The operations are logically concurrent, even if one physically precedes the other. In this
case, no order constraints apply. Two messages sent by concurrent threads can be
received in any order. Similarly, if two receive operations that are logically concurrent receive two successively sent messages, then the two messages can match the
receives in either order.

It is important to understand what is guaranteed by the ordering property and
what is not. Between any pair of communicating processes, messages flow in order. This does not imply a consistent, total order on communication events in the
system. Consider the following example.

Example 2.10 Order preserving is not transitive.

```
CALL MPI_COMM_RANK(comm, rank, ierr)
IF (rank.EQ.0) THEN
    CALL MPI_SEND(buf1, count, MPI_REAL, 2, tag, comm, ierr)
    CALL MPI_SEND(buf2, count, MPI_REAL, 1, tag, comm, ierr)
ELSE IF (rank.EQ.1) THEN
    CALL MPI_RECV(buf2, count, MPI_REAL, 0, tag, comm, status, ierr)
    CALL MPI_SEND(buf2, count, MPI_REAL, 2, tag, comm, ierr)
ELSE IF (rank.EQ.2)
    CALL MPI_RECV(buf1, count, MPI_REAL, MPI_ANY_SOURCE, tag,
                                       comm, status, ierr)
    CALL MPI_RECV(buf2, count, MPI_REAL, MPI_ANY_SOURCE, tag,
                                       comm, status, ierr)
END IF
```

Process zero sends a message to process two and next sends a message to process one. Process one receives the message from process zero, then sends a message to process two. Process two receives two messages, with source = dontcare. The two incoming messages can be received by process two in any order, even though process one sent its message after it received the second message sent by process zero. The reason is that communication delays can be arbitrary and MPI does not enforce global serialization of communications. Thus, the somewhat paradoxical outcome illustrated in Figure 2.2 can occur. If process zero had sent directly two messages to process two then these two messages would have been received in order. Since it relayed the second message via process one, then the messages may now arrive out of order. In practice, such an occurrence is unlikely.

2.4.4 Progress

If a pair of matching send and receives have been initiated on two processes, then at least one of these two operations will complete, independently of other actions in the system. The send operation will complete, unless the receive is satisfied by another message. The receive operation will complete, unless the message sent is consumed by another matching receive posted at the same destination process.

Advice to implementors. This requirement imposes constraints on implementation strategies. Suppose, for example, that a process executes two successive blocking send calls. The message sent by the first call is buffered, and the second call starts. Then, if a receive is posted that matches this second send, the second message should be able to overtake the first buffered one. (*End of advice to implementors.*)

Process 0

Figure 2.2
Order preserving is not transitive.

2.4.5   Fairness

MPI makes no guarantee of *fairness* in the handling of communication. Suppose that a send is posted. Then it is possible that the destination process repeatedly posts a receive that matches this send, yet the message is never received, because it is repeatedly overtaken by other messages, sent from other sources. The scenario requires that the receive used the wildcard MPI_ANY_SOURCE as its source argument.

Similarly, suppose that a receive is posted by a multi-threaded process. Then it is possible that messages that match this receive are repeatedly consumed, yet the receive is never satisfied, because it is overtaken by other receives posted at this node by other threads. It is the programmer's responsibility to prevent starvation in such situations.

2.5   Example — Jacobi iteration

We shall use the following example to illustrate the material introduced so far, and to motivate new functions.

Example 2.11 Jacobi iteration – sequential code
```
REAL A(0:n+1,0:n+1), B(1:n,1:n)
...


! Main Loop
DO WHILE(.NOT.converged)
   ! perform 4 point stencil
   DO j=1, n
     DO i=1, n
        B(i,j) =0.25*(A(i-1,j)+A(i+1,j)+A(i,j-1)+A(i,j+1))
     END DO
   END DO

   ! copy result back into array A
   DO j=1,n
     DO i=1,n
        A(i,j) = B(i,j)
     END DO
   END DO
...
! Convergence test omitted
END DO
```
The code fragment describes the main loop of an iterative solver where, at each iteration, the value at a point is replaced by the average of the North, South, East and West neighbors (a four point stencil is used to keep the example simple). Boundary values do not change. We focus on the inner loop, where most of the computation is done, and use Fortran 90 syntax, for clarity.

Since this code has a simple structure, a data-parallel approach can be used to derive an equivalent parallel code. The array is distributed across processes, and each process is assigned the task of updating the entries on the part of the array it owns.

A parallel algorithm is derived from a choice of data distribution. The distribution should be balanced, allocating (roughly) the same number of entries to each processor; and it should minimize communication. Figure 2.3 illustrates two possible distributions: a 1D (block) distribution, where the matrix is partitioned in one dimension, and a 2D (block,block) distribution, where the matrix is partitioned in two dimensions.

1D partition   **2D partition**

Figure 2.3
Block partitioning of a matrix.

Since the communication occurs at block boundaries, communication volume is minimized by the 2D partition which has a better area to perimeter ratio. However, in this partition, each processor communicates with four neighbors, rather than two neighbors in the 1D partition. When the ratio of n/P (P number of processors) is small, communication time will be dominated by the fixed overhead per message, and the first partition will lead to better performance. When the ratio is large, the second partition will result in better performance. In order to keep the example simple, we shall use the first partition; a realistic code would use a "polyalgorithm" that selects one of the two partitions, according to problem size, number of processors, and communication performance parameters.

The value of each point in the array B is computed from the value of the four neighbors in array A. Communications are needed at block boundaries in order to receive values of neighbor points which are owned by another processor. Communications are simplified if an overlap area is allocated at each processor for storing the values to be received from the neighbor processor. Essentially, storage is allocated for each entry both at the producer and at the consumer of that entry. If an entry is produced by one processor and consumed by another, then storage is allocated for this entry at both processors. With such scheme there is no need for dynamic allocation of communication buffers, and the location of each variable is fixed. Such scheme works whenever the data dependencies in the computation are fixed and simple. In our case, they are described by a four point stencil. Therefore, a one-column overlap is needed, for a 1D partition.

We shall partition array **A** with one column overlap. No such overlap is required for array **B**. Figure 2.4 shows the extra columns in **A** and how data is transfered for each iteration.

We shall use an algorithm where all values needed from a neighbor are brought in one message. Coalescing of communications in this manner reduces the number of messages and generally improves performance.

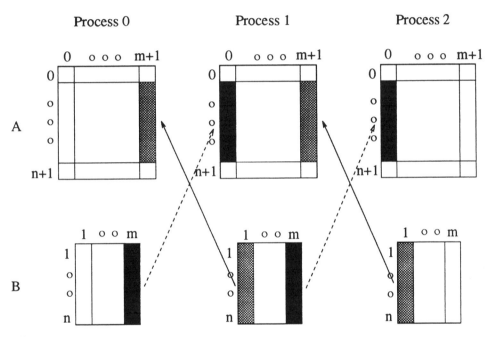

Figure 2.4
1D block partitioning with overlap and communication pattern for jacobi iteration.

The resulting parallel algorithm is shown below.

Example 2.12 Jacobi iteration – first version of parallel code

```
...
REAL, ALLOCATABLE A(:,:), B(:,:)
...
! Compute number of processes and myrank
CALL MPI_COMM_SIZE(comm, p, ierr)
CALL MPI_COMM_RANK(comm, myrank, ierr)
```

```
! Compute size of local block
m = n/p
IF (myrank.LT.(n-p*m)) THEN
   m = m+1
END IF

! Allocate local arrays
ALLOCATE (A(0:n+1,0:m+1), B(n,m))
...
! Main loop
DO WHILE (.NOT. converged)
   ! Compute
   DO j=1,m
      DO i=1,n
         B(i,j) = 0.25*(A(i-1,j)+A(i+1,j)+A(i,j-1)+A(i,j+1))
      END DO
   END DO
   DO j=1,m
      DO i=1,n
         A(i,j) = B(i,j)
      END DO
   END DO

   ! Communicate
   IF (myrank.GT.0) THEN
      CALL MPI_SEND(B(1,1), n, MPI_REAL, myrank-1, tag, comm, ierr)
      CALL MPI_RECV(A(1,0), n, MPI_REAL, myrank-1, tag, comm,
                                                  status, ierr)
   END IF
   IF (myrank.LT.p-1) THEN
      CALL MPI_SEND(B(1,m), n, MPI_REAL, myrank+1, tag, comm, ierr)
      CALL MPI_RECV(A(1,m+1), n, MPI_REAL, myrank+1, tag, comm,
                                                  status, ierr)
   END IF
   ...
END DO
```

This code has a communication pattern similar to the code in Example 2.9. It is unsafe, since each processor first sends messages to its two neighbors, next receives the messages they have sent.

One way to get a safe version of this code is to alternate the order of sends and receives: odd rank processes will first send, next receive, and even rank processes will first receive, next send. Thus, one achieves the communication pattern of Example 2.7.

The modified main loop is shown below. We shall later see simpler ways of dealing with this problem.

Example 2.13 Main loop of Jacobi iteration – safe version of parallel code

```
...
! Main loop
DO WHILE(.NOT. converged)
   ! Compute
   DO j=1,m
      DO i=1,n
         B(i,j) = 0.25*(A(i-1,j)+A(i+1,j)+A(i,j-1)+A(i,j+1))
      END DO
   END DO
   DO j=1,m
      DO i=1,n
         A(i,j) = B(i,j)
      END DO
   END DO

   ! Communicate
   IF (MOD(myrank,2).EQ.1) THEN
      CALL MPI_SEND(B(1,1), n, MPI_REAL, myrank-1, tag,
                                             comm, ierr)
      CALL MPI_RECV(A(1,0), n, MPI_REAL, myrank-1, tag,
                                             comm, status, ierr)
      IF (myrank.LT.p-1) THEN
         CALL MPI_SEND(B(1,m), n, MPI_REAL, myrank+1, tag,
                                             comm, ierr)
         CALL MPI_RECV(A(1,m+1), n, MPI_REAL, myrank+1, tag,
                                             comm, status, ierr)
      END IF
   ELSE    ! myrank is even
      IF (myrank.GT.0) THEN
```

```
        CALL MPI_RECV(A(1,0), n, MPI_REAL, myrank-1, tag,
                                       comm, status, ierr)
        CALL MPI_SEND(B(1,1), n, MPI_REAL, myrank-1, tag,
                                             comm, ierr)
    END IF
    IF (myrank.LT.p-1) THEN
        CALL MPI_RECV(A(1,m+1), n, MPI_REAL, myrank+1, tag,
                                       comm, status, ierr)
        CALL MPI_SEND(B(1,m), n, MPI_REAL, myrank+1, tag,
                                           comm, ierr)
    END IF
  END IF
...
END DO
```

2.6   Send-Receive

The exchange communication pattern exhibited by the last example is sufficiently frequent to justify special support. The **send-receive** operation combines, in one call, the sending of one message to a destination and the receiving of another message from a source. The source and destination are possibly the same. Send-receive is useful for communications patterns where each node both sends and receives messages. One example is an exchange of data between two processes. Another example is a shift operation across a chain of processes. A safe program that implements such shift will need to use an odd/even ordering of communications, similar to the one used in Example 2.13. When send-receive is used, data flows simultaneously in both directions (logically, at least) and cycles in the communication pattern do not lead to deadlock.

Send-receive can be used in conjunction with the functions described in Chapter 6 to perform shifts on logical topologies. Also, send-receive can be used for implementing remote procedure calls: one blocking send-receive call can be used for sending the input parameters to the callee and receiving back the output parameters.

There is compatibility between send-receive and normal sends and receives. A message sent by a send-receive can be received by a regular receive or probed by a regular probe, and a send-receive can receive a message sent by a regular send.

MPI_SENDRECV(sendbuf, sendcount, sendtype, dest, sendtag, recvbuf, recvcount, recvtype, source, recvtag, comm, status)

IN	sendbuf	initial address of send buffer
IN	sendcount	number of entries to send
IN	sendtype	type of entries in send buffer
IN	dest	rank of destination
IN	sendtag	send tag
OUT	recvbuf	initial address of receive buffer
IN	recvcount	max number of entries to receive
IN	recvtype	type of entries in receive buffer
IN	source	rank of source
IN	recvtag	receive tag
IN	comm	communicator
OUT	status	return status

```
int MPI_Sendrecv(void *sendbuf, int sendcount, MPI_Datatype sendtype,
          int dest, int sendtag, void *recvbuf, int recvcount,
          MPI_Datatype recvtype, int source,
          MPI_Datatype recvtag, MPI_Comm comm, MPI_Status *status)
```

```
MPI_SENDRECV(SENDBUF, SENDCOUNT, SENDTYPE, DEST, SENDTAG, RECVBUF,
          RECVCOUNT, RECVTYPE, SOURCE, RECVTAG, COMM, STATUS,
          IERROR)
    <type> SENDBUF(*), RECVBUF(*)
    INTEGER SENDCOUNT, SENDTYPE, DEST, SENDTAG, RECVCOUNT, RECVTYPE,
    SOURCE, RECV TAG, COMM, STATUS(MPI_STATUS_SIZE), IERROR
```

MPI_SENDRECV executes a blocking send and receive operation. Both the send and receive use the same communicator, but have distinct tag arguments. The send buffer and receive buffers must be disjoint, and may have different lengths and datatypes. The next function handles the case where the buffers are not disjoint.

The semantics of a send-receive operation is what would be obtained if the caller forked two concurrent threads, one to execute the send, and one to execute the receive, followed by a join of these two threads.

MPI_SENDRECV_REPLACE(buf, count, datatype, dest, sendtag, source, recvtag, comm, status)

INOUT	buf	initial address of send and receive buffer
IN	count	number of entries in send and receive buffer
IN	datatype	type of entries in send and receive buffer
IN	dest	rank of destination
IN	sendtag	send message tag
IN	source	rank of source
IN	recvtag	receive message tag
IN	comm	communicator
OUT	status	status object

```
int MPI_Sendrecv_replace(void* buf, int count, MPI_Datatype datatype,
            int dest, int sendtag, int source, int recvtag,
            MPI_Comm comm, MPI_Status *status)
```

```
MPI_SENDRECV_REPLACE(BUF, COUNT, DATATYPE, DEST, SENDTAG, SOURCE,
            RECVTAG, COMM, STATUS, IERROR)
    <type> BUF(*)
    INTEGER COUNT, DATATYPE, DEST, SENDTAG, SOURCE, RECVTAG, COMM,
    STATUS(MPI_STATUS_SIZE), IERROR
```

MPI_SENDRECV_REPLACE executes a blocking send and receive. The same buffer is used both for the send and for the receive, so that the message sent is replaced by the message received.

The example below shows the main loop of the parallel Jacobi code, reimplemented using send-receive.

Example 2.14 Main loop of Jacobi code – version using send-receive.

```
...
! Main loop
DO WHILE(.NOT.converged)
   ! Compute
   DO j=1,m
     DO i=1,n
        B(i,j) = 0.25*(A(i-1,j)+A(i+1,j)+A(i,j-1)+A(i,j+1))
     END DO
   END DO
```

```
DO j=1,m
   DO i=1,n
      A(i,j) = B(i,j)
   END DO
END DO

! Communicate
IF (myrank.GT.0) THEN
   CALL MPI_SENDRECV(B(1,1), n, MPI_REAL, myrank-1, tag,
      A(1,0), n, MPI_REAL, myrank-1, tag, comm, status, ierr)
END IF
IF (myrank.LT.p-1) THEN
   CALL MPI_SENDRECV(B(1,m), n, MPI_REAL, myrank+1, tag,
      A(1,m+1), n, MPI_REAL, myrank+1, tag, comm, status, ierr)
END IF
...
END DO
```
This code is safe, notwithstanding the cyclic communication pattern.

Advice to implementors. Additional, intermediate buffering is needed for the replace variant. Only a fixed amount of buffer space should be used, otherwise send-receive will not be more robust then the equivalent pair of blocking send and receive calls. (*End of advice to implementors.*)

2.7 Null Processes

In many instances, it is convenient to specify a "dummy" source or destination for communication.

In the Jacobi example, this will avoid special handling of boundary processes. This also simplifies handling of boundaries in the case of a non-circular shift, when used in conjunction with the functions described in Chapter 6.

The special value MPI_PROC_NULL can be used instead of a rank wherever a source or a destination argument is required in a communication function. A communication with process MPI_PROC_NULL has no effect. A send to MPI_PROC_NULL succeeds and returns as soon as possible. A receive from MPI_PROC_NULL succeeds and returns as soon as possible with no modifications to the receive buffer. When a receive with source = MPI_PROC_NULL is executed then the status object returns source = MPI_PROC_NULL, tag = MPI_ANY_TAG and count = 0.

We take advantage of null processes to further simplify the parallel Jacobi code.

Example 2.15 Jacobi code – version of parallel code using sendrecv and null processes.

```
...
REAL, ALLOCATABLE A(:,:), B(:,:)
...
! Compute number of processes and myrank
CALL MPI_COMM_SIZE(comm, p, ierr)
CALL MPI_COMM_RANK(comm, myrank, ierr)

! Compute size of local block
m = n/p
IF (myrank.LT.(n-p*m)) THEN
   m = m+1
END IF

! Compute neighbors
IF (myrank.EQ.0) THEN
   left = MPI_PROC_NULL
ELSE
   left = myrank -1
END IF
IF (myrank.EQ.p-1) THEN
   right = MPI_PROC_NULL
ELSE
   right = myrank+1
END IF

! Allocate local arrays
ALLOCATE (A(0:n+1,0:m+1), B(n,m))
...
! Main loop
DO WHILE(.NOT. converged)
   ! Compute
   DO j=1,m
      DO i=1,n
```

```
        B(i,j) = 0.25*(A(i-1,j)+A(i+1,j)+A(i,j-1)+A(i,j+1))
      END DO
   END DO
   DO j=1,m
      DO i=1,n
         A(i,j) = B(i,j)
      END DO
   END DO

   ! Communicate
   CALL MPI_SENDRECV(B(1,1), n, MPI_REAL, left, tag,
            A(1,0), n, MPI_REAL, left, tag, comm, status, ierr)
   CALL  MPI_SENDRECV(B(1,m), n, MPI_REAL, right, tag,
         A(1,m+1), n, MPI_REAL, right, tag, comm, status, ierr)
...
END DO
```

The boundary test that was previously executed inside the loop has been effectively moved outside the loop. Although this is not expected to change performance significantly, the code is simplified.

2.8   Nonblocking Communication

One can improve performance on many systems by overlapping communication and computation. This is especially true on systems where communication can be executed autonomously by an intelligent communication controller. Multi-threading is one mechanism for achieving such overlap. While one thread is blocked, waiting for a communication to complete, another thread may execute on the same processor. This mechanism is efficient if the system supports light-weight threads that are integrated with the communication subsystem. An alternative mechanism that often gives better performance is to use **nonblocking communication**. A nonblocking **post-send** initiates a send operation, but does not complete it. The post-send will return before the message is copied out of the send buffer. A separate **complete-send** call is needed to complete the communication, that is, to verify that the data has been copied out of the send buffer. With suitable hardware, the transfer of data out of the sender memory may proceed concurrently with computations done at the sender after the send was initiated and before it completed. Similarly, a nonblocking **post-receive** initiates a receive operation, but does not complete it.

The call will return before a message is stored into the receive buffer. A separate **complete-receive** is needed to complete the receive operation and verify that the data has been received into the receive buffer.

A nonblocking send can be posted whether a matching receive has been posted or not. The post-send call has local completion semantics: it returns immediately, irrespective of the status of other processes. If the call causes some system resource to be exhausted, then it will fail and return an error code. Quality implementations of MPI should ensure that this happens only in "pathological" cases. That is, an MPI implementation should be able to support a large number of pending nonblocking operations.

The complete-send returns when data has been copied out of the send buffer. The complete-send has non-local completion semantics. The call may return before a matching receive is posted, if the message is buffered. On the other hand, the complete-send may not return until a matching receive is posted.

There is compatibility between blocking and nonblocking communication functions. Nonblocking sends can be matched with blocking receives, and vice-versa.

Advice to users. The use of nonblocking sends allows the sender to proceed ahead of the receiver, so that the computation is more tolerant of fluctuations in the speeds of the two processes.

The MPI message-passing model fits a "push" model, where communication is initiated by the sender. The communication will generally have lower overhead if a receive buffer is already posted when the sender initiates the communication. The use of nonblocking receives allows one to post receives "early" and so achieve lower communication overheads without blocking the receiver while it waits for the send. (*End of advice to users.*)

2.8.1 Request Objects

Nonblocking communications use **request** objects to identify communication operations and link the posting operation with the completion operation. Request objects are allocated by MPI and reside in MPI "system" memory. The request object is opaque in the sense that the type and structure of the object is not visible to users. The application program can only manipulate handles to request objects, not the objects themselves. The system may use the request object to identify various properties of a communication operation, such as the communication buffer that is associated with it, or to store information about the status of the pending communication operation. The user may access request objects through various MPI calls to inquire about the status of pending communication operations.

The special value **MPI_REQUEST_NULL** is used to indicate an invalid request handle. Operations that deallocate request objects set the request handle to this value.

2.8.2 Posting Operations

Calls that post send or receive operations have the same names as the corresponding blocking calls, except that an additional prefix of I (for immediate) indicates that the call is nonblocking.

MPI_ISEND(buf, count, datatype, dest, tag, comm, request)

IN	buf	initial address of send buffer
IN	count	number of entries in send buffer
IN	datatype	datatype of each send buffer entry
IN	dest	rank of destination
IN	tag	message tag
IN	comm	communicator
OUT	request	request handle

```
int MPI_Isend(void* buf, int count, MPI_Datatype datatype, int dest,
              int tag, MPI_Comm comm, MPI_Request *request)
```

```
MPI_ISEND(BUF, COUNT, DATATYPE, DEST, TAG, COMM, REQUEST, IERROR)
    <type> BUF(*)
    INTEGER COUNT, DATATYPE, DEST, TAG, COMM, REQUEST, IERROR
```

MPI_ISEND posts a standard-mode, nonblocking send.

MPI_IRECV (buf, count, datatype, source, tag, comm, request)

OUT	buf	initial address of receive buffer
IN	count	number of entries in receive buffer
IN	datatype	datatype of each receive buffer entry
IN	source	rank of source
IN	tag	message tag
IN	comm	communicator
OUT	request	request handle

```
int MPI_Irecv(void* buf, int count, MPI_Datatype datatype,
              int source, int tag, MPI_Comm comm,
              MPI_Request *request)
```

```
MPI_IRECV(BUF, COUNT, DATATYPE, SOURCE, TAG, COMM, REQUEST, IERROR)
   <type> BUF(*)
   INTEGER COUNT, DATATYPE, SOURCE, TAG, COMM, REQUEST, IERROR
```

MPI_IRECV posts a nonblocking receive.

These calls allocate a request object and return a handle to it in **request**. The request is used to query the status of the communication or wait for its completion.

A nonblocking post-send call indicates that the system may start copying data out of the send buffer. The sender must not access any part of the send buffer (neither for loads nor for stores) after a nonblocking send operation is posted, until the complete-send returns.

A nonblocking post-receive indicates that the system may start writing data into the receive buffer. The receiver must not access any part of the receive buffer after a nonblocking receive operation is posted, until the complete-receive returns.

Rationale. We prohibit read accesses to a send buffer while it is being used, even though the send operation is not supposed to alter the content of this buffer. This may seem more stringent than necessary, but the additional restriction causes little loss of functionality and allows better performance on some systems — consider the case where data transfer is done by a DMA engine that is not cache-coherent with the main processor. (*End of rationale.*)

2.8.3   Completion Operations

The functions MPI_WAIT and MPI_TEST are used to complete nonblocking sends and receives. The completion of a send indicates that the sender is now free to access the send buffer. The completion of a receive indicates that the receive buffer contains the message, the receiver is free to access it, and that the status object is set.

MPI_WAIT(request, status)

INOUT	request	request handle
OUT	status	status object

```
int MPI_Wait(MPI_Request *request, MPI_Status *status)
```

```
MPI_WAIT(REQUEST, STATUS, IERROR)
   INTEGER REQUEST, STATUS(MPI_STATUS_SIZE), IERROR
```

A call to MPI_WAIT returns when the operation identified by **request** is complete. If the system object pointed to by **request** was originally created by a nonblocking send or receive, then the object is deallocated by MPI_WAIT and **request** is set to MPI_REQUEST_NULL. The status object is set to contain information on the completed operation. MPI_WAIT has non-local completion semantics.

MPI_TEST(request, flag, status)

INOUT	request	request handle
OUT	flag	true if operation completed
OUT	status	status object

```
int MPI_Test(MPI_Request *request, int *flag, MPI_Status *status)
```

```
MPI_TEST(REQUEST, FLAG, STATUS, IERROR)
    LOGICAL FLAG
    INTEGER REQUEST, STATUS(MPI_STATUS_SIZE), IERROR
```

A call to MPI_TEST returns flag = true if the operation identified by **request** is complete. In this case, the status object is set to contain information on the completed operation. If the system object pointed to by **request** was originally created by a nonblocking send or receive, then the object is deallocated by MPI_TEST and request is set to MPI_REQUEST_NULL. The call returns flag = false, otherwise. In this case, the value of the status object is undefined. MPI_TEST has local completion semantics.

For both MPI_WAIT and MPI_TEST, information on the completed operation is returned in **status**. The content of the status object for a receive operation is accessed as described in Section 2.2.8. The contents of a status object for a send operation is undefined, except that the query function MPI_TEST_CANCELLED (Section 2.10) can be applied to it.

Advice to users. The use of MPI_TEST allows one to schedule alternative activities within a single thread of execution. (*End of advice to users.*)

Advice to implementors. In a multi-threaded environment, a call to MPI_WAIT should block only the calling thread, allowing another thread to be scheduled for execution. (*End of advice to implementors.*)

Rationale. MPI_WAIT and MPI_TEST are defined so that MPI_TEST returns successfully (with flag = true) exactly in those situation where MPI_WAIT returns.

In those cases, both return the same information in **status**. This allows one to replace a blocking call to MPI_WAIT with a nonblocking call to MPI_TEST with few changes in the program. The same design logic will be followed for the multi-completion operations of Section 2.9. (*End of rationale.*)

2.8.4 Examples

We illustrate the use of nonblocking communication for the same Jacobi computation used in previous examples (Example 2.11–2.15). To achieve maximum overlap between computation and communication, communications should be started as soon as possible and completed as late as possible. That is, sends should be posted as soon as the data to be sent is available; receives should be posted as soon as the receive buffer can be reused; sends should be completed just before the send buffer is to be reused; and receives should be completed just before the data in the receive buffer is to be used. Sometimes, the overlap can be increased by reordering computations.

Example 2.16 Use of nonblocking communications in Jacobi computation.

```
...
REAL, ALLOCATABLE A(:,:), B(:,:)
INTEGER req(4)
INTEGER status(MPI_STATUS_SIZE,4)
...
! Compute number of processes and myrank
CALL MPI_COMM_SIZE(comm, p, ierr)
CALL MPI_COMM_RANK(comm, myrank, ierr)

! Compute size of local block
m = n/p
IF (myrank.LT.(n-p*m)) THEN
   m = m+1
END IF

! Compute neighbors
IF (myrank.EQ.0) THEN
   left = MPI_PROC_NULL
ELSE
   left = myrank -1
END IF
```

```
IF (myrank.EQ.p-1) THEN
   right = MPI_PROC_NULL
ELSE
   right = myrank+1
ENDIF

! Allocate local arrays
ALLOCATE (A(0:n+1,0:m+1), B(n,m))
...
! Main loop
DO WHILE(.NOT.converged)

   ! Compute boundary columns
   DO i=1,n
      B(i,1) = 0.25*(A(i-1,1)+A(i+1,1)+A(i,0)+A(i,2))
      B(i,m) = 0.25*(A(i-1,m)+A(i+1,m)+A(i,m-1)+A(i,m+1))
   END DO

   ! Start communication
   CALL MPI_ISEND(B(1,1), n, MPI_REAL, left, tag, comm, req(1), ierr)
   CALL MPI_ISEND(B(1,m), n, MPI_REAL, right, tag, comm, req(2), ierr)
   CALL MPI_IRECV(A(1,0), n, MPI_REAL, left, tag, comm, req(3), ierr)
   CALL MPI_IRECV(A(1,m+1), n, MPI_REAL, right, tag, comm, req(4), ierr)

   ! Compute interior
   DO j=2,m-1
      DO i=1,n
         B(i,j) = 0.25*(A(i-1,j)+A(i+1,j)+A(i,j-1)+A(i,j+1))
      END DO
   END DO
   DO j=1,m
      DO i=1,n
         A(i,j) = B(i,j)
      END DO
   END DO

   ! Complete communication
   DO i=1,4
```

```
      CALL MPI_WAIT(req(i), status(1,i), ierr)
   END DO
...
END DO
```

The communication calls use the leftmost and rightmost columns of local array
B and set the leftmost and rightmost columns of local array A. The send buffers
are made available early by separating the update of the leftmost and rightmost
columns of B from the update of the interior of B. Since this is also where the
leftmost and rightmost columns of A are used, the communication can be started
immediately after these columns are updated and can be completed just before the
next iteration.

The next example shows a multiple-producer, single-consumer code. The last
process in the group consumes messages sent by the other processes.

Example 2.17 Multiple-producer, single-consumer code using nonblocking communication

```
...
typedef struct {
  char data[MAXSIZE];
  int datasize;
  MPI_Request req;
} Buffer;
Buffer buffer[];
MPI_Status status;
...

MPI_Comm_rank(comm, &rank);
MPI_Comm_size(comm, &size);
if(rank != size-1) {  /* producer code  */
   /* initialization - producer allocates one buffer */
   buffer = (Buffer *)malloc(sizeof(Buffer));
   while(1) {  /* main loop */
      /* producer fills data buffer and returns
         number of bytes stored in buffer */
      produce( buffer->data, &buffer->datasize);
      /* send data */
      MPI_Send(buffer->data, buffer->datasize, MPI_CHAR,
               size-1, tag, comm);
```

```
      }
   }
else { /* rank == size-1; consumer code */
   /* initialization - consumer allocates one buffer
                     per producer */
   buffer = (Buffer *)malloc(sizeof(Buffer)*(size-1));
   for(i=0;  i< size-1; i++)
      /* post a receive from each producer */
      MPI_Irecv(buffer[i].data, MAXSIZE, MPI_CHAR, i, tag,
                                    comm, &(buffer[i].req));

   for(i=0;  ; i=(i+1)%(size-1)) { /* main loop */
      MPI_Wait(&(buffer[i].req), &status);
      /* find number of bytes actually received */
      MPI_Get_count(&status, MPI_CHAR, &(buffer[i].datasize));
      /* consume empties data buffer */
      consume(buffer[i].data, buffer[i].datasize);
      /* post new receive */
      MPI_Irecv(buffer[i].data, MAXSIZE, MPI_CHAR, i, tag,
                comm, &(buffer[i].req));
   }
   }
}
```

Each producer runs an infinite loop where it repeatedly produces one message and sends it. The consumer serves each producer in turn, by receiving its message and consuming it.

The example imposes a strict round-robin discipline, since the consumer receives one message from each producer, in turn. In some cases it is preferable to use a "first-come-first-served" discipline. This is achieved by using MPI_TEST, rather than MPI_WAIT, as shown below. Note that MPI can only offer an approximation to first-come-first-served, since messages do not necessarily arrive in the order they were sent.

Example 2.18 Multiple-producer, single-consumer code, modified to use test calls.
```
...
typedef struct {
  char data[MAXSIZE];
  int datasize;
```

```
   MPI_Request req;
} Buffer;
Buffer buffer[];
MPI_Status status;
...
MPI_Comm_rank(comm, &rank);
MPI_Comm_size(comm, &size);
if(rank != size-1)  {  /* producer code  */
   buffer = (Buffer *)malloc(sizeof(Buffer));
   while(1) {  /* main loop */
      produce( buffer->data, &buffer->datasize);
      MPI_Send(buffer->data, buffer->datasize, MPI_CHAR,
                                    size-1, tag, comm);
   }
}
else { /* rank == size-1; consumer code */
   buffer = (Buffer *)malloc(sizeof(Buffer)*(size-1));
   for(i=0;  i< size-1; i++)
      MPI_Irecv(buffer[i].data, MAXSIZE, MPI_CHAR, i, tag,
                                    comm, &buffer[i].req);
   i = 0;
   while(1) { /* main loop */
      for (flag=0; !flag; i= (i+1)%(size-1))
         /* busy-wait for completed receive */
         MPI_Test(&(buffer[i].req), &flag, &status);
      MPI_Get_count(&status, MPI_CHAR, &buffer[i].datasize);
      consume(buffer[i].data, buffer[i].datasize);
      MPI_Irecv(buffer[i].data, MAXSIZE, MPI_CHAR, i, tag,
                                    comm, &buffer[i].req);
   }
}
```

If there is no message pending from a producer, then the consumer process skips to the next producer. A more efficient implementation that does not require multiple test calls and busy-waiting will be presented in Section 2.9.

2.8.5   Freeing Requests

A request object is deallocated automatically by a successful call to MPI_WAIT or MPI_TEST. In addition, a request object can be explicitly deallocated by using the following operation.

MPI_REQUEST_FREE(request)

    INOUT   **request**   request handle

```
int MPI_Request_free(MPI_Request *request)
```

```
MPI_REQUEST_FREE(REQUEST, IERROR)
    INTEGER REQUEST, IERROR
```

MPI_REQUEST_FREE marks the request object for deallocation and sets **request** to MPI_REQUEST_NULL. An ongoing communication associated with the request will be allowed to complete. The request becomes unavailable after it is deallocated, as the handle is reset to MPI_REQUEST_NULL. However, the request object itself need not be deallocated immediately. If the communication associated with this object is still ongoing, and the object is required for its correct completion, then MPI will not deallocate the object until after its completion.

MPI_REQUEST_FREE cannot be used for cancelling an ongoing communication. For that purpose, one should use MPI_CANCEL, described in Section 2.10. One should use MPI_REQUEST_FREE when the logic of the program is such that a nonblocking communication is known to have terminated and, therefore, a call to MPI_WAIT or MPI_TEST is superfluous. For example, the program could be such that a send command generates a reply from the receiver. If the reply has been successfully received, then the send is known to be complete.

Example 2.19 An example using MPI_REQUEST_FREE.
```
CALL MPI_COMM_RANK(MPI_COMM_WORLD, rank, ierr)
IF(rank.EQ.0) THEN
    DO i=1, n
      CALL MPI_ISEND(outval, 1, MPI_REAL, 1, 0, comm, req, ierr)
      CALL MPI_REQUEST_FREE(req, ierr)
      CALL MPI_IRECV(inval, 1, MPI_REAL, 1, 0, comm, req, ierr)
      CALL MPI_WAIT(req, status, ierr)
    END DO
ELSE IF (rank.EQ.1) THEN
    CALL MPI_IRECV(inval, 1, MPI_REAL, 0, 0, comm, req, ierr)
    CALL MPI_WAIT(req, status, ierr)
    DO i=1, n-1
```

```
      CALL MPI_ISEND(outval, 1, MPI_REAL, 0, 0, comm, req, ierr)
      CALL MPI_REQUEST_FREE(req, ierr)
      CALL MPI_IRECV(inval, 1, MPI_REAL, 0, 0, comm, req, ierr)
      CALL MPI_WAIT(req, status, ierr)
   END DO
   CALL MPI_ISEND(outval, 1, MPI_REAL, 0, 0, comm, req, ierr)
   CALL MPI_WAIT(req, status)
END IF
```

Advice to users. Requests should not be freed explicitly unless the communication is known to complete. Receive requests should never be freed without a call to MPI_WAIT or MPI_TEST, since only such a call can guarantee that a nonblocking receive operation has completed. This is explained in Section 2.8.6. If an error occurs during a communication after the request object has been freed, then an error code cannot be returned to the user (the error code would normally be returned to the MPI_TEST or MPI_WAIT request). Therefore, such an error will be treated by MPI as fatal. (*End of advice to users.*)

2.8.6 Semantics of Nonblocking Communications

The semantics of nonblocking communication is defined by suitably extending the definitions in Section 2.4.

Order Nonblocking communication operations are ordered according to the execution order of the posting calls. The non-overtaking requirement of Section 2.4 is extended to nonblocking communication.

Example 2.20 Message ordering for nonblocking operations.
```
CALL MPI_COMM_RANK(comm, rank, ierr)
IF (rank.EQ.0) THEN
      CALL MPI_ISEND(a, 1, MPI_REAL, 1, 0, comm, r1, ierr)
      CALL MPI_ISEND(b, 1, MPI_REAL, 1, 0, comm, r2, ierr)
ELSE IF (rank.EQ.1) THEN
      CALL MPI_IRECV(a, 1, MPI_REAL, 0, 0, comm, r1, ierr)
      CALL MPI_IRECV(b, 1, MPI_REAL, 0, 0, comm, r2, ierr)
END IF
CALL MPI_WAIT(r2,status)
CALL MPI_WAIT(r1,status)
```

The first send of process zero will match the first receive of process one, even if both messages are sent before process one executes either receive.

The order requirement specifies how post-send calls are matched to post-receive calls. There are no restrictions on the order in which operations complete. Consider the code in Example 2.21.

Example 2.21 Order of completion for nonblocking communications.

```
CALL MPI_COMM_RANK(comm, rank, ierr)
flag1 = .FALSE.
flag2 = .FALSE.
IF (rank.EQ.0) THEN
   CALL MPI_ISEND(a, n, MPI_REAL, 1, 0, comm, r1, ierr)
   CALL MPI_ISEND(b, 1, MPI_REAL, 1, 0, comm, r2, ierr)
   DO WHILE (.NOT.(flag1.AND.flag2))
      IF (.NOT.flag1) CALL MPI_TEST(r1, flag1, s, ierr)
      IF (.NOT.flag2) CALL MPI_TEST(r2, flag2, s, ierr)
   END DO
ELSE IF (rank.EQ.1) THEN
   CALL MPI_IRECV(a, n, MPI_REAL, 0, 0, comm, r1, ierr)
   CALL MPI_IRECV(b, 1, MPI_REAL, 0, 0, comm, r2, ierr)
   DO WHILE (.NOT.(flag1.AND.flag2))
      IF (.NOT.flag1) CALL MPI_TEST(r1, flag1, s, ierr)
      IF (.NOT.flag2) CALL MPI_TEST(r2, flag2, s, ierr)
   END DO
END IF
```

As in Example 2.20, the first send of process zero will match the first receive of process one. However, the second receive may complete ahead of the first receive, and the second send may complete ahead of the first send, especially if the first communication involves more data than the second.

Since the completion of a receive can take an arbitrary amount of time, there is no way to infer that the receive operation completed, short of executing a complete-receive call. On the other hand, the completion of a send operation can be inferred indirectly from the completion of a matching receive.

Progress A communication is *enabled* once a send and a matching receive have been posted by two processes. The progress rule requires that once a communication is enabled, then either the send or the receive will proceed to completion (they might not both complete as the send might be matched by another receive or the receive might be matched by another send). Thus, a call to MPI_WAIT that completes a receive will eventually return if a matching send has been started, unless the send is satisfied by another receive. In particular, if the matching send is nonblocking, then the receive completes even if no complete-send call is made on the sender side.

Similarly, a call to MPI_WAIT that completes a send eventually returns if a matching receive has been started, unless the receive is satisfied by another send, and even if no complete-receive call is made on the receiving side.

Example 2.22 An illustration of progress semantics.
```
CALL MPI_COMM_RANK(comm, rank, ierr)
IF (rank.EQ.0) THEN
      CALL MPI_SEND(a, count, MPI_REAL, 1, 0, comm, ierr)
      CALL MPI_SEND(b, count, MPI_REAL, 1, 1, comm, ierr)
ELSE IF (rank.EQ.1) THEN
      CALL MPI_IRECV(a, count, MPI_REAL, 0, 0, comm, r, ierr)
      CALL MPI_RECV(b, count, MPI_REAL, 0, 1, comm, status, ierr)
      CALL MPI_WAIT(r, status, ierr)
END IF
```

This program is safe and should not deadlock. The first send of process zero must complete after process one posts the matching (nonblocking) receive even if process one has not yet reached the call to MPI_WAIT. Thus, process zero will continue and execute the second send, allowing process one to complete execution.

If a call to MPI_TEST that completes a receive is repeatedly made with the same arguments, and a matching send has been started, then the call will eventually return flag = true, unless the send is satisfied by another receive. If a call to MPI_TEST that completes a send is repeatedly made with the same arguments, and a matching receive has been started, then the call will eventually return flag = true, unless the receive is satisfied by another send.

Fairness The statement made in Section 2.4 concerning fairness applies to nonblocking communications. Namely, MPI does not guarantee fairness.

Buffering and resource limitations The use of nonblocking communication alleviates the need for buffering, since a sending process may progress after it has posted a send. Therefore, the constraints of safe programming can be relaxed. However, some amount of storage is consumed by a pending communication. At a minimum, the communication subsystem needs to copy the parameters of a posted send or receive before the call returns. If this storage is exhausted, then a call that posts a new communication will fail, since post-send or post-receive calls are not allowed to block. A high quality implementation will consume only a fixed amount of storage per posted, nonblocking communication, thus supporting a large number of pending communications. The failure of a parallel program that exceeds the bounds on the number of pending nonblocking communications, like the failure of a sequential program that exceeds the bound on stack size, should be seen as a pathological case, due either to a pathological program or a pathological MPI implementation.

Example 2.23 An illustration of buffering for nonblocking messages.

```
CALL MPI_COMM_RANK(comm, rank, ierr)
IF (rank.EQ.0) THEN
    CALL MPI_ISEND(sendbuf, count, MPI_REAL, 1, tag, comm, req, ierr)
    CALL MPI_RECV(recvbuf, count, MPI_REAL, 1, tag, comm, status, ierr)
    CALL MPI_WAIT(req, status, ierr)
ELSE    ! rank.EQ.1
    CALL MPI_ISEND(sendbuf, count, MPI_REAL, 0, tag, comm, req, ierr)
    CALL MPI_RECV(recvbuf, count, MPI_REAL, 0, tag, comm, status, ierr)
    CALL MPI_WAIT(req, status, ierr)
END IF
```

This program is similar to the program shown in Example 2.9, page 34: two processes exchange messages, by first executing a send, next a receive. However, unlike Example 2.9, a nonblocking send is used. This program is safe, since it is not necessary to buffer any of the messages data.

Example 2.24 Out of order communication with nonblocking messages.

```
CALL MPI_COMM_RANK(comm, rank, ierr)
IF (rank.EQ.0) THEN
    CALL MPI_SEND(sendbuf1, count, MPI_REAL, 1, 1, comm, ierr)
    CALL MPI_SEND(sendbuf2, count, MPI_REAL, 1, 2, comm, ierr)
ELSE    ! rank.EQ.1
    CALL MPI_IRECV(recvbuf2, count, MPI_REAL, 0, 2, comm, req1, ierr)
```

```
    CALL MPI_IRECV(recvbuf1, count, MPI_REAL, 0, 1, comm, req2, ierr)
    CALL MPI_WAIT(req1, status, ierr)
    CALL MPI_WAIT(req2, status, ierr)
END IF
```

In this program process zero sends two messages to process one, while process one receives these two messages in the reverse order. If blocking send and receive operations were used, the program would be unsafe: the first message has to be copied and buffered before the second send can proceed; the first receive can complete only after the second send executes. However, since we used nonblocking receive operations, the program is safe. The MPI implementation will store a small, fixed amount of information about the first receive call before it proceeds to the second receive call. Once the second post-receive call occurred at process one and the first (blocking) send occurred at process zero then the transfer of buffer sendbuf1 is enabled and is guaranteed to complete. At that point, the second send at process zero is started, and is also guaranteed to complete.

The approach illustrated in the last two examples can be used, in general, to transform unsafe programs into safe ones. Assume that the program consists of successive communication phases, where processes exchange data, followed by computation phases. The communication phase should be rewritten as two sub-phases, the first where each process posts all its communication, and the second where the process waits for the completion of all its communications. The order in which the communications are posted is not important, as long as the total number of messages sent or received at any node is moderate. This is further discussed in Section 9.2.

2.8.7 Comments on Semantics of Nonblocking Communications

Advice to users. Typically, a posted send will consume storage both at the sending and at the receiving process. The sending process has to keep track of the posted send, and the receiving process needs the message envelope, so as to be able to match it to posted receives. Thus, storage for pending communications can be exhausted not only when any one node executes a large number of post-send or post-receive calls, but also when any one node is the destination of a large number of messages. In a large system, such a "hot-spot" may occur even if each individual process has only a small number of pending posted sends or receives, if the communication pattern is very unbalanced. (*End of advice to users.*)

Advice to implementors.   In most MPI implementations, sends and receives are matched at the receiving process node. This is because the receive may specify a wildcard source parameter. When a post-send returns, the MPI implementation must guarantee not only that it has stored the parameters of the call, but also that it can forward the envelope of the posted message to the destination. Otherwise, no progress might occur on the posted send, even though a matching receive was posted. This imposes restrictions on implementations strategies for MPI.

Assume, for example, that each pair of communicating processes is connected by one ordered, flow-controlled channel. A naïve MPI implementation may eagerly send down the channel any posted send message; the back pressure from the flow-control mechanism will prevent loss of data and will throttle the sender if the receiver is not ready to receive the incoming data. Unfortunately, with this *short protocol*, a long message sent by a nonblocking send operation may fill the channel, and prevent moving to the receiver any information on subsequently posted sends. This might occur, for example, with the program in Example 2.24, page 63. The data sent by the first send call might clog the channel, and prevent process zero from informing process one that the second send was posted.

The problem can be remedied by using a *long protocol*: when a send is posted, it is only the message envelope that is sent to the receiving process. The receiving process buffers the fixed-size envelope. When a matching receive is posted, it sends back a "ready-to-receive" message to the sender. The sender can now transmit the message data, without clogging the communication channel. The two protocols are illustrated in Figure 2.5.

While safer, this protocol requires two additional transactions, as compared to the simpler, eager protocol. A possible compromise is to use the short protocol for short messages, and the long protocol for long messages. An early-arriving short message is buffered at the destination. The amount of storage consumed per pending communication is still bounded by a (reasonably small) constant and the hand-shaking overhead can be amortized over the transfer of larger amounts of data.

(*End of advice to implementors.*)

Rationale.   When a process runs out of space and cannot handle a new post-send operation, would it not be better to block the sender, rather than declare failure? If one merely blocks the post-send, then it is possible that the messages that clog the communication subsystem will be consumed, allowing the computation to proceed. Thus, blocking would allow more programs to run successfully.

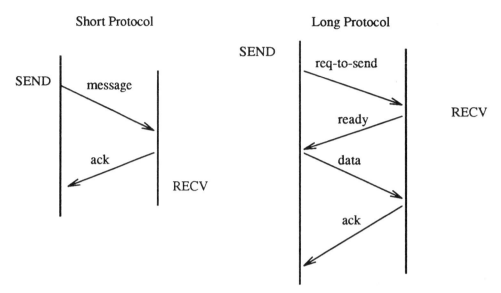

Figure 2.5
Message passing protocols.

The counterargument is that, in a well-designed system, the large majority of programs that exceed the system bounds on the number of pending communications do so because of program errors. Rather then artificially prolonging the life of a program that is doomed to fail, and then have it fail in an obscure deadlock mode, it may be better to cleanly terminate it, and have the programmer correct the program. Also, when programs run close to the system limits, they "thrash" and waste resources, as processes repeatedly block. Finally, the claim of a more lenient behavior should not be used as an excuse for a deficient implementation that cannot support a large number of pending communications.

A different line of argument against the current design is that MPI should not force implementors to use more complex communication protocols, in order to support out-of-order receives with a large number of pending communications. Rather, users should be encouraged to order their communications so that, for each pair of communicating processes, receives are posted in the same order as the matching sends.

This argument is made by implementors, not users. Many users perceive this ordering restriction as too constraining. The design of MPI encourages virtualization of communication, as one process can communicate through several, separate communication spaces. One can expect that users will increasingly take advantage of this feature, especially on multi-threaded systems. A process may support multiple threads, each with its own separate communication domain. The communication subsystem should provide robust multiplexing of these communications, and minimize the chances that one thread is blocked because of communications initiated by another thread, in another communication domain.

Users should be aware that different MPI implementations differ not only in their bandwidth or latency, but also in their ability to support out-of-order delivery of messages. (*End of rationale.*)

2.9 Multiple Completions

It is convenient and efficient to complete in one call a list of multiple pending communication operations, rather than completing only one. MPI_WAITANY or MPI_TESTANY are used to complete one out of several operations. MPI_WAITALL or MPI_TESTALL are used to complete all operations in a list. MPI_WAITSOME or MPI_TESTSOME are used to complete all enabled operations in a list. The behavior of these functions is described in this section and in Section 2.12.

MPI_WAITANY (count, array_of_requests, index, status)

IN	count	list length
INOUT	array_of_requests	array of request handles
OUT	index	index of request handle that completed
OUT	status	status object

```
int MPI_Waitany(int count, MPI_Request *array_of_requests,
            int *index, MPI_Status *status)
```

```
MPI_WAITANY(COUNT, ARRAY_OF_REQUESTS, INDEX, STATUS, IERROR)
    INTEGER COUNT, ARRAY_OF_REQUESTS(*), INDEX,
    STATUS(MPI_STATUS_SIZE), IERROR
```

MPI_WAITANY blocks until one of the communication operations associated with requests in the array has completed. If more then one operation can be completed, MPI_WAITANY arbitrarily picks one and completes it. MPI_WAITANY returns in index the array location of the completed request and returns in status the status of the completed communication. The request object is deallocated and the request handle is set to MPI_REQUEST_NULL. MPI_WAITANY has non-local completion semantics.

MPI_TESTANY(count, array_of_requests, index, flag, status)

IN	count	list length
INOUT	array_of_requests	array of request handles
OUT	index	index of request handle that completed
OUT	flag	true if one has completed
OUT	status	status object

```
int MPI_Testany(int count, MPI_Request *array_of_requests,
          int *index, int *flag, MPI_Status *status)
```

```
MPI_TESTANY(COUNT, ARRAY_OF_REQUESTS, INDEX, FLAG, STATUS, IERROR)
   LOGICAL FLAG
   INTEGER COUNT, ARRAY_OF_REQUESTS(*), INDEX,
   STATUS(MPI_STATUS_SIZE), IERROR
```

MPI_TESTANY tests for completion of the communication operations associated with requests in the array. MPI_TESTANY has local completion semantics.

If an operation has completed, it returns flag = true, returns in index the array location of the completed request, and returns in status the status of the completed communication. The request is deallocated and the handle is set to MPI_REQUEST_NULL.

If no operation has completed, it returns flag = false, returns MPI_UNDEFINED in index and status is undefined.

The execution of MPI_Testany(count, array_of_requests, &index, &flag, &status) has the same effect as the execution of MPI_Test(&array_of_requests[i], &flag, &status), for i=0, 1 ,...., count-1, in some arbitrary order, until one call returns flag = true, or all fail. In the former case, index is set to the last value of i, and in the latter case, it is set to MPI_UNDEFINED.

Example 2.25 Producer-consumer code using waitany.

```
...
typedef struct {
  char data[MAXSIZE];
  int datasize;
} Buffer;
Buffer buffer[];
MPI_Request req[];
MPI_Status status;
...

MPI_Comm_rank(comm, &rank);
MPI_Comm_size(comm, &size);
if(rank != size-1)  {  /* producer code */
   buffer = (Buffer *)malloc(sizeof(Buffer));
   while(1) {  /* main loop */
      produce( buffer->data, &buffer->datasize);
      MPI_Send(buffer->data, buffer->datasize, MPI_CHAR,
                                    size-1, tag, comm);
   }
}
else { /* rank == size-1; consumer code */
   buffer = (Buffer *)malloc(sizeof(Buffer)*(size-1));
   req = (MPI_Request *)malloc(sizeof(MPI_Request)*(size-1));
   for(i=0;  i< size-1; i++)
      MPI_Irecv(buffer[i].data, MAXSIZE, MPI_CHAR, i, tag,
                                          comm, &req[i]);
   while(1) { /* main loop */
      MPI_Waitany(size-1, req, &i, &status);
      MPI_Get_count(&status, MPI_CHAR, &buffer[i].datasize);
      consume(buffer[i].data, buffer[i].datasize);
      MPI_Irecv(buffer[i].data, MAXSIZE, MPI_CHAR, i, tag,
                                          comm, &req[i]);
   }
}
```

This program implements the same producer-consumer protocol as the program in Example 2.18, page 57. The use of MPI_WAIT_ANY avoids the execution of multiple tests to find a communication that completed, resulting in more compact

and more efficient code. However, this code, unlike the code in Example 2.18, does
not prevent starvation of producers.   It is possible that the consumer repeatedly
consumes messages sent from process zero, while ignoring messages sent by the
other processes. Example 2.27 below shows how to implement a fair server, using
MPI_WAITSOME.

MPI_WAITALL(count, array_of_requests, array_of_statuses)

IN	count	list length
INOUT	array_of_requests	array of request handles
OUT	array_of_statuses	array of status objects

```
int MPI_Waitall(int count, MPI_Request *array_of_requests,
        MPI_Status *array_of_statuses)
```

```
MPI_WAITALL(COUNT, ARRAY_OF_REQUESTS, ARRAY_OF_STATUSES, IERROR)
    INTEGER COUNT, ARRAY_OF_REQUESTS(*)
    INTEGER ARRAY_OF_STATUSES(MPI_STATUS_SIZE,*), IERROR
```

MPI_WAITALL blocks until all communications, associated with requests in the
array, complete. The i-th entry in array_of_statuses is set to the return status of the
i-th operation. All request objects are deallocated and the corresponding handles in
the array are set to MPI_REQUEST_NULL. MPI_WAITALL has non-local completion
semantics.

The execution of MPI_Waitall(count, array_of_requests, array_of_statuses) has the
same effect as the execution of MPI_Wait(&array_of_requests[i],&array_of_statuses[i]),
for i=0 ,..., count-1, in some arbitrary order.

When one or more of the communications completed by a call to MPI_WAITALL
fail, MPI_WAITALL will return the error code MPI_ERR_IN_STATUS and will set the
error field of each status to a specific error code. This code will be MPI_SUCCESS,
if the specific communication completed; it will be another specific error code,
if it failed; or it will be MPI_PENDING if it has not failed nor completed. The
function MPI_WAITALL will return MPI_SUCCESS if it completed successfully, or will
return another error code if it failed for other reasons (such as invalid arguments).
MPI_WAITALL updates the error fields of the status objects only when it returns
MPI_ERR_IN_STATUS.

Rationale.   This design streamlines error handling in the application. The application code need only test the (single) function result to determine if an error has

occurred. It needs to check individual statuses only when an error occurred. (*End of rationale.*)

MPI_TESTALL(count, array_of_requests, flag, array_of_statuses)

IN	count	list length
INOUT	array_of_requests	array of request handles
OUT	flag	true if all have completed
OUT	array_of_statuses	array of status objects

```
int MPI_Testall(int count, MPI_Request *array_of_requests, int *flag,
          MPI_Status *array_of_statuses)
```

```
MPI_TESTALL(COUNT, ARRAY_OF_REQUESTS, FLAG, ARRAY_OF_STATUSES,
          IERROR)
    LOGICAL FLAG
    INTEGER COUNT, ARRAY_OF_REQUESTS(*),
    ARRAY_OF_STATUSES(MPI_STATUS_SIZE,*), IERROR
```

MPI_TESTALL tests for completion of all communications associated with requests in the array. MPI_TESTALL has local completion semantics.

If all operations have completed, it returns flag = true, sets the corresponding entries in status, deallocates all requests and sets all request handles to MPI_REQUEST_NULL.

If all operations have not completed, flag = false is returned, no request is modified and the values of the status entries are undefined.

Errors that occurred during the execution of MPI_TEST_ALL are handled in the same way as errors in MPI_WAIT_ALL.

Example 2.26 Main loop of Jacobi computation using waitall.

```
...
! Main loop
DO WHILE(.NOT. converged)
   ! Compute boundary columns
   DO i=1,n
      B(i,1) = 0.25*(A(i-1,1)+A(i+1,1)+A(i,0)+A(i,2))
      B(i,m) = 0.25*(A(i-1,m)+A(i+1,m)+A(i,m-1)+A(i,m+1))
   END DO
```

```
! Start communication
CALL MPI_ISEND(B(1,1), n, MPI_REAL, left, tag, comm, req(1), ierr)
CALL MPI_ISEND(B(1,m), n, MPI_REAL, right, tag, comm, req(2), ierr)
CALL MPI_IRECV(A(1,0), n, MPI_REAL, left, tag, comm, req(3), ierr)
CALL MPI_IRECV(A(1,m+1), n, MPI_REAL, right, tag, comm, req(4), ierr)

! Compute interior
DO j=2,m-1
   DO i=1,n
      B(i,j) = 0.25*(A(i-1,j)+A(i+1,j)+A(i,j-1)+A(i,j+1))
   END DO
END DO
DO j=1,m
   DO i=1,n
      A(i,j) = B(i,j)
   END DO
END DO

! Complete communication
CALL MPI_WAITALL(4, req, status, ierr)
...
```

This code solves the same problem as the code in Example 2.16, page 54. We replaced four calls to MPI_WAIT by one call to MPI_WAITALL. This saves function calls and context switches.

MPI_WAITSOME(incount, array_of_requests, outcount, array_of_indices, array_of_statuses)

IN	incount	length of array_of_requests
INOUT	array_of_requests	array of request handles
OUT	outcount	number of completed requests
OUT	array_of_indices	array of indices of completed operations
OUT	array_of_statuses	array of status objects for completed operations

```
int MPI_Waitsome(int incount, MPI_Request *array_of_requests,
          int *outcount, int *array_of_indices,
          MPI_Status *array_of_statuses)
```

```
MPI_WAITSOME(INCOUNT, ARRAY_OF_REQUESTS, OUTCOUNT, ARRAY_OF_INDICES,
          ARRAY_OF_STATUSES, IERROR)
    INTEGER INCOUNT, ARRAY_OF_REQUESTS(*), OUTCOUNT,
    ARRAY_OF_INDICES(*), ARRAY_OF_STATUSES(MPI_STATUS_SIZE,*), IERROR
```

MPI_WAITSOME waits until at least one of the communications, associated with requests in the array, completes. MPI_WAITSOME returns in outcount the number of completed requests. The first outcount locations of the array array_of_indices are set to the indices of these operations. The first outcount locations of the array array_of_statuses are set to the status for these completed operations. Each request that completed is deallocated, and the associated handle is set to MPI_REQUEST_NULL. MPI_WAITSOME has non-local completion semantics.

If one or more of the communications completed by MPI_WAITSOME fail then the arguments outcount, array_of_indices and array_of_statuses will be adjusted to indicate completion of all communications that have succeeded or failed. The call will return the error code MPI_ERR_IN_STATUS and the error field of each status returned will be set to indicate success or to indicate the specific error that occurred. The call will return MPI_SUCCESS if it succeeded, and will return another error code if it failed for for other reasons (such as invalid arguments). MPI_WAITSOME updates the status fields of the request objects only when it returns MPI_ERR_IN_STATUS.

MPI_TESTSOME(incount, array_of_requests, outcount, array_of_indices, array_of_statuses)

IN	incount	length of array_of_requests
INOUT	array_of_requests	array of request handles
OUT	outcount	number of completed requests
OUT	array_of_indices	array of indices of completed operations
OUT	array_of_statuses	array of status objects for completed operations

```
int MPI_Testsome(int incount, MPI_Request *array_of_requests,
          int *outcount, int *array_of_indices,
          MPI_Status *array_of_statuses)
```

```
MPI_TESTSOME(INCOUNT, ARRAY_OF_REQUESTS, OUTCOUNT, ARRAY_OF_INDICES,
          ARRAY_OF_STATUSES, IERROR)
    INTEGER INCOUNT, ARRAY_OF_REQUESTS(*), OUTCOUNT,
    ARRAY_OF_INDICES(*), ARRAY_OF_STATUSES(MPI_STATUS_SIZE,*), IERROR
```

MPI_TESTSOME behaves like MPI_WAITSOME, except that it returns immediately. If no operation has completed it returns outcount = 0. MPI_TESTSOME has local completion semantics.

Errors that occur during the execution of MPI_TESTSOME are handled as for MPI_WAIT_SOME.

Both MPI_WAITSOME and MPI_TESTSOME fulfill a fairness requirement: if a request for a receive repeatedly appears in a list of requests passed to MPI_WAITSOME or MPI_TESTSOME, and a matching send has been posted, then the receive will eventually complete, unless the send is satisfied by another receive. A similar fairness requirement holds for send requests.

Example 2.27 A client-server code where starvation is prevented.

```
...
typedef struct {
  char data[MAXSIZE];
  int datasize;
} Buffer;
Buffer buffer[];
MPI_Request req[];
MPI_Status status[];
int index[];
...

MPI_Comm_rank(comm, &rank);
MPI_Comm_size(comm, &size);
if(rank != size-1) {  /* producer code */
   buffer = (Buffer *)malloc(sizeof(Buffer));
   while(1) {  /* main loop */
      produce( buffer->data, &buffer->datasize);
      MPI_Send(buffer->data, buffer->datasize, MPI_CHAR,
                                    size-1, tag, comm);
      }
   }
else { /* rank == size-1; consumer code */
   buffer = (Buffer *)malloc(sizeof(Buffer)*(size-1));
   req = (MPI_Request *)malloc(sizeof(MPI_Request)*(size-1));
   status = (MPI_Status *)malloc(sizeof(MPI_Status)*(size-1));
   index = (int *)malloc(sizeof(int)*(size-1));
```

```
for(i=0;  i< size-1; i++)
   MPI_Irecv(buffer[i].data, MAXSIZE, MPI_CHAR, i, tag,
                                       comm, &req[i]);
while(1) { /* main loop */
   MPI_Waitsome(size-1, req, &count, index, status);
   for(i=0; i < count; i++) {
      j = index[i];
      MPI_Get_count(&status[i], MPI_CHAR, &(buffer[j].datasize));
      consume(buffer[j].data, buffer[j].datasize);
      MPI_Irecv(buffer[j].data, MAXSIZE, MPI_CHAR, j, tag,
                                       comm, &req[j]);
   }
}
}
```

This code solves the starvation problem of the code in Example 2.25, page 69. We replaced the consumer call to MPI_WAITANY by a call to MPI_WAITSOME. This achieves two goals. The number of communication calls is reduced, since one call now can complete multiple communications. Secondly, the consumer will not starve any of the consumers, since it will receive any posted send.

Advice to implementors. MPI_WAITSOME and MPI_TESTSOME should complete as many pending communications as possible. It is expected that both will complete all receive operations for which information on matching sends has reached the receiver node. This will ensure that they satisfy their fairness requirement. (*End of advice to implementors.*)

2.10   Probe and Cancel

MPI_PROBE and MPI_IPROBE allow polling of incoming messages without actually receiving them. The application can then decide how to receive them, based on the information returned by the probe (in a status variable). For example, the application might allocate memory for the receive buffer according to the length of the probed message.

MPI_CANCEL allows pending communications to be canceled. This is required for cleanup in some situations. Suppose an application has posted nonblocking sends or receives and then determines that these operations will not complete. Posting a send or a receive ties up application resources (send or receive buffers), and a cancel allows these resources to be freed.

MPI_IPROBE(source, tag, comm, flag, status)

IN	source	rank of source
IN	tag	message tag
IN	comm	communicator
OUT	flag	true if there is a message
OUT	status	status object

```
int MPI_Iprobe(int source, int tag, MPI_Comm comm, int *flag,
          MPI_Status *status)
```

```
MPI_IPROBE(SOURCE, TAG, COMM, FLAG, STATUS, IERROR)
    LOGICAL FLAG
    INTEGER SOURCE, TAG, COMM, STATUS(MPI_STATUS_SIZE), IERROR
```

MPI_IPROBE is a nonblocking operation that returns flag = true if there is a message that can be received and that matches the message envelope specified by source, tag, and comm. The call matches the same message that would have been received by a call to MPI_RECV (with these arguments) executed at the same point in the program, and returns in status the same value. Otherwise, the call returns flag = false, and leaves status undefined. MPI_IPROBE has local completion semantics.

If MPI_IPROBE(source, tag, comm, flag, status) returns flag = true, then the first, subsequent receive executed with the communicator comm, and with the source and tag returned in status, will receive the message that was matched by the probe.

The argument source can be MPI_ANY_SOURCE, and tag can be MPI_ANY_TAG, so that one can probe for messages from an arbitrary source and/or with an arbitrary tag. However, a specific communicator must be provided in comm.

It is not necessary to receive a message immediately after it has been probed for, and the same message may be probed for several times before it is received.

MPI_PROBE(source, tag, comm, status)

IN	source	rank of source
IN	tag	message tag
IN	comm	communicator
OUT	status	status object

```
int MPI_Probe(int source, int tag, MPI_Comm comm, MPI_Status *status)
```

```
MPI_PROBE(SOURCE, TAG, COMM, STATUS, IERROR)
    INTEGER SOURCE, TAG, COMM, STATUS(MPI_STATUS_SIZE), IERROR
```

MPI_PROBE behaves like MPI_IPROBE except that it blocks and returns only after a matching message has been found. MPI_PROBE has non-local completion semantics.

The semantics of MPI_PROBE and MPI_IPROBE guarantee progress, in the same way as a corresponding receive executed at the same point in the program. If a call to MPI_PROBE has been issued by a process, and a send that matches the probe has been initiated by some process, then the call to MPI_PROBE will return, unless the message is received by another, concurrent receive operation, irrespective of other activities in the system. Similarly, if a process busy waits with MPI_IPROBE and a matching message has been issued, then the call to MPI_IPROBE will eventually return flag = true unless the message is received by another concurrent receive operation, irrespective of other activities in the system.

Example 2.28 Use a blocking probe to wait for an incoming message.

```
        CALL MPI_COMM_RANK(comm, rank, ierr)
        IF (rank.EQ.0) THEN
            CALL MPI_SEND(i, 1, MPI_INTEGER, 2, 0, comm, ierr)
        ELSE IF (rank.EQ.1) THEN
            CALL MPI_SEND(x, 1, MPI_REAL, 2, 0, comm, ierr)
        ELSE IF (rank.EQ.2) THEN
            DO i=1, 2
              CALL MPI_PROBE(MPI_ANY_SOURCE, 0,
                             comm, status, ierr)
              IF (status(MPI_SOURCE) = 0) THEN
100               CALL MPI_RECV(i, 1, MPI_INTEGER, 0, 0, comm,
    $                 .      status, ierr)
              ELSE
200               CALL MPI_RECV(x, 1, MPI_REAL, 1, 0, comm,
    $                     status, ierr)
              END IF
            END DO
        END IF
```

Each message is received with the right type.

Example 2.29 A similar program to the previous example, but with a problem.

```
      CALL MPI_COMM_RANK(comm, rank, ierr)
      IF (rank.EQ.0) THEN
          CALL MPI_SEND(i, 1, MPI_INTEGER, 2, 0, comm, ierr)
      ELSE IF (rank.EQ.1) THEN
          CALL MPI_SEND(x, 1, MPI_REAL, 2, 0, comm, ierr)
      ELSE IF (rank.EQ.2) THEN
        DO i=1, 2
          CALL MPI_PROBE(MPI_ANY_SOURCE, 0,
                            comm, status, ierr)
          IF (status(MPI_SOURCE) = 0) THEN
100           CALL MPI_RECV(i, 1, MPI_INTEGER, MPI_ANY_SOURCE,
                            0, comm, status, ierr)
          ELSE
200           CALL MPI_RECV(x, 1, MPI_REAL, MPI_ANY_SOURCE,
                            0, comm, status, ierr)
          END IF
        END DO
      END IF
```

We slightly modified example 2.28, using MPI_ANY_SOURCE as the source argument in the two receive calls in statements labeled 100 and 200. The program now has different behavior: the receive operation may receive a message that is distinct from the message probed.

Advice to implementors.   A call to MPI_PROBE(source, tag, comm, status) will match the message that would have been received by a call to MPI_RECV(..., source, tag, comm, status) executed at the same point. Suppose that this message has source s, tag t and communicator c. If the tag argument in the probe call has value MPI_ANY_TAG then the message probed will be the earliest pending message from source s with communicator c and any tag; in any case, the message probed will be the earliest pending message from source s with tag t and communicator c (this is the message that would have been received, so as to preserve message order). This message continues as the earliest pending message from source s with tag t and communicator c, until it is received. The first receive operation subsequent to the probe that uses the same communicator as the probe and uses the tag and source values returned by the probe, must receive this message. (*End of advice to implementors.*)

MPI_CANCEL(request)

    IN   **request**   request handle

```
int MPI_Cancel(MPI_Request *request)
```

```
MPI_CANCEL(REQUEST, IERROR)
    INTEGER REQUEST, IERROR
```

MPI_CANCEL marks for cancelation a pending, nonblocking communication operation (send or receive). MPI_CANCEL has local completion semantics. It returns immediately, possibly before the communication is actually canceled. After this, it is still necessary to complete a communication that has been marked for cancelation, using a call to MPI_REQUEST_FREE, MPI_WAIT, MPI_TEST or one of the functions in Section 2.9. If the communication was not cancelled (that is, if the communication happened to start before the cancelation could take effect), then the completion call will complete the communication, as usual. If the communication was successfully cancelled, then the completion call will deallocate the request object and will return in status the information that the communication was canceled. The application should then call MPI_TEST_CANCELLED, using status as input, to test whether the communication was actually canceled.

Either the cancelation succeeds, and no communication occurs, or the communication completes, and the cancelation fails. If a send is marked for cancelation, then it must be the case that either the send completes normally, and the message sent is received at the destination process, or that the send is successfully canceled, and no part of the message is received at the destination. If a receive is marked for cancelation, then it must be the case that either the receive completes normally, or that the receive is successfully canceled, and no part of the receive buffer is altered.

If a communication is marked for cancelation, then a completion call for that communication is guaranteed to return, irrespective of the activities of other processes. In this case, MPI_WAIT behaves as a local function. Similarly, if MPI_TEST is repeatedly called in a busy wait loop for a canceled communication, then MPI_TEST will eventually succeed.

MPI_TEST_CANCELLED(status, flag)

IN	status	status object
OUT	flag	true if canceled

```
int MPI_Test_cancelled(MPI_Status *status, int *flag)
```

```
MPI_TEST_CANCELLED(STATUS, FLAG, IERROR)
   LOGICAL FLAG
   INTEGER STATUS(MPI_STATUS_SIZE), IERROR
```

MPI_TEST_CANCELLED is used to test whether the communication operation was actually canceled by MPI_CANCEL. It returns flag = true if the communication associated with the status object was canceled successfully. In this case, all other fields of status are undefined. It returns flag = false, otherwise.

Example 2.30 Code using MPI_CANCEL
```
MPI_Comm_rank(comm, &rank);
if (rank == 0)
   MPI_Send(a, 1, MPI_CHAR, 1, tag, comm);
else if (rank==1) {
   MPI_Irecv(a, 1, MPI_CHAR, 0, tag, comm, &req);
   MPI_Cancel(&req);
   MPI_Wait(&req, &status);
   MPI_Test_cancelled(&status, &flag);
   if (flag) /* cancel succeeded -- need to post new receive */
      MPI_Recv(a, 1, MPI_CHAR, 0, tag, comm, &req);
   }
```

Advice to users. MPI_CANCEL can be an expensive operation that should be used only exceptionally. (*End of advice to users.*)

Advice to implementors. A communication operation cannot be cancelled once the receive buffer has been partly overwritten. In this situation, the communication should be allowed to complete. In general, a communication may be allowed to complete, if send and receive have already been matched. The implementation should take care of the possible race between cancelation and matching.

The cancelation of a send operation will internally require communication with the intended receiver, if information on the send operation has already been forwarded to the destination. Note that, while communication may be needed to implement

MPI_CANCEL, this is still a local operation, since its completion does not depend on the application code executed by other processes. (*End of advice to implementors.*)

2.11   Persistent Communication Requests

Often a communication with the same argument list is repeatedly executed within the inner loop of a parallel computation. In such a situation, it may be possible to optimize the communication by binding the list of communication arguments to a **persistent** communication request once and then, repeatedly, using the request to initiate and complete messages. A persistent request can be thought of as a communication port or a "half-channel." It does not provide the full functionality of a conventional channel, since there is no binding of the send port to the receive port. This construct allows reduction of the overhead for communication between the process and communication controller, but not of the overhead for communication between one communication controller and another.

It is not necessary that messages sent with a persistent request be received by a receive operation using a persistent request, or vice-versa. Persistent communication requests are associated with nonblocking send and receive operations.

A persistent communication request is created using the following functions. They involve no communication and thus have local completion semantics.

MPI_SEND_INIT(buf, count, datatype, dest, tag, comm, request)

IN	buf	initial address of send buffer
IN	count	number of entries to send
IN	datatype	datatype of each entry
IN	dest	rank of destination
IN	tag	message tag
IN	comm	communicator
OUT	request	request handle

```
int MPI_Send_init(void* buf, int count, MPI_Datatype datatype,
            int dest, int tag, MPI_Comm comm, MPI_Request *request)
```

```
MPI_SEND_INIT(BUF, COUNT, DATATYPE, DEST, TAG, COMM, REQUEST, IERROR)
    <type> BUF(*)
    INTEGER REQUEST, COUNT, DATATYPE, DEST, TAG, COMM, REQUEST,
    IERROR
```

MPI_SEND_INIT creates a persistent communication request for a standard-mode, nonblocking send operation, and binds to it all the arguments of a send operation.

MPI_RECV_INIT(buf, count, datatype, source, tag, comm, request)

OUT	buf	initial address of receive buffer
IN	count	max number of entries to receive
IN	datatype	datatype of each entry
IN	source	rank of source
IN	tag	message tag
IN	comm	communicator
OUT	request	request handle

```
int MPI_Recv_init(void* buf, int count, MPI_Datatype datatype,
          int source, int tag, MPI_Comm comm,
          MPI_Request *request)
```

```
MPI_RECV_INIT(BUF, COUNT, DATATYPE, SOURCE, TAG, COMM, REQUEST,
          IERROR)
    <type> BUF(*)
    INTEGER COUNT, DATATYPE, SOURCE, TAG, COMM, REQUEST, IERROR
```

MPI_RECV_INIT creates a persistent communication request for a nonblocking receive operation. The argument buf is marked as OUT because the application gives permission to write on the receive buffer.

Persistent communication requests are created by the preceding functions, but they are, so far, inactive. They are activated, and the associated communication operations started, by MPI_START or MPI_STARTALL.

MPI_START(request)

INOUT	request	request handle

```
int MPI_Start(MPI_Request *request)
```

```
MPI_START(REQUEST, IERROR)
    INTEGER REQUEST, IERROR
```

MPI_START activates request and initiates the associated communication. Since all persistent requests are associated with nonblocking communications, MPI_START has local completion semantics. The semantics of communications done with persistent requests are identical to the corresponding operations without persistent requests. That is, a call to MPI_START with a request created by MPI_SEND_INIT starts a communication in the same manner as a call to MPI_ISEND; a call to MPI_START with a request created by MPI_RECV_INIT starts a communication in the same manner as a call to MPI_IRECV.

A send operation initiated with MPI_START can be matched with any receive operation (including MPI_PROBE) and a receive operation initiated with MPI_START can receive messages generated by any send operation.

MPI_STARTALL(count, array_of_requests)

| IN | count | list length |
| INOUT | array_of_requests | array of request handles |

```
int MPI_Startall(int count, MPI_Request *array_of_requests)
```

```
MPI_STARTALL(COUNT, ARRAY_OF_REQUESTS, IERROR)
    INTEGER COUNT, ARRAY_OF_REQUESTS(*), IERROR
```

MPI_STARTALL starts all communications associated with persistent requests in array_of_requests. A call to MPI_STARTALL(count, array_of_requests) has the same effect as calls to MPI_START(array_of_requests[i]), executed for i=0 ,..., count-1, in some arbitrary order.

A communication started with a call to MPI_START or MPI_STARTALL is completed by a call to MPI_WAIT, MPI_TEST, or one of the other completion functions described in Section 2.9. The persistent request becomes inactive after the completion of such a call, but it is not deallocated and it can be re-activated by another MPI_START or MPI_STARTALL.

Persistent requests are explicitly deallocated by a call to MPI_REQUEST_FREE (Section 2.8.5). The call to MPI_REQUEST_FREE can occur at any point in the program after the persistent request was created. However, the request will be deallocated only after it becomes inactive. Active receive requests should not be freed. Otherwise, it will not be possible to check that the receive has completed. It is preferable to free requests when they are inactive. If this rule is followed, then the functions described in this section will be invoked in a sequence of the form,

Create (Start Complete)* Free ,

where * indicates zero or more repetitions. If the same communication request is used in several concurrent threads, it is the user's responsibility to coordinate calls so that the correct sequence is obeyed.

MPI_CANCEL can be used to cancel a communication that uses a persistent request, in the same way it is used for nonpersistent requests. A successful cancelation cancels the active communication, but does not deallocate the request. After the call to MPI_CANCEL and the subsequent call to MPI_WAIT or MPI_TEST (or other completion function), the request becomes inactive and can be activated for a new communication.

Example 2.31 Jacobi computation, using persistent requests.

```
...
REAL, ALLOCATABLE A(:,:), B(:,:)
INTEGER req(4)
INTEGER status(MPI_STATUS_SIZE,4)
...
! Compute number of processes and myrank
CALL MPI_COMM_SIZE(comm, p, ierr)
CALL MPI_COMM_RANK(comm, myrank, ierr)

! Compute size of local block
m = n/p
IF (myrank.LT.(n-p*m)) THEN
   m = m+1
END IF

! Compute neighbors
IF (myrank.EQ.0) THEN
   left = MPI_PROC_NULL
ELSE
   left = myrank -1
END IF
IF (myrank.EQ.p-1) THEN
   right = MPI_PROC_NULL
ELSE
   right = myrank+1
ENDIF

! Allocate local arrays
```

```fortran
ALLOCATE (A(n,0:m+1), B(n,m))
...
! Create persistent requests
CALL MPI_SEND_INIT(B(1,1), n, MPI_REAL, left, tag, comm, req(1), ierr)
CALL MPI_SEND_INIT(B(1,m), n, MPI_REAL, right, tag, comm, req(2), ierr)
CALL MPI_RECV_INIT(A(1,0), n, MPI_REAL, left, tag, comm, req(3), ierr)
CALL MPI_RECV_INIT(A(1,m+1), n, MPI_REAL, right, tag, comm, req(4), ierr)
....

! Main loop
DO WHILE(.NOT.converged)

   ! Compute boundary columns
   DO i=1,n
      B(i,1) = 0.25*(A(i-1,1)+A(i+1,1)+A(i,0)+A(i,2))
      B(i,m) = 0.25*(A(i-1,m)+A(i+1,m)+A(i,m-1)+A(i,m+1))
   END DO

   ! Start communication
   CALL MPI_STARTALL(4, req, ierr)

   ! Compute interior
   DO j=2,m-1
      DO i=1,n
         B(i,j) = 0.25*(A(i-1,j)+A(i+1,j)+A(i,j-1)+A(i,j+1))
      END DO
   END DO
   DO j=1,m
      DO i=1,n
         A(i,j) = B(i,j)
      END DO
   END DO

   ! Complete communication
      CALL MPI_WAITALL(4, req, status, ierr)
   ...
END DO
```

We come back (for a last time!) to our Jacobi example (Example 2.12, page 41).

The communication calls in the main loop are reduced to two: one to start all four communications and one to complete all four communications.

2.12   Communication-Complete Calls with Null Request Handles

Normally, an invalid handle to an MPI object is not a valid argument for a call that expects an object. There is one exception to this rule: communication-complete calls can be passed request handles with value MPI_REQUEST_NULL. A communication complete call with such an argument is a "no-op": the null handles are ignored. The same rule applies to persistent handles that are not associated with an active communication operation.

We shall use the following terminology. A **null** request handle is a handle with value MPI_REQUEST_NULL. A handle to a persistent request is **inactive** if the request is not currently associated with an ongoing communication. A handle is **active**, if it is neither null nor inactive. An **empty** status is a status that is set to tag = MPI_ANY_TAG, source = MPI_ANY_SOURCE, and is also internally configured so that calls to MPI_GET_COUNT and MPI_GET_ELEMENT return count = 0. We set a status variable to empty in cases when the value returned is not significant. Status is set this way to prevent errors due to access of stale information.

A call to MPI_WAIT with a null or inactive request argument returns immediately with an empty status.

A call to MPI_TEST with a null or inactive request argument returns immediately with flag = true and an empty status.

The list of requests passed to MPI_WAITANY may contain null or inactive requests. If some of the requests are active, then the call returns when an active request has completed. If all the requests in the list are null or inactive then the call returns immediately, with index = MPI_UNDEFINED and an empty status.

The list of requests passed to MPI_TESTANY may contain null or inactive requests. The call returns flag = false if there are active requests in the list, and none have completed. It returns flag = true if an active request has completed, or if all the requests in the list are null or inactive. In the later case, it returns index = MPI_UNDEFINED and an empty status.

The list of requests passed to MPI_WAITALL may contain null or inactive requests. The call returns as soon as all active requests have completed. The call sets to empty each status associated with a null or inactive request.

The list of requests passed to MPI_TESTALL may contain null or inactive requests. The call returns flag = true if all active requests have completed. In this case, the call sets to empty each status associated with a null or inactive request. Otherwise, the call returns flag = false.

The list of requests passed to MPI_WAITSOME may contain null or inactive requests. If the list contains active requests, then the call returns when some of the active requests have completed. If all requests were null or inactive, then the call returns immediately, with outcount = MPI_UNDEFINED.

The list of requests passed to MPI_TESTSOME may contain null or inactive requests. If the list contains active requests and some have completed, then the call returns in outcount the number of completed request. If it contains active requests, and none have completed, then it returns outcount = 0. If the list contains no active requests, then it returns outcount = MPI_UNDEFINED.

In all these cases, null or inactive request handles are not modified by the call.

Example 2.32 Starvation-free producer-consumer code

```
...
typedef struct {
  char data[MAXSIZE];
  int datasize;
} Buffer;
Buffer buffer[];
MPI_Request req[];
MPI_Status status;
...

MPI_Comm_rank(comm, &rank);
MPI_Comm_size(comm, &size);
if(rank != size-1) {   /* producer code  */
   buffer = (Buffer *)malloc(sizeof(Buffer));
   while(1) {  /* main loop */
      produce( buffer->data, &buffer->datasize);
      MPI_Send(buffer->data, buffer->datasize, MPI_CHAR,
               size-1, tag, comm, &status);
   }
}
else { /* rank == size-1; consumer code */
   buffer = (Buffer *)malloc(sizeof(Buffer)*(size-1));
   req = (MPI_Request *)malloc(sizeof(MPI_Request)*(size-1));
   for (i=0; i<size-1; i++)
```

```
    req[i] = MPI_REQUEST_NULL;
while (1) { /* main loop */
   MPI_Waitany(size-1, req, &i, &status);
   if (i == MPI_UNDEFINED) { /* no pending receive left */
      for(j=0;   j< size-1; j++)
         MPI_Irecv(buffer[j].data, MAXSIZE, MPI_CHAR, j, tag,
                   comm, &req[j]);
   else {
      MPI_Get_count(&status, MPI_CHAR, &buffer[i].datasize);
      consume(buffer[i].data, buffer[i].datasize);
      }
   }
}
```

This is our last remake of the producer-consumer code from Example 2.17, page 56. As in Example 2.17, the computation proceeds in phases, where at each phase the consumer consumes one message from each producer. Unlike Example 2.17, messages need not be consumed in order within each phase but, rather, can be consumed as soon as arrived.

Rationale. The acceptance of null or inactive requests in communication-complete calls facilitate the use of multiple completion calls (Section 2.9). As in the example above, the user need not delete each request from the list as soon as it has completed, but can reuse the same list until all requests in the list have completed. Checking for null or inactive requests is not expected to add a significant overhead, since quality implementations will check parameters, anyhow. However, most implementations will suffer some performance loss if they often traverse mostly empty request lists, looking for active requests.

The behavior of the multiple completion calls was defined with the following structure.

- Test returns with flag = true whenever Wait would return; both calls return same information in this case.

- A call to Wait, Waitany, Waitsome or Waitall will return if all requests in the list are null or inactive, thus avoiding deadlock.

- The information returned by a Test, Testany, Testsome or Testall call distinguishes between the case "no operation completed" and the case "there is no operation to complete."

(*End of rationale.*)

2.13   Communication Modes

The send call described in Section 2.2.1 used the **standard** communication mode. In this mode, it is up to MPI to decide whether outgoing messages will be buffered. MPI may buffer outgoing messages. In such a case, the send call may complete before a matching receive is invoked. On the other hand, buffer space may be unavailable, or MPI may choose not to buffer outgoing messages, for performance reasons. In this case, the send call will not complete until a matching receive has been posted, and the data has been moved to the receiver. (A blocking send completes when the call returns; a nonblocking send completes when the matching Wait or Test call returns successfully.)

Thus, a send in standard mode can be started whether or not a matching receive has been posted. It may complete before a matching receive is posted. The standard-mode send has non-local completion semantics, since successful completion of the send operation may depend on the occurrence of a matching receive.

A **buffered**-mode send operation can be started whether or not a matching receive has been posted. It may complete before a matching receive is posted. Buffered-mode send has local completion semantics: its completion does not depend on the occurrence of a matching receive. In order to complete the operation, it may be necessary to buffer the outgoing message locally. For that purpose, buffer space is provided by the application (Section 2.13.4). An error will occur if a buffered-mode send is called and there is insufficient buffer space. The buffer space occupied by the message is freed when the message is transferred to its destination or when the buffered send is cancelled.

A **synchronous**-mode send can be started whether or not a matching receive was posted. However, the send will complete successfully only if a matching receive is posted, and the receive operation has started to receive the message sent by the synchronous send. Thus, the completion of a synchronous send not only indicates that the send buffer can be reused, but also indicates that the receiver has reached a certain point in its execution, namely that it has started executing the matching receive. Synchronous mode provides synchronous communication semantics: a communication does not complete at either end before both processes rendezvous at the communication. A synchronous-mode send has non-local completion semantics.

A **ready**-mode send may be started *only* if the matching receive has already been posted. Otherwise, the operation is erroneous and its outcome is undefined. On some systems, this allows the removal of a hand-shake operation and results in improved performance. A ready-mode send has the same semantics as a standard-mode send. In a correct program, therefore, a ready-mode send could be replaced by a standard-mode send with no effect on the behavior of the program other than performance.

Three additional send functions are provided for the three additional communication modes. The communication mode is indicated by a one letter prefix: B for buffered, S for synchronous, and R for ready. There is only one receive mode and it matches any of the send modes.

All send and receive operations use the buf, count, datatype, source, dest, tag, comm, status and request arguments in the same way as the standard-mode send and receive operations.

2.13.1 Blocking Calls

MPI_BSEND (buf, count, datatype, dest, tag, comm)

IN	buf	initial address of send buffer
IN	count	number of entries in send buffer
IN	datatype	datatype of each send buffer entry
IN	dest	rank of destination
IN	tag	message tag
IN	comm	communicator

```
int MPI_Bsend(void* buf, int count, MPI_Datatype datatype, int dest,
            int tag, MPI_Comm comm)
```

```
MPI_BSEND(BUF, COUNT, DATATYPE, DEST, TAG, COMM, IERROR)
    <type> BUF(*)
    INTEGER COUNT, DATATYPE, DEST, TAG, COMM, IERROR
```

MPI_BSEND performs a buffered-mode, blocking send.

MPI_SSEND (buf, count, datatype, dest, tag, comm)

IN	buf	initial address of send buffer
IN	count	number of entries in send buffer
IN	datatype	datatype of each send buffer entry
IN	dest	rank of destination
IN	tag	message tag
IN	comm	communicator

```
int MPI_Ssend(void* buf, int count, MPI_Datatype datatype, int dest,
```

```
        int tag, MPI_Comm comm)
MPI_SSEND(BUF, COUNT, DATATYPE, DEST, TAG, COMM, IERROR)
    <type> BUF(*)
    INTEGER COUNT, DATATYPE, DEST, TAG, COMM, IERROR
```

MPI_SSEND performs a synchronous-mode, blocking send.

MPI_RSEND (buf, count, datatype, dest, tag, comm)

IN	buf	initial address of send buffer
IN	count	number of entries in send buffer
IN	datatype	datatype of each send buffer entry
IN	dest	rank of destination
IN	tag	message tag
IN	comm	communicator

```
int MPI_Rsend(void* buf, int count, MPI_Datatype datatype, int dest,
            int tag, MPI_Comm comm)

MPI_RSEND(BUF, COUNT, DATATYPE, DEST, TAG, COMM, IERROR)
    <type> BUF(*)
    INTEGER COUNT, DATATYPE, DEST, TAG, COMM, IERROR
```

MPI_RSEND performs a ready-mode, blocking send.

2.13.2 Nonblocking Calls

We use the same naming conventions as for blocking communication: a prefix of B, S, or R is used for buffered, synchronous or ready mode. In addition, a prefix of I (for immediate) indicates that the call is nonblocking. There is only one nonblocking receive call, MPI_IRECV. Nonblocking send operations are completed with the same Wait and Test calls as for standard-mode send.

MPI_IBSEND(buf, count, datatype, dest, tag, comm, request)

IN	buf	initial address of send buffer
IN	count	number of elements in send buffer
IN	datatype	datatype of each send buffer element
IN	dest	rank of destination
IN	tag	message tag
IN	comm	communicator
OUT	request	request handle

```
int MPI_Ibsend(void* buf, int count, MPI_Datatype datatype, int dest,
            int tag, MPI_Comm comm, MPI_Request *request)
```

```
MPI_IBSEND(BUF, COUNT, DATATYPE, DEST, TAG, COMM, REQUEST, IERROR)
    <type> BUF(*)
    INTEGER COUNT, DATATYPE, DEST, TAG, COMM, REQUEST, IERROR
```

MPI_IBSEND posts a buffered-mode, nonblocking send.

MPI_ISSEND(buf, count, datatype, dest, tag, comm, request)

IN	buf	initial address of send buffer
IN	count	number of elements in send buffer
IN	datatype	datatype of each send buffer element
IN	dest	rank of destination
IN	tag	message tag
IN	comm	communicator
OUT	request	request handle

```
int MPI_Issend(void* buf, int count, MPI_Datatype datatype, int dest,
            int tag, MPI_Comm comm, MPI_Request *request)
```

```
MPI_ISSEND(BUF, COUNT, DATATYPE, DEST, TAG, COMM, REQUEST, IERROR)
    <type> BUF(*)
    INTEGER COUNT, DATATYPE, DEST, TAG, COMM, REQUEST, IERROR
```

MPI_ISSEND posts a synchronous-mode, nonblocking send.

MPI_IRSEND(buf, count, datatype, dest, tag, comm, request)

IN	buf	initial address of send buffer
IN	count	number of elements in send buffer
IN	datatype	datatype of each send buffer element
IN	dest	rank of destination
IN	tag	message tag
IN	comm	communicator
OUT	request	request handle

```
int MPI_Irsend(void* buf, int count, MPI_Datatype datatype, int dest,
            int tag, MPI_Comm comm, MPI_Request *request)
```

```
MPI_IRSEND(BUF, COUNT, DATATYPE, DEST, TAG, COMM, REQUEST, IERROR)
    <type> BUF(*)
    INTEGER COUNT, DATATYPE, DEST, TAG, COMM, REQUEST, IERROR
```

MPI_IRSEND posts a ready-mode, nonblocking send.

2.13.3 Persistent Requests

MPI_BSEND_INIT(buf, count, datatype, dest, tag, comm, request)

IN	buf	initial address of send buffer
IN	count	number of entries to send
IN	datatype	datatype of each entry
IN	dest	rank of destination
IN	tag	message tag
IN	comm	communicator
OUT	request	request handle

```
int MPI_Bsend_init(void* buf, int count, MPI_Datatype datatype,
            int dest, int tag, MPI_Comm comm, MPI_Request *request)
```

```
MPI_BSEND_INIT(BUF, COUNT, DATATYPE, DEST, TAG, COMM, REQUEST,
            IERROR)
    <type> BUF(*)
    INTEGER REQUEST, COUNT, DATATYPE, DEST, TAG, COMM, REQUEST,
    IERROR
```

MPI_BSEND_INIT creates a persistent communication request for a buffered-mode, nonblocking send, and binds to it all the arguments of a send operation.

MPI_SSEND_INIT(buf, count, datatype, dest, tag, comm, request)

IN	buf	initial address of send buffer
IN	count	number of entries to send
IN	datatype	datatype of each entry
IN	dest	rank of destination
IN	tag	message tag
IN	comm	communicator
OUT	request	request handle

```
int MPI_Ssend_init(void* buf, int count, MPI_Datatype datatype,
            int dest, int tag, MPI_Comm comm, MPI_Request *request)
```

```
MPI_SSEND_INIT(BUF, COUNT, DATATYPE, DEST, TAG, COMM, REQUEST,
            IERROR)
    <type> BUF(*)
    INTEGER COUNT, DATATYPE, DEST, TAG, COMM, REQUEST, IERROR
```

MPI_SSEND_INIT creates a persistent communication object for a synchronous-mode, nonblocking send, and binds to it all the arguments of a send operation.

MPI_RSEND_INIT(buf, count, datatype, dest, tag, comm, request)

IN	buf	initial address of send buffer
IN	count	number of entries to send
IN	datatype	datatype of each entry
IN	dest	rank of destination
IN	tag	message tag
IN	comm	communicator
OUT	request	request handle

```
int MPI_Rsend_init(void* buf, int count, MPI_Datatype datatype,
            int dest, int tag, MPI_Comm comm, MPI_Request *request)
```

```
MPI_RSEND_INIT(BUF, COUNT, DATATYPE, DEST, TAG, COMM, REQUEST,
            IERROR)
    <type> BUF(*)
    INTEGER COUNT, DATATYPE, DEST, TAG, COMM, REQUEST, IERROR
```

MPI_RSEND_INIT creates a persistent communication object for a ready-mode, nonblocking send, and binds to it all the arguments of a send operation.

Example 2.33 Use of ready-mode and synchronous-mode
```
INTEGER req(2), status(MPI_STATUS_SIZE,2), comm, ierr
REAL buff(1000,2)
...
CALL MPI_COMM_RANK(comm, rank, ierr)
IF (rank.EQ.0) THEN
   CALL MPI_IRECV(buff(1,1), 1000, MPI_REAL, 1, 1,
                              comm, req(1), ierr)
   CALL MPI_IRECV(buff(1,2), 1000, MPI_REAL, 1, 2,
                              comm, req(2), ierr)
   CALL MPI_WAITALL(2, req, status, ierr)
ELSE IF (rank.EQ.1) THEN
   CALL MPI_SSEND(buff(1,2), 1000, MPI_REAL, 0, 2,
                          comm, status(1,1), ierr)
   CALL MPI_RSEND(buff(1,1), 1000, MPI_REAL, 0, 1,
                          comm, status(1,2), ierr)
END IF
```
The first, synchronous-mode send of process one matches the second receive of
process zero. This send operation will complete only after the second receive of
process zero has started, and after the completion of the first post-receive of process
zero. Therefore, the second, ready-mode send of process one starts, correctly, after
a matching receive is posted.

2.13.4   Buffer Allocation and Usage

An application must specify a buffer to be used for buffering messages sent in
buffered mode. Buffering is done by the sender.

MPI_BUFFER_ATTACH(buffer, size)

IN	buffer	initial buffer address
IN	size	buffer size, in bytes

```
int MPI_Buffer_attach( void* buffer, int size)
```

```
MPI_BUFFER_ATTACH( BUFFER, SIZE, IERROR)
   <type> BUFFER(*)
   INTEGER SIZE, IERROR
```

MPI_BUFFER_ATTACH provides to MPI a buffer in the application's memory to be used for buffering outgoing messages. The buffer is used only by messages sent in buffered mode. Only one buffer can be attached at a time (per process).

MPI_BUFFER_DETACH(buffer, size)

OUT	buffer	initial buffer address
OUT	size	buffer size, in bytes

```
int MPI_Buffer_detach( void* buffer, int* size)
```

```
MPI_BUFFER_DETACH( BUFFER, SIZE, IERROR)
    <type> BUFFER(*)
    INTEGER SIZE, IERROR
```

MPI_BUFFER_DETACH detaches the buffer currently associated with MPI. The call returns the address and the size of the detached buffer. This operation will block until all messages currently in the buffer have been transmitted. Upon return of this function, the user may reuse or deallocate the space taken by the buffer.

Example 2.34 Calls to attach and detach buffers.
```
#define BUFFSIZE 10000
int size
char *buff;
buff = (char *)malloc(BUFFSIZE);
MPI_Buffer_attach(buff, BUFFSIZE);
/* a buffer of 10000 bytes can now be used by MPI_Bsend */
MPI_Buffer_detach( &buff, &size);
/* Buffer size reduced to zero */
MPI_Buffer_attach( buff, size);
/* Buffer of 10000 bytes available again */
```

Advice to users. Even though the C functions MPI_Buffer_attach and MPI_Buffer-_detach both have a first argument of type void*, these arguments are used differently: A pointer to the buffer is passed to MPI_Buffer_attach; the address of the pointer is passed to MPI_Buffer_detach, so that this call can return the pointer value. (*End of advice to users.*)

Rationale. Both arguments are defined to be of type void* (rather than void* and void**, respectively), so as to avoid complex type casts. E.g., in the last example, &buff, which is of type char**, can be passed as an argument to MPI_Buffer_detach without type casting. If the formal parameter had type void** then one would need a type cast before and after the call. (*End of rationale.*)

Now the question arises: how is the attached buffer to be used? The answer is that MPI must behave *as if* outgoing message data were buffered by the sending process, in the specified buffer space, using a circular, contiguous-space allocation policy. We outline below a model implementation that defines this policy. MPI may provide more buffering, and may use a better buffer allocation algorithm than described below. On the other hand, MPI may signal an error whenever the simple buffering allocator described below would run out of space.

2.13.5   Model Implementation of Buffered Mode

The model implementation uses the packing and unpacking functions described in Section 3.8 and the nonblocking communication functions described in Section 2.8.

We assume that a circular queue of pending message entries (PME) is maintained. Each entry contains a communication request that identifies a pending nonblocking send, a pointer to the next entry and the packed message data. The entries are stored in successive locations in the buffer. Free space is available between the queue tail and the queue head.

A buffered send call results in the execution of the following algorithm.

- Traverse sequentially the PME queue from head towards the tail, deleting all entries for communications that have completed, up to the first entry with an uncompleted request; update queue head to point to that entry.
- Compute the number, n, of bytes needed to store entries for the new message. An upper bound on n can be computed as follows: A call to the function MPI_PACK_SIZE(count, datatype, comm, size), with the count, datatype and comm arguments used in the MPI_BSEND call, returns an upper bound on the amount of space needed to buffer the message data (see Section 3.8). The MPI constant MPI_BSEND_OVERHEAD provides an upper bound on the additional space consumed by the entry (e.g., for pointers or envelope information).
- Find the next contiguous, empty space of n bytes in buffer (space following queue tail, or space at start of buffer if queue tail is too close to end of buffer). If space is not found then raise buffer overflow error.
- Copy request, next pointer and packed message data into empty space; MPI_PACK

is used to pack data. Set pointers so that this entry is at tail of PME queue.

- Post nonblocking send (standard mode) for packed data.
- Return

2.13.6   Comments on Communication Modes

Advice to users.   When should one use each mode?

Most of the time, it is preferable to use the standard-mode send: implementers are likely to provide the best and most robust performance for this mode.

Users that do not trust the buffering policy of standard-mode may use the buffered-mode, and control buffer allocation themselves. With this authority comes responsibility: it is the user responsibility to ensure that buffers never overflow.

The synchronous mode is convenient in cases where an acknowledgment would be otherwise required, e.g., when communication with rendezvous semantics is desired. Also, use of the synchronous-mode is a hint to the system that buffering should be avoided, since the sender cannot progress anyhow, even if the data is buffered.

The ready-mode is error prone and should be used with care. (*End of advice to users.*)

Advice to implementors.   Since a synchronous-mode send cannot complete before a matching receive is posted, one will not normally buffer messages sent by such an operation.

It is usually preferable to choose buffering over blocking the sender, for standard-mode sends. The programmer can get the non-buffered protocol by using synchronous mode.

A possible choice of communication protocols for the various communication modes is outlined below.

standard-mode send: Short protocol is used for short messages, and long protocol is used for long messages (see Figure 2.5, page 66).

ready-mode send: The message is sent with the short protocol (that is, ready-mode messages are always "short").

synchronous-mode send: The long protocol is used (that is, synchronous-mode messages are always "long").

buffered-mode send: The send copies the message into the application-provided buffer and then sends it with a standard-mode, nonblocking send.

Ready-mode send can be implemented as a standard-mode send. In this case there will be no performance advantage (or disadvantage) for the use of ready-mode send.

A standard-mode send could be implemented as a synchronous-mode send, so that no data buffering is needed. This is consistent with the MPI specification. However, many users would be surprised by this choice, since standard-mode is the natural place for system-provided buffering. (*End of advice to implementors.*)

3 User-Defined Datatypes and Packing

3.1 Introduction

The MPI communication mechanisms introduced in the previous chapter allows one to send or receive a sequence of identical elements that are contiguous in memory. It is often desirable to send data that is not homogeneous, such as a structure, or that is not contiguous in memory, such as an array section. This allows one to amortize the fixed overhead of sending and receiving a message over the transmittal of many elements, even in these more general circumstances. MPI provides two mechanisms to achieve this.

- The user can define *derived* datatypes, that specify more general data layouts. User-defined datatypes can be used in MPI communication functions, in place of the basic, predefined datatypes.
- A sending process can explicitly pack noncontiguous data into a contiguous buffer, and next send it; a receiving process can explicitly unpack data received in a contiguous buffer and store in noncontiguous locations.

The construction and use of derived datatypes is described in Section 3.2-3.7. The use of Pack and Unpack functions is described in Section 3.8. It is often possible to achieve the same data transfer using either mechanisms. We discuss the pros and cons of each approach at the end of this chapter.

3.2 Introduction to User-Defined Datatypes

All MPI communication functions take a datatype argument. In the simplest case this will be a primitive type, such as an integer or floating-point number. An important and powerful generalization results by allowing user-defined (or "derived") types wherever the primitive types can occur. These are not "types" as far as the programming language is concerned. They are only "types" in that MPI is made aware of them through the use of type-constructor functions, and they describe the layout, in memory, of sets of primitive types. Through user-defined types, MPI supports the communication of complex data structures such as array sections and structures containing combinations of primitive datatypes. Example 3.1 shows how a user-defined datatype is used to send the upper-triangular part of a matrix, and Figure 3.1 diagrams the memory layout represented by the user-defined datatype.

Example 3.1 MPI code that sends an upper triangular matrix.

```
double a[100][100]
disp[100],blocklen[100],i;
MPI_Datatype upper;
...
 /* compute start and size of each row */
for (i=0; i<100; ++i) {
   disp[i] = 100 * i + i;
   blocklen[i] = 100 - i;
}
 /* create datatype for upper triangular part */
MPI_Type_indexed(100, blocklen, disp, MPI_DOUBLE, &upper);
MPI_Type_commit(&upper);
 /* .. and send it */
MPI_Send(a, 1, upper, dest, tag, MPI_COMM_WORLD);
```

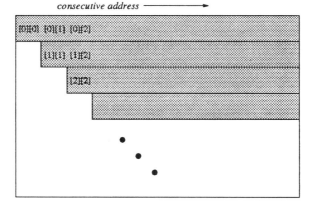

Figure 3.1
A diagram of the memory cells represented by the user-defined datatype **upper**. The shaded cells are the locations of the array that will be sent.

Derived datatypes are constructed from basic datatypes using the constructors described in Section 3.3. The constructors can be applied recursively.

A **derived datatype** is an opaque object that specifies two things:

• A sequence of primitive datatypes and,
• A sequence of integer (byte) displacements.

The displacements are not required to be positive, distinct, or in increasing order. Therefore, the order of items need not coincide with their order in memory, and an item may appear more than once. We call such a pair of sequences (or sequence of pairs) a **type map**. The sequence of primitive datatypes (displacements ignored) is the **type signature** of the datatype.

Let

$$Typemap = \{(type_0, disp_0), \ldots, (type_{n-1}, disp_{n-1})\},$$

be such a type map, where $type_i$ are primitive types, and $disp_i$ are displacements. Let

$$Typesig = \{type_0, \ldots, type_{n-1}\}$$

be the associated type signature. This type map, together with a base address *buf*, specifies a communication buffer: the communication buffer that consists of n entries, where the i-th entry is at address $buf + disp_i$ and has type $type_i$. A message assembled from a single type of this sort will consist of n values, of the types defined by $Typesig$.

A handle to a derived datatype can appear as an argument in a send or receive operation, instead of a primitive datatype argument. The operation MPI_SEND(buf, 1, datatype,...) will use the send buffer defined by the base address buf and the derived datatype associated with datatype. It will generate a message with the type signature determined by the datatype argument. MPI_RECV(buf, 1, datatype,...) will use the receive buffer defined by the base address buf and the derived datatype associated with datatype.

Derived datatypes can be used in all send and receive operations including collective. We discuss, in Section 3.4.3, the case where the second argument count has value > 1.

The primitive datatypes presented in Section 2.2.2 are special cases of a derived datatype, and are predefined. Thus, MPI_INT is a predefined handle to a datatype with type map $\{(int, 0)\}$, with one entry of type int and displacement zero. The other primitive datatypes are similar.

The **extent** of a datatype is defined to be the span from the first byte to the last byte occupied by entries in this datatype, rounded up to satisfy alignment requirements. That is, if

$$Typemap = \{(type_0, disp_0), \ldots, (type_{n-1}, disp_{n-1})\},$$

then

$$
\begin{aligned}
lb(Typemap) &= \min_j disp_j, \\
ub(Typemap) &= \max_j(disp_j + sizeof(type_j)) + \epsilon, \text{ and}
\end{aligned}
$$

$$extent(Typemap) \quad = \quad ub(Typemap) - lb(Typemap).$$

where $j = 0, \ldots, n-1$. lb is the **lower bound** and ub is the **upper bound** of the datatype. If $type_i$ requires alignment to a byte address that is a multiple of k_i, then ϵ is the least nonnegative increment needed to round $extent(Typemap)$ to the next multiple of $\max_i k_i$. (The definition of extent is expanded in Section 3.6.)

Example 3.2 Assume that $Type = \{(\text{double}, 0), (\text{char}, 8)\}$ (a **double** at displacement zero, followed by a **char** at displacement eight). Assume, furthermore, that doubles have to be strictly aligned at addresses that are multiples of eight. Then, the extent of this datatype is 16 (9 rounded to the next multiple of 8). A datatype that consists of a character immediately followed by a double will also have an extent of 16.

Rationale. The rounding term that appears in the definition of upper bound is to facilitate the definition of datatypes that correspond to arrays of structures. The extent of a datatype defined to describe a structure will be the extent of memory a compiler will normally allocate for this structure entry in an array.

More explicit control of the extent is described in Section 3.6. Such explicit control is needed in cases where this assumption does not hold, for example, where the compiler offers different alignment options for structures. (*End of rationale.*)

Advice to implementors. Implementors should provide information on the "default" alignment option used by the MPI library to define upper bound and extent. This should match, whenever possible, the "default" alignment option of the compiler. (*End of advice to implementors.*)

The following functions return information on datatypes.

MPI_TYPE_EXTENT(datatype, extent)

| IN | datatype | datatype |
| OUT | extent | datatype extent |

```
int MPI_Type_extent(MPI_Datatype datatype, MPI_Aint *extent)
```

```
MPI_TYPE_EXTENT(DATATYPE, EXTENT, IERROR)
    INTEGER DATATYPE, EXTENT, IERROR
```

MPI_TYPE_EXTENT returns the extent of a datatype. In addition to its use with derived datatypes, it can be used to inquire about the extent of primitive datatypes.

For example, MPI_TYPE_EXTENT(MPI_INT, extent) will return in extent the size, in bytes, of an int – the same value that would be returned by the C call sizeof(int).

Advice to users. Since datatypes in MPI are opaque handles, it is important to use the function MPI_TYPE_EXTENT to determine the "size" of the datatype. As an example, it may be tempting (in C) to use sizeof(datatype), e.g., sizeof(MPI_DOUBLE). However, this will return the size of the opaque handle, which is most likely the size of a pointer, and usually a different value than sizeof(double). (*End of advice to users.*)

MPI_TYPE_SIZE(datatype, size)

IN	datatype	datatype
OUT	size	datatype size

```
int MPI_Type_size(MPI_Datatype datatype, int *size)
```

```
MPI_TYPE_SIZE(DATATYPE, SIZE, IERROR)
    INTEGER DATATYPE, SIZE, IERROR
```

MPI_TYPE_SIZE returns the total size, in bytes, of the entries in the type signature associated with datatype; that is, the total size of the data in a message that would be created with this datatype. Entries that occur multiple times in the datatype are counted with their multiplicity. For primitive datatypes, this function returns the same information as MPI_TYPE_EXTENT.

Example 3.3 Let datatype have the Type map *Type* defined in Example 3.2. Then a call to MPI_TYPE_EXTENT(datatype, i) will return i = 16; a call to MPI_TYPE_SIZE(datatype, i) will return i = 9.

3.3 Datatype Constructors

This section presents the MPI functions for constructing derived datatypes. The functions are presented in an order from simplest to most complex.

3.3.1 Contiguous

MPI_TYPE_CONTIGUOUS(count, oldtype, newtype)

IN	count	replication count
IN	oldtype	old datatype
OUT	newtype	new datatype

```
int MPI_Type_contiguous(int count, MPI_Datatype oldtype,
        MPI_Datatype *newtype)
```

```
MPI_TYPE_CONTIGUOUS(COUNT, OLDTYPE, NEWTYPE, IERROR)
    INTEGER COUNT, OLDTYPE, NEWTYPE, IERROR
```

MPI_TYPE_CONTIGUOUS is the simplest datatype constructor. It constructs a typemap consisting of the replication of a datatype into contiguous locations. The argument newtype is the datatype obtained by concatenating count copies of oldtype. Concatenation is defined using *extent(oldtype)* as the size of the concatenated copies. The action of the Contiguous constructor is represented schematically in Figure 3.2.

Figure 3.2
Effect of datatype constructor MPI_TYPE_CONTIGUOUS.

Example 3.4 Let oldtype have type map $\{(double, 0), (char, 8)\}$, with extent 16, and let count $= 3$. The type map of the datatype returned by newtype is

$$\{(double, 0), (char, 8), (double, 16), (char, 24), (double, 32), (char, 40)\},$$

that is, alternating double and char elements, with displacements $0, 8, 16, 24, 32, 40$.

In general, assume that the type map of **oldtype** is

$$\{(type_0, disp_0), \ldots, (type_{n-1}, disp_{n-1})\},$$

with extent ex. Then **newtype** has a type map with count $\cdot\, n$ entries defined by:

$$\{(type_0, disp_0), \ldots, (type_{n-1}, disp_{n-1}),$$

$$(type_0, disp_0 + ex), \ldots, (type_{n-1}, disp_{n-1} + ex),$$

$$\ldots, (type_0, disp_0 + ex \cdot (\mathsf{count} - 1)), \ldots, (type_{n-1}, disp_{n-1} + ex \cdot (\mathsf{count} - 1))\}.$$

3.3.2   Vector

MPI_TYPE_VECTOR(count, blocklength, stride, oldtype, newtype)

IN	count	number of blocks
IN	blocklength	number of elements in each block
IN	stride	spacing between start of each block, measured as number of elements
IN	oldtype	old datatype
OUT	newtype	new datatype

```
int MPI_Type_vector(int count, int blocklength, int stride,
            MPI_Datatype oldtype, MPI_Datatype *newtype)
```

```
MPI_TYPE_VECTOR(COUNT, BLOCKLENGTH, STRIDE, OLDTYPE, NEWTYPE, IERROR)
    INTEGER COUNT, BLOCKLENGTH, STRIDE, OLDTYPE, NEWTYPE, IERROR
```

MPI_TYPE_VECTOR is a constructor that allows replication of a datatype into locations that consist of equally spaced blocks. Each block is obtained by concatenating the same number of copies of the old datatype. The spacing between blocks is a multiple of the extent of the old datatype. The action of the Vector constructor is represented schematically in Figure 3.3.

Example 3.5 As before, assume that oldtype has type map $\{(\mathsf{double}, 0), (\mathsf{char}, 8)\}$, with extent 16. A call to MPI_TYPE_VECTOR(2, 3, 4, oldtype, newtype) will create the datatype with type map

Figure 3.3
Datatype constructor MPI_TYPE_VECTOR.

$\{(\text{double}, 0), (\text{char}, 8), (\text{double}, 16), (\text{char}, 24), (\text{double}, 32), (\text{char}, 40),$

$(\text{double}, 64), (\text{char}, 72), (\text{double}, 80), (\text{char}, 88), (\text{double}, 96), (\text{char}, 104)\}.$

That is, two blocks with three copies each of the old type, with a stride of 4 elements $(4 \times 16$ bytes) between the blocks.

Example 3.6 A call to MPI_TYPE_VECTOR(3, 1, -2, oldtype, newtype) will create the datatype with type map

$\{(\text{double}, 0), (\text{char}, 8), (\text{double}, -32), (\text{char}, -24), (\text{double}, -64), (\text{char}, -56)\}.$

In general, assume that oldtype has type map

$\{(type_0, disp_0), \ldots, (type_{n-1}, disp_{n-1})\},$

with extent ex. Let bl be the blocklength. The new datatype has a type map with count $\cdot$ bl $\cdot n$ entries:

$\{(type_0, disp_0), \ldots, (type_{n-1}, disp_{n-1}),$

$(type_0, disp_0 + ex), \ldots, (type_{n-1}, disp_{n-1} + ex), \ldots,$

$(type_0, disp_0 + (\text{bl} - 1) \cdot ex), \ldots, (type_{n-1}, disp_{n-1} + (\text{bl} - 1) \cdot ex),$

$(type_0, disp_0 + \text{stride} \cdot ex), \ldots, (type_{n-1}, disp_{n-1} + \text{stride} \cdot ex), \ldots,$

$(type_0, disp_0 + (\text{stride} + \text{bl} - 1) \cdot ex), \ldots, (type_{n-1}, disp_{n-1} + (\text{stride} + \text{bl} - 1) \cdot ex),$

$\ldots, (type_0, disp_0 + \text{stride} \cdot (\text{count} - 1) \cdot ex), \ldots,$

$(type_{n-1}, disp_{n-1} + \mathsf{stride} \cdot (\mathsf{count} - 1) \cdot ex), \ldots,$

$(type_0, disp_0 + (\mathsf{stride} \cdot (\mathsf{count} - 1) + \mathsf{bl} - 1) \cdot ex), \ldots,$

$(type_{n-1}, disp_{n-1} + (\mathsf{stride} \cdot (\mathsf{count} - 1) + \mathsf{bl} - 1) \cdot ex)\}.$

A call to MPI_TYPE_CONTIGUOUS(count, oldtype, newtype) is equivalent to a call to MPI_TYPE_VECTOR(count, 1, 1, oldtype, newtype), or to a call to MPI-_TYPE_VECTOR(1, count, num, oldtype, newtype), with num arbitrary.

3.3.3   Hvector

The Vector type constructor assumes that the stride between successive blocks is a multiple of the oldtype extent. This avoids, most of the time, the need for computing stride in bytes. Sometimes it is useful to relax this assumption and allow a stride which consists of an arbitrary number of bytes. The Hvector type constructor below achieves this purpose. The usage of both Vector and Hvector is illustrated in Examples 3.7–3.10.

MPI_TYPE_HVECTOR(count, blocklength, stride, oldtype, newtype)

IN	count	number of blocks
IN	blocklength	number of elements in each block
IN	stride	spacing between start of each block, measured as bytes
IN	oldtype	old datatype
OUT	newtype	new datatype

```
int MPI_Type_hvector(int count, int blocklength, MPI_Aint stride,
            MPI_Datatype oldtype, MPI_Datatype *newtype)
```

```
MPI_TYPE_HVECTOR(COUNT, BLOCKLENGTH, STRIDE, OLDTYPE, NEWTYPE,
            IERROR)
    INTEGER COUNT, BLOCKLENGTH, STRIDE, OLDTYPE, NEWTYPE, IERROR
```

MPI_TYPE_HVECTOR is identical to MPI_TYPE_VECTOR, except that stride is given in bytes, rather than in elements. (H stands for "heterogeneous"). The action of the Hvector constructor is represented schematically in Figure 3.4.

Figure 3.4
Datatype constructor MPI_TYPE_HVECTOR.

Example 3.7 Consider a call to MPI_TYPE_HVECTOR, using the same arguments as in the call to MPI_TYPE_VECTOR in Example 3.5. As before, assume that oldtype has type map $\{(\text{double}, 0), (\text{char}, 8)\}$, with extent 16.

A call to MPI_TYPE_HVECTOR(2, 3, 4, oldtype, newtype) will create the datatype with type map

$\{(\text{double}, 0), (\text{char}, 8), (\text{double}, 16), (\text{char}, 24), (\text{double}, 32), (\text{char}, 40),$

$(\text{double}, 4), (\text{char}, 12), (\text{double}, 20), (\text{char}, 28), (\text{double}, 36), (\text{char}, 44)\}.$

This derived datatype specifies overlapping entries. Since a **DOUBLE** cannot start both at displacement zero and at displacement four, the use of this datatype in a send operation will cause a type match error. In order to define the same type map as in Example 3.5, one would use here stride = 64 (4×16).

In general, assume that oldtype has type map

$\{(type_0, disp_0), \ldots, (type_{n-1}, disp_{n-1})\},$

with extent ex. Let bl be the blocklength. The new datatype has a type map with count $\cdot$ bl $\cdot$ n entries:

$\{(type_0, disp_0), \ldots, (type_{n-1}, disp_{n-1}),$

$(type_0, disp_0 + ex), \ldots, (type_{n-1}, disp_{n-1} + ex), \ldots,$

$(type_0, disp_0 + (\text{bl} - 1) \cdot ex), \ldots, (type_{n-1}, disp_{n-1} + (\text{bl} - 1) \cdot ex),$

$(type_0, disp_0 + \text{stride}), \ldots, (type_{n-1}, disp_{n-1} + \text{stride}), \ldots,$

$(type_0, disp_0 + \text{stride} + (\text{bl} - 1) \cdot ex), \ldots,$

$(type_{n-1}, disp_{n-1} + \text{stride} + (\text{bl} - 1) \cdot ex), \ldots,$

$(type_0, disp_0 + \text{stride} \cdot (\text{count} - 1)), \ldots, (type_{n-1}, disp_{n-1} + \text{stride} \cdot (\text{count} - 1)), \ldots,$

$(type_0, disp_0 + \text{stride} \cdot (\text{count} - 1) + (\text{bl} - 1) \cdot ex), \ldots,$

$(type_{n-1}, disp_{n-1} + \text{stride} \cdot (\text{count} - 1) + (\text{bl} - 1) \cdot ex)\}.$

Example 3.8 Send and receive a section of a 2D array. The layout of the 2D array section is shown in Fig 3.5. The first call to MPI_TYPE_VECTOR defines a datatype that describes one column of the section: the 1D array section (1:6:2) which consists of three REAL's, spaced two apart. The second call to MPI_TYPE_HVECTOR defines a datatype that describes the 2D array section (1:6:2, 1:5:2): three copies of the previous 1D array section, with a stride of 12*sizeofreal; the stride is not a multiple of the extent of the 1D section, which is 5*sizeofreal. The usage of MPI_TYPE_COMMIT is explained later, in Section 3.4.

```
      REAL a(6,5), e(3,3)
      INTEGER oneslice, twoslice, sizeofreal, myrank, ierr
      INTEGER status(MPI_STATUS_SIZE)

C     extract the section a(1:6:2,1:5:2)
C     and store it in e(:,:).

      CALL MPI_COMM_RANK(MPI_COMM_WORLD, myrank, ierr)

      CALL MPI_TYPE_EXTENT(MPI_REAL, sizeofreal, ierr)

C     create datatype for a 1D section
      CALL MPI_TYPE_VECTOR(3, 1, 2, MPI_REAL, oneslice, ierr)

C     create datatype for a 2D section
      CALL MPI_TYPE_HVECTOR(3, 1, 12*sizeofreal, oneslice, twoslice, ierr)
```

```
        CALL MPI_TYPE_COMMIT( twoslice, ierr)

C       send and recv on same process
        CALL MPI_SENDRECV(a(1,1,1), 1, twoslice, myrank, 0, e, 9,
                          MPI_REAL, myrank, 0, MPI_COMM_WORLD, status, ierr)
```

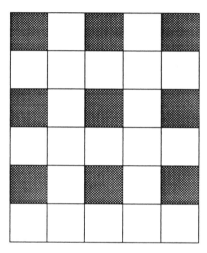

Figure 3.5
Memory layout of 2D array section for Example 3.8. The shaded blocks are sent.

Example 3.9 Transpose a matrix. To do so, we create a datatype that describes
the matrix layout in row-major order; we send the matrix with this datatype and
receive the matrix in natural, column-major order.

```
        REAL a(100,100), b(100,100)
        INTEGER row, xpose, sizeofreal, myrank, ierr
        INTEGER status(MPI_STATUS_SIZE)

C       transpose matrix a into b

        CALL MPI_COMM_RANK(MPI_COMM_WORLD, myrank, ierr)

        CALL MPI_TYPE_EXTENT(MPI_REAL, sizeofreal, ierr)
```

```
C     create datatype for one row
C     (vector with 100 real entries and stride 100)
      CALL MPI_TYPE_VECTOR(100, 1, 100, MPI_REAL, row, ierr)

C     create datatype for matrix in row-major order
C     (one hundred copies of the row datatype, strided one word
C     apart; the successive row datatypes are interleaved)
      CALL MPI_TYPE_HVECTOR(100, 1, sizeofreal, row, xpose, ierr)

      CALL MPI_TYPE_COMMIT(xpose, ierr)

C     send matrix in row-major order and receive in column major order
      CALL MPI_SENDRECV(a, 1, xpose, myrank, 0, b, 100*100,
                MPI_REAL, myrank, 0, MPI_COMM_WORLD, status, ierr)
```

Example 3.10 Each entry in the array particle is a structure which contains several fields. One of this fields consists of six coordinates (location and velocity). One needs to extract the first three (location) coordinates of all particles and send them in one message. The relative displacement between successive triplets of coordinates may not be a multiple of sizeof(double); therefore, the Hvector datatype constructor is used.

```
struct Partstruct
   {
   char   class;  /* particle class */
   double d[6];   /* particle coordinates */
   char   b[7];   /* some additional information */
   };
struct Partstruct    particle[1000];
int                  i, dest, rank;
MPI_Comm      comm;
MPI_Datatype Locationtype;  /* datatype for locations */

MPI_Type_hvector(1000, 3, sizeof(Partstruct),
                MPI_DOUBLE, &Locationtype);
MPI_Type_commit(&Locationtype);

MPI_Send(particle[0].d, 1, Locationtype, dest, tag, comm);
```

3.3.4 Indexed

The Indexed constructor allows one to specify a noncontiguous data layout where displacements between successive blocks need not be equal. This allows one to gather arbitrary entries from an array and send them in one message, or receive one message and scatter the received entries into arbitrary locations in an array.

MPI_TYPE_INDEXED(count, array_of_blocklengths, array_of_displacements, oldtype, newtype)

IN	count	number of blocks
IN	array_of_blocklengths	number of elements per block
IN	array_of_displacements	displacement for each block, measured
		as number of elements
IN	oldtype	old datatype
OUT	newtype	new datatype

```
int MPI_Type_indexed(int count, int *array_of_blocklengths,
          int *array_of_displacements, MPI_Datatype oldtype,
          MPI_Datatype *newtype)
```

```
MPI_TYPE_INDEXED(COUNT, ARRAY_OF_BLOCKLENGTHS, ARRAY_OF_DISPLACEMENTS,
          OLDTYPE, NEWTYPE, IERROR)
   INTEGER COUNT, ARRAY_OF_BLOCKLENGTHS(*),
   ARRAY_OF_DISPLACEMENTS(*), OLDTYPE, NEWTYPE, IERROR
```

MPI_TYPE_INDEXED allows replication of an old datatype into a sequence of blocks (each block is a concatenation of the old datatype), where each block can contain a different number of copies of oldtype and have a different displacement. All block displacements are measured in units of the oldtype extent. The action of the Indexed constructor is represented schematically in Figure 3.6.

Example 3.11 Let oldtype have type map
{(double, 0), (char, 8)},
with extent 16. Let B = (3, 1) and let D = (4, 0). A call to MPI_TYPE_INDEXED(2, B, D, oldtype, newtype) returns a datatype with type map

{(double, 64), (char, 72), (double, 80), (char, 88), (double, 96), (char, 104),

(double, 0), (char, 8)}.

oldtype

count = 3, blocklength = (2,3,1), displacement = (0,3,8)

newtype

Figure 3.6
Datatype constructor MPI_TYPE_INDEXED.

That is, three copies of the old type starting at displacement $4 \times 16 = 64$, and one copy starting at displacement 0.

In general, assume that oldtype has type map

$$\{(type_0, disp_0), \ldots, (type_{n-1}, disp_{n-1})\},$$

with extent ex. Let B be the array_of_blocklengths argument and D be the array_of__displacements argument. The new datatype has a type map with $n \cdot \sum_{i=0}^{count-1} B[i]$ entries:

$$\{(type_0, disp_0 + D[0] \cdot ex), \ldots, (type_{n-1}, disp_{n-1} + D[0] \cdot ex), \ldots,$$

$$(type_0, disp_0 + (D[0] + B[0] - 1) \cdot ex), \ldots,$$

$$(type_{n-1}, disp_{n-1} + (D[0] + B[0] - 1) \cdot ex), \ldots,$$

$$(type_0, disp_0 + D[count - 1] \cdot ex), \ldots, (type_{n-1}, disp_{n-1} + D[count - 1] \cdot ex), \ldots,$$

$$(type_0, disp_0 + (D[count - 1] + B[count - 1] - 1) \cdot ex), \ldots,$$

$$(type_{n-1}, disp_{n-1} + (D[count - 1] + B[count - 1] - 1) \cdot ex)\}.$$

A call to MPI_TYPE_VECTOR(count, blocklength, stride, oldtype, newtype) is equivalent to a call to MPI_TYPE_INDEXED(count, B, D, oldtype, newtype) where

$$D[j] = j \cdot stride, \; j = 0, \ldots, count - 1,$$

and

$B[j] = \text{blocklength}, \ j = 0, \ldots, \text{count} - 1.$

The use of the MPI_TYPE_INDEXED function was illustrated in Example 3.1, on page 102; the function was used to transfer the upper triangular part of a square matrix.

3.3.5   Hindexed

As with the Vector and Hvector constructors, it is usually convenient to measure displacements in multiples of the extent of the oldtype, but sometimes necessary to allow for arbitrary displacements. The Hindexed constructor satisfies the later need.

MPI_TYPE_HINDEXED(count, array_of_blocklengths, array_of_displacements, oldtype, newtype)

IN	count	number of blocks
IN	array_of_blocklengths	number of elements per block
IN	array_of_displacements	byte displacement for each block
IN	oldtype	old datatype
OUT	newtype	new datatype

```
int MPI_Type_hindexed(int count, int *array_of_blocklengths,
          MPI_Aint *array_of_displacements, MPI_Datatype oldtype,
          MPI_Datatype *newtype)
```

```
MPI_TYPE_HINDEXED(COUNT, ARRAY_OF_BLOCKLENGTHS,
          ARRAY_OF_DISPLACEMENTS, OLDTYPE, NEWTYPE, IERROR)
    INTEGER COUNT, ARRAY_OF_BLOCKLENGTHS(*),
    ARRAY_OF_DISPLACEMENTS(*), OLDTYPE, NEWTYPE, IERROR
```

MPI_TYPE_HINDEXED is identical to MPI_TYPE_INDEXED, except that block displacements in array_of_displacements are specified in bytes, rather than in multiples of the oldtype extent. The action of the Hindexed constructor is represented schematically in Figure 3.7.

count = 3, blocklength = (2,3,1), displacement = (0,7,18)

Figure 3.7
Datatype constructor MPI_TYPE_HINDEXED.

Example 3.12 We use the same arguments as for MPI_TYPE_INDEXED, in Example 3.11. Thus, oldtype has type map, $\{(double, 0), (char, 8)\}$, with extent 16; B = (3, 1), and D = (4, 0). A call to MPI_TYPE_HINDEXED(2, B, D, oldtype, newtype) returns a datatype with type map

$\{(double, 4), (char, 12), (double, 20), (char, 28), (double, 36), (char, 44),$

$(double, 0), (char, 8)\}$.

The partial overlap between the entries of type DOUBLE implies that a type matching error will occur if this datatype is used in a send operation. To get the same datatype as in Example 3.11, the call would have D = (64, 0).

In general, assume that oldtype has type map

$\{(type_0, disp_0), \ldots, (type_{n-1}, disp_{n-1})\},$

with extent ex. Let B be the array_of_blocklength argument and D be the array_of__displacements argument. The new datatype has a type map with $n \cdot \sum_{i=0}^{count-1} B[i]$ entries:

$\{(type_0, disp_0 + D[0]), \ldots, (type_{n-1}, disp_{n-1} + D[0]), \ldots,$

$(type_0, disp_0 + D[0] + (B[0] - 1) \cdot ex), \ldots,$

$(type_{n-1}, disp_{n-1} + D[0] + (B[0] - 1) \cdot ex), \ldots,$

$(type_0, disp_0 + D[count - 1]), \ldots, (type_{n-1}, disp_{n-1} + D[count - 1]), \ldots,$

$$(type_0, disp_0 + \text{D}[\text{count} - 1] + (\text{B}[\text{count} - 1] - 1) \cdot ex), \ldots,$$

$$(type_{n-1}, disp_{n-1} + \text{D}[\text{count} - 1] + (\text{B}[\text{count} - 1] - 1) \cdot ex)\}.$$

3.3.6   Struct

MPI_TYPE_STRUCT(count, array_of_blocklengths, array_of_displacements, array_of_types, newtype)

IN	count	number of blocks
IN	array_of_blocklengths	number of elements per block
IN	array_of_displacements	byte displacement for each block
IN	array_of_types	type of elements in each block
OUT	newtype	new datatype

```
int MPI_Type_struct(int count, int *array_of_blocklengths,
            MPI_Aint *array_of_displacements,
            MPI_Datatype *array_of_types, MPI_Datatype *newtype)
```

```
MPI_TYPE_STRUCT(COUNT, ARRAY_OF_BLOCKLENGTHS, ARRAY_OF_DISPLACEMENTS,
            ARRAY_OF_TYPES, NEWTYPE, IERROR)
    INTEGER COUNT, ARRAY_OF_BLOCKLENGTHS(*),
    ARRAY_OF_DISPLACEMENTS(*), ARRAY_OF_TYPES(*), NEWTYPE, IERROR
```

MPI_TYPE_STRUCT is the most general type constructor. It further generalizes MPI_TYPE_HINDEXED in that it allows each block to consist of replications of different datatypes. The intent is to allow descriptions of arrays of structures, as a single datatype. The action of the Struct constructor is represented schematically in Figure 3.8.

oldtypes

count = 3, blocklength = (2,3,4), displacement = (0,7,16)

newtype

Figure 3.8
Datatype constructor MPI_TYPE_STRUCT.

Example 3.13 Let type1 have type map
$\{(double, 0), (char, 8)\}$,
with extent 16. Let B = (2, 1, 3), D = (0, 16, 26), and T = (MPI_FLOAT, type1, MPI_CHAR). Then a call to MPI_TYPE_STRUCT(3, B, D, T, newtype) returns a datatype with type map

$$\{(float, 0), (float, 4), (double, 16), (char, 24), (char, 26), (char, 27), (char, 28)\}.$$

That is, two copies of MPI_FLOAT starting at 0, followed by one copy of type1 starting at 16, followed by three copies of MPI_CHAR, starting at 26. (We assume that a float occupies four bytes.)

In general, let T be the array_of_types argument, where T[i] is a handle to,

$$typemap_i = \{(type_0^i, disp_0^i), \dots, (type_{n_i-1}^i, disp_{n_i-1}^i)\},$$

with extent ex_i. Let B be the array_of_blocklength argument and D be the array_of_displacements argument. Let c be the count argument. Then the new datatype has a type map with $\sum_{i=0}^{c-1} B[i] \cdot n_i$ entries:

$$\{(type_0^0, disp_0^0 + D[0]), \dots, (type_{n_0}^0, disp_{n_0}^0 + D[0]), \dots,$$

$$(type_0^0, disp_0^0 + D[0] + (B[0] - 1) \cdot ex_0), \dots,$$

$$(type_{n_0}^0, disp_{n_0}^0 + D[0] + (B[0] - 1) \cdot ex_0), \dots,$$

$$(type_0^{c-1}, disp_0^{c-1} + D[c-1]), \dots, (type_{n_{c-1}-1}^{c-1}, disp_{n_{c-1}-1}^{c-1} + D[c-1]), \dots,$$

$$(type_0^{c-1}, disp_0^{c-1} + D[c-1] + (B[c-1] - 1) \cdot ex_{c-1}), \dots,$$

$$(type^{c-1}_{n_{c-1}-1}, disp^{c-1}_{n_{c-1}-1} + D[c-1] + (B[c-1]-1) \cdot ex_{c-1})\}.$$

A call to MPI_TYPE_HINDEXED(count, B, D, oldtype, newtype) is equivalent to a call to MPI_TYPE_STRUCT(count, B, D, T, newtype), where each entry of T is equal to oldtype.

Example 3.14 Sending an array of structures.

```
struct Partstruct
    {
    char    class;   /* particle class */
    double d[6];     /* particle coordinates */
    char    b[7];    /* some additional information */
    };

struct Partstruct      particle[1000];
int                    i, dest, rank;
MPI_Comm       comm;

/* build datatype describing structure */

MPI_Datatype Particletype;
MPI_Datatype type[3] = {MPI_CHAR, MPI_DOUBLE, MPI_CHAR};
int          blocklen[3] = {1, 6, 7};
MPI_Aint     disp[3] = {0, sizeof(double}, 7*sizeof(double)};

MPI_Type_struct(3, blocklen, disp, type, &Particletype);
MPI_Type_commit(&Particletype);

/* send the array */

MPI_Send(particle, 1000, Particletype, dest, tag, comm);
```

The array disp was initialized assuming that a double is double-word aligned. If double's are single-word aligned, then disp should be initialized to (0, sizeof(int), sizeof(int)+6*sizeof(double)). We show in Example 3.21 on page 129, how to avoid this machine dependence.

Example 3.15 A more complex example, using the same array of structures as in Example 3.14: process zero sends a message that consists of all particles of class zero. Process one receives these particles in contiguous locations.

```
struct Partstruct
   {
   char    class;  /* particle class */
   double d[6];    /* particle coordinates */
   char    b[7];   /* some additional information */
   };
struct Partstruct    particle[1000];
int                  i, j, myrank;
MPI_Status           status;
MPI_Datatype Particletype;
MPI_Datatype type[3] = {MPI_CHAR, MPI_DOUBLE, MPI_CHAR};
int          blocklen[3] = {1, 6, 7};
MPI_Aint     disp[3] = {0, sizeof(double), 7*sizeof(double)}, sizeaint;
int          base;
MPI_Datatype Zparticles;    /* datatype describing all particles
                               with class zero (needs to be recomputed
                               if classes change) */
MPI_Aint     *zdisp;
int          *zblocklen;

MPI_Type_struct(3, blocklen, disp, type, &Particletype);
MPI_Comm_rank(comm, &myrank);

if(myrank == 0) {

/* send message consisting of all class zero particles */

   /* allocate data structures for datatype creation */

   MPI_Type_extent(MPI_Aint, &sizeaint)
   zdisp = (MPI_Aint*)malloc(1000*sizeaint);
   zblocklen = (int*)malloc(1000*sizeof(int));

   /* compute displacements of class zero particles */
```

```
    j = 0;
    for(i=0; i < 1000; i++)
       if (particle[i].class==0) {
          zdisp[j] = i;
          zblocklen[j] = 1;
          j++;
          }

    /* create datatype for class zero particles  */

    MPI_Type_indexed(j, zblocklen, zdisp, Particletype, &Zparticles);
    MPI_Type_commit(&Zparticles);

    /* send */

    MPI_Send(particle, 1, Zparticles, 1, 0, comm);
 }

else if (myrank == 1)

/* receive class zero particles in contiguous locations */

    MPI_recv(particle, 1000, Particletype, 0, 0,
                                 comm, &status);
```

Example 3.16 An optimization for the last example: rather than handling each class zero particle as a separate block, it is more efficient to compute largest consecutive blocks of class zero particles and use these blocks in the call to MPI_Type_indexed. The modified loop that computes zblock and zdisp is shown below.

...

```
j=0;
for (i=0; i < 1000; i++)
  if (particle[i].class==0) {
    for (k=i+1; (k < 1000)&&(particle[k].class == 0); k++);
    zdisp[j] = i;
    zblocklen[j] = k-i;
    j++;
```

```
    i = k;
    }
MPI_Type_indexed(j, zblocklen, zdisp, Particletype, &Zparticles);
...
```

3.4 Use of Derived Datatypes

3.4.1 Commit

A derived datatype must be **committed** before it can be used in a communication. A committed datatype can continue to be used as an input argument in datatype constructors (so that other datatypes can be derived from the committed datatype). There is no need to commit primitive datatypes.

MPI_TYPE_COMMIT(datatype)

INOUT	datatype	datatype that is to be committed

```
int MPI_Type_commit(MPI_Datatype *datatype)
```

```
MPI_TYPE_COMMIT(DATATYPE, IERROR)
    INTEGER DATATYPE, IERROR
```

MPI_TYPE_COMMIT commits the datatype. Commit should be thought of as a possible "flattening" or "compilation" of the formal description of a type map into an efficient representation. Commit does not imply that the datatype is bound to the current content of a communication buffer. After a datatype has been committed, it can be repeatedly reused to communicate different data.

Advice to implementors. The system may "compile" at commit time an internal representation for the datatype that facilitates communication. (*End of advice to implementors.*)

3.4.2 Deallocation

A datatype object is deallocated by a call to MPI_TYPE_FREE.

MPI_TYPE_FREE(datatype)

    INOUT   datatype   datatype to be freed

```
int MPI_Type_free(MPI_Datatype *datatype)
```

```
MPI_TYPE_FREE(DATATYPE, IERROR)
    INTEGER DATATYPE, IERROR
```

MPI_TYPE_FREE marks the datatype object associated with datatype for deallocation and sets datatype to MPI_DATATYPE_NULL. Any communication that is currently using this datatype will complete normally. Derived datatypes that were defined from the freed datatype are not affected.

Advice to implementors. An implementation may keep a reference count of active communications that use the datatype, in order to decide when to free it. Also, one may implement constructors of derived datatypes so that they keep pointers to their datatype arguments, rather then copying them. In this case, one needs to keep track of active datatype definition references in order to know when a datatype object can be freed. (*End of advice to implementors.*)

Example 3.17 The following code fragment gives examples of using MPI_TYPE-_COMMIT and MPI_TYPE_FREE.

```
INTEGER type1, type2
CALL MPI_TYPE_CONTIGUOUS(5, MPI_REAL, type1, ierr)
            ! new type object created
CALL MPI_TYPE_COMMIT(type1, ierr)
            ! now type1 can be used for communication
type2 = type1
            ! type2 can be used for communication
            ! (it is a handle to same object as type1)
CALL MPI_TYPE_VECTOR(3, 5, 4, MPI_REAL, type1, ierr)
            ! new uncommitted type object created
CALL MPI_TYPE_COMMIT(type1, ierr)
            ! now type1 can be used anew for communication
CALL MPI_TYPE_FREE(type2, ierr)
            ! free before overwrite handle
type2 = type1
            ! type2 can be used for communication
CALL MPI_TYPE_FREE(type2, ierr)
```

```
                    ! both type1 and type2 are unavailable; type2
                    ! has value MPI_DATATYPE_NULL and type1 is
                    ! undefined
```

3.4.3   Relation to count

A call of the form MPI_SEND(buf, count, datatype , ...), where count > 1, is interpreted as if the call was passed a new datatype which is the concatenation of count copies of datatype. Thus, MPI_SEND(buf, count, datatype, dest, tag, comm) is equivalent to,

```
MPI_TYPE_CONTIGUOUS(count, datatype, newtype)
MPI_TYPE_COMMIT(newtype)
MPI_SEND(buf, 1, newtype, dest, tag, comm).
```

Similar statements apply to all other communication functions that have a count and datatype argument.

3.4.4   Type Matching

Suppose that a send operation MPI_SEND(buf, count, datatype, dest, tag, comm) is executed, where datatype has type map
$\{(type_0, disp_0), \ldots, (type_{n-1}, disp_{n-1})\}$,
and extent $extent$. The send operation sends $n \cdot$count entries, where entry (i, j) is at location $addr_{i,j} = $ buf $+ extent \cdot i + disp_j$ and has type $type_j$, for $i = 0, \ldots,$ count -1 and $j = 0, \ldots, n - 1$. The variable stored at address $addr_{i,j}$ in the calling program should be of a type that matches $type_j$, where type matching is defined as in Section 2.3.1.

Similarly, suppose that a receive operation MPI_RECV(buf, count, datatype, source, tag, comm, status) is executed. The receive operation receives up to $n \cdot$count entries, where entry (i, j) is at location buf $+ extent \cdot i + disp_j$ and has type $type_j$. Type matching is defined according to the type signature of the corresponding datatypes, that is, the sequence of primitive type components. Type matching does not depend on other aspects of the datatype definition, such as the displacements (layout in memory) or the intermediate types used to define the datatypes.

For sends, a datatype may specify overlapping entries. This is not true for receives. If the datatype used in a receive operation specifies overlapping entries then the call is erroneous.

Example 3.18 This example shows that type matching is defined only in terms of the primitive types that constitute a derived type.

```
...
CALL MPI_TYPE_CONTIGUOUS( 2, MPI_REAL, type2, ...)
CALL MPI_TYPE_CONTIGUOUS( 4, MPI_REAL, type4, ...)
CALL MPI_TYPE_CONTIGUOUS( 2, type2, type22, ...)
...
CALL MPI_SEND( a, 4, MPI_REAL, ...)
CALL MPI_SEND( a, 2, type2, ...)
CALL MPI_SEND( a, 1, type22, ...)
CALL MPI_SEND( a, 1, type4, ...)
...
CALL MPI_RECV( a, 4, MPI_REAL, ...)
CALL MPI_RECV( a, 2, type2, ...)
CALL MPI_RECV( a, 1, type22, ...)
CALL MPI_RECV( a, 1, type4, ...)
```

Each of the sends matches *any* of the receives.

3.4.5   Message Length

If a message was received using a user-defined datatype, then a subsequent call to
MPI_GET_COUNT(status, datatype, count) (Section 2.2.8) will return the number
of "copies" of datatype received (count). That is, if the receive operation was
MPI_RECV(buff, count,datatype,...) then MPI_GET_COUNT may return any integer
value k, where $0 \leq k \leq$ count. If MPI_GET_COUNT returns k, then the number of
primitive elements received is $n \cdot k$, where n is the number of primitive elements in
the type map of datatype. The received message need not fill an integral number of
"copies" of datatype. If the number of primitive elements received is not a multiple
of n, that is, if the receive operation has not received an integral number of datatype
"copies," then MPI_GET_COUNT returns the value MPI_UNDEFINED.

The function MPI_GET_ELEMENTS below can be used to determine the number
of primitive elements received.

MPI_GET_ELEMENTS(status, datatype, count)

IN	status	status of receive
IN	datatype	datatype used by receive operation
OUT	count	number of primitive elements received

```
int MPI_Get_elements(MPI_Status *status, MPI_Datatype datatype,
```

```
                    int *count)
MPI_GET_ELEMENTS(STATUS, DATATYPE, COUNT, IERROR)
    INTEGER STATUS(MPI_STATUS_SIZE), DATATYPE, COUNT, IERROR
```

Example 3.19 Usage of MPI_GET_COUNT and MPI_GET_ELEMENT.

```
...
CALL MPI_TYPE_CONTIGUOUS(2, MPI_REAL, Type2, ierr)
CALL MPI_TYPE_COMMIT(Type2, ierr)
...
CALL MPI_COMM_RANK(comm, rank, ierr)
IF(rank.EQ.0) THEN
      CALL MPI_SEND(a, 2, MPI_REAL, 1, 0, comm, ierr)
      CALL MPI_SEND(a, 3, MPI_REAL, 1, 1, comm, ierr)
ELSE
      CALL MPI_RECV(a, 2, Type2, 0, 0, comm, stat, ierr)
      CALL MPI_GET_COUNT(stat, Type2, i, ierr)      ! returns i=1
      CALL MPI_GET_ELEMENTS(stat, Type2, i, ierr)  ! returns i=2
      CALL MPI_RECV(a, 2, Type2, 0, 1, comm, stat, ierr)
      CALL MPI_GET_COUNT(stat, Type2, i, ierr)
                                        ! returns i=MPI_UNDEFINED
      CALL MPI_GET_ELEMENTS(stat, Type2, i, ierr)  ! returns i=3
END IF
```

The function MPI_GET_ELEMENTS can also be used after a probe to find the number of primitive datatype elements in the probed message. Note that the two functions MPI_GET_COUNT and MPI_GET_ELEMENTS return the same values when they are used with primitive datatypes.

Rationale. The definition of MPI_GET_COUNT is consistent with the use of the count argument in the receive call: the function returns the value of the count argument, when the receive buffer is filled. Sometimes datatype represents a basic unit of data one wants to transfer. One should be able to find out how many components were received without bothering to divide by the number of elements in each component. The MPI_GET_COUNT is used in such cases. However, on other occasions, datatype is used to define a complex layout of data in the receiver memory, and does not represent a basic unit of data for transfers. In such cases, one must use MPI_GET_ELEMENTS. (*End of rationale.*)

Advice to implementors. Structures often contain padding space used to align entries correctly. Assume that data is moved from a send buffer that describes a structure into a receive buffer that describes an identical structure on another process. In such a case, it is probably advantageous to copy the structure, together with the padding, as one contiguous block. The user can "force" this optimization by explicitly including padding as part of the message. The implementation is free to do this optimization when it does not impact the outcome of the computation. However, it may be hard to detect when this optimization applies, since data sent from a structure may be received into a set of disjoint variables. Also, padding will differ when data is communicated in a heterogeneous environment, or even on the same architecture, when different compiling options are used. The MPI-2 forum is considering options to alleviate this problem and support more efficient transfer of structures. (*End of advice to implementors.*)

3.5 Address Function

As shown in Example 3.14, page 120, one sometimes needs to be able to find the displacement, in bytes, of a structure component relative to the structure start. In C, one can use the sizeof operator to find the size of C objects; and one will be tempted to use the & operator to compute addresses and then displacements. However, the C standard does not require that (int)&v be the byte address of variable v: the mapping of pointers to integers is implementation dependent. Some systems may have "word" pointers and "byte" pointers; other systems may have a segmented, noncontiguous address space. Therefore, a portable mechanism has to be provided by MPI to compute the "address" of a variable. Such a mechanism is certainly needed in Fortran, which has no dereferencing operator.

MPI_ADDRESS(location, address)

IN	location	variable representing a memory location
OUT	address	address of location

```
int MPI_Address(void* location, MPI_Aint *address)
```

```
MPI_ADDRESS(LOCATION, ADDRESS, IERROR)
    <type> LOCATION(*)
    INTEGER ADDRESS, IERROR
```

MPI_ADDRESS is used to find the address of a location in memory. It returns the byte address of location.

Example 3.20 Using MPI_ADDRESS for an array. The value of DIFF is set to 909*sizeofreal, while the values of I1 and I2 are implementation dependent.

```
REAL A(100,100)
INTEGER I1, I2, DIFF
CALL MPI_ADDRESS(A(1,1), I1, IERROR)
CALL MPI_ADDRESS(A(10,10), I2, IERROR)
DIFF = I2 - I1
```

Example 3.21 We modify the code in Example 3.14, page 120, so as to avoid architectural dependencies. Calls to MPI_ADDRESS are used to compute the displacements of the structure components.

```
struct Partstruct
   {
   char    class;  /* particle class */
   double d[6];   /* particle coordinates */
   char    b[7];   /* some additional information */
   };
struct Partstruct    particle[1000];
int                  i, dest, rank;
MPI_Comm    comm;
MPI_Datatype Particletype;
MPI_Datatype type[3] = {MPI_CHAR, MPI_DOUBLE, MPI_CHAR};
int          blocklen[3] = {1, 6, 7};
MPI_Aint    disp[3];

/* compute displacements */

MPI_Address(particle, &disp[0]);
MPI_Address(particle[0].d, &disp[1]);
MPI_Address(particle[0].b, &disp[2]);

for (i=2; i >= 0; i--)
   disp[i] -= disp[0];

/* build datatype */
```

```
MPI_Type_struct(3, blocklen, disp, type, &Particletype);
MPI_Type_commit(&Particletype);

...

/*  send the entire array */

MPI_Send(particle, 1000, Particletype, dest, tag, comm);
...
```

Advice to implementors. The absolute value returned by MPI_ADDRESS is not significant; only relative displacements, that is differences between addresses of different variables, are significant. Therefore, the implementation may pick an arbitrary "starting point" as location zero in memory. (*End of advice to implementors.*)

3.6   Lower-bound and Upper-bound Markers

Sometimes it is necessary to override the definition of extent given in Section 3.2. Consider, for example, the code in Example 3.21 in the previous section. Assume that a double occupies 8 bytes and must be double-word aligned. There will be 7 bytes of padding after the first field and one byte of padding after the last field of the structure Partstruct, and the structure will occupy 64 bytes. If, on the other hand, a double can be word aligned only, then there will be only 3 bytes of padding after the first field, and Partstruct will occupy 60 bytes. The MPI library will follow the alignment rules used on the target systems so that the extent of datatype Particletype equals the amount of storage occupied by Partstruct. The catch is that different alignment rules may be specified, on the same system, using different compiler options. An even more difficult problem is that some compilers allow the use of pragmas in order to specify different alignment rules for different structures within the same program. (Many architectures can correctly handle misaligned values, but with lower performance; different alignment rules trade speed of access for storage density.) The MPI library will assume the default alignment rules. However, the user should be able to overrule this assumption if structures are packed otherwise.

To allow this capability, MPI has two additional "pseudo-datatypes," MPI_LB and MPI_UB, that can be used, respectively, to mark the lower bound or the upper bound of a datatype. These pseudo-datatypes occupy no space ($extent$(MPI_LB) = $extent$(MPI_UB) = 0). They do not affect the size or count of a datatype, and do not affect the the content of a message created with this datatype. However, they do change the extent of a datatype and, therefore, affect the outcome of a replication of this datatype by a datatype constructor.

Example 3.22 Let D = (-3, 0, 6); T = (MPI_LB, MPI_INT, MPI_UB), and B = (1, 1, 1). Then a call to MPI_TYPE_STRUCT(3, B, D, T, type1) creates a new datatype that has an extent of 9 (from -3 to 5, 5 included), and contains an integer at displacement 0. This datatype has type map: {(lb, -3), (int, 0), (ub, 6)} . If this type is replicated twice by a call to MPI_TYPE_CONTIGUOUS(2, type1, type2) then **type2** has type map: {(lb, -3), (int, 0), (int,9), (ub, 15)} . (An entry of type lb can be deleted if there is another entry of type lb at a lower address; and an entry of type ub can be deleted if there is another entry of type ub at a higher address.)

In general, if

$$Typemap = \{(type_0, disp_0), \ldots, (type_{n-1}, disp_{n-1})\},$$

then the **lower bound** of $Typemap$ is defined to be

$$lb(Typemap) = \begin{cases} \min_j disp_j & \text{if no entry has basic type lb} \\ \min_j\{disp_j \text{ such that } type_j = \text{lb}\} & \text{otherwise} \end{cases}$$

Similarly, the **upper bound** of $Typemap$ is defined to be

$$ub(Typemap) = \begin{cases} \max_j disp_j + sizeof(type_j) + \epsilon & \text{if no entry has basic type ub} \\ \max_j\{disp_j \text{ such that } type_j = \text{ub}\} & \text{otherwise} \end{cases}$$

And

$$extent(Typemap) = ub(Typemap) - lb(Typemap)$$

If $type_i$ requires alignment to a byte address that is a multiple of k_i, then ϵ is the least nonnegative increment needed to round $extent(Typemap)$ to the next multiple of $\max_i k_i$. The formal definitions given for the various datatype constructors continue to apply, with the amended definition of **extent**. Also, MPI_TYPE_EXTENT returns the above as its value for extent.

Example 3.23 We modify Example 3.21, so that the code explicitly sets the extent of Particletype to the right value, rather than trusting MPI to compute fills correctly.

```
struct Partstruct
    {
    char    class; /* particle class */
    double d[6];   /* particle coordinates */
    char    b[7];  /* some additional information */
    };
struct Partstruct    particle[1000];
int                  i, dest, rank;
```

```
MPI_Comm      comm;
MPI_Datatype Particletype;
MPI_Datatype type[4] = {MPI_CHAR, MPI_DOUBLE, MPI_CHAR, MPI_UB};
int           blocklen[4] = {1, 6, 7, 1};
MPI_Aint      disp[4];

/* compute displacements of structure components */

MPI_Address(particle, &disp[0]);
MPI_Address(particle[0].d, &disp[1]);
MPI_Address(particle[0].b, &disp[2]);
MPI_Address(particle[1], &disp[3]);

for (i=3; i >= 0; i--) disp[i] -= disp[0];

/* build datatype for structure */

MPI_Type_struct(4, blocklen, disp, type, &Particletype);
MPI_Type_commit(&Particletype);

/*  send the entire array */

MPI_Send(particle, 1000, Particletype, dest, tag, comm);
```

The two functions below can be used for finding the lower bound and the upper
bound of a datatype.

MPI_TYPE_LB(datatype, displacement)

IN	datatype	datatype
OUT	displacement	displacement of lower bound

```
int MPI_Type_lb(MPI_Datatype datatype, MPI_Aint* displacement)
```

```
MPI_TYPE_LB(DATATYPE, DISPLACEMENT, IERROR)
    INTEGER DATATYPE, DISPLACEMENT, IERROR
```

MPI_TYPE_LB returns the lower bound of a datatype, in bytes, relative to the
datatype origin.

MPI_TYPE_UB(datatype, displacement)

IN	datatype	datatype
OUT	displacement	displacement of upper bound

```
int MPI_Type_ub(MPI_Datatype datatype, MPI_Aint* displacement)
```

```
MPI_TYPE_UB(DATATYPE, DISPLACEMENT, IERROR)
    INTEGER DATATYPE, DISPLACEMENT, IERROR
```

MPI_TYPE_UB returns the upper bound of a datatype, in bytes, relative to the datatype origin.

3.7 Absolute Addresses

Consider Example 3.21 on page 129. One computes the "absolute address" of the structure components, using calls to MPI_ADDRESS, then subtracts the starting address of the array to compute relative displacements. When the send operation is executed, the starting address of the array is added back, in order to compute the send buffer location. These superfluous arithmetics could be avoided if "absolute" addresses were used in the derived datatype, and "address zero" was passed as the buffer argument in the send call.

MPI supports the use of such "absolute" addresses in derived datatypes. The displacement arguments used in datatype constructors can be "absolute addresses", i.e., addresses returned by calls to MPI_ADDRESS. Address zero is indicated to communication functions by passing the constant MPI_BOTTOM as the buffer argument. Unlike derived datatypes with relative displacements, the use of "absolute" addresses restricts the use to the specific structure for which it was created.

Example 3.24 The code in Example 3.21 on page 129 is modified to use absolute addresses, rather than relative displacements.

```
struct Partstruct
    {
    char   class;  /* particle class */
    double d[6];   /* particle coordinates */
    char   b[7];   /* some additional information */
    };
struct Partstruct    particle[1000];
int                  i, dest, rank;
```

```
MPI_Comm       comm;

/* build datatype describing structure */

MPI_Datatype Particletype;
MPI_Datatype type[3] = {MPI_CHAR, MPI_DOUBLE, MPI_CHAR};
int          blocklen[3] = {1, 6, 7};
MPI_Aint     disp[3];

/* compute addresses of components in 1st structure*/

MPI_Address(particle, disp);
MPI_Address(particle[0].d, disp+1);
MPI_Address(particle[0].b, disp+2);

/* build datatype for 1st structure */

MPI_Type_struct(3, blocklen, disp, type, &Particletype);
MPI_Type_commit(&Particletype);

/*  send the entire array */

MPI_Send(MPI_BOTTOM, 1000, Particletype, dest, tag, comm);
```

Advice to implementors.   On systems with a flat address space, the implementation may pick an arbitrary address as the value of MPI_BOTTOM in C (or the address of the variable MPI_BOTTOM in Fortran). All that is needed is that calls to MPI_ADDRESS(location, address) return the displacement of location, relative to MPI_BOTTOM. (*End of advice to implementors.*)

The use of addresses and displacements in MPI is best understood in the context of a flat address space. Then, the "address" of a location, as computed by calls to MPI_ADDRESS can be the regular address of that location (or a shift of it), and integer arithmetic on MPI "addresses" yields the expected result. However, the use of a flat address space is not mandated by C or Fortran. Another potential source of problems is that Fortran **INTEGER**'s may be too short to store full addresses.

Variables belong to the same **sequential storage** if they belong to the same array, to the same **COMMON** block in Fortran, or to the same structure in C. Implementations may restrict the use of addresses so that arithmetic on addresses is confined within sequential storage. Namely, in a communication call, either

- The communication buffer specified by the buff, count and datatype arguments is all within the same sequential storage.

- The initial buffer address argument buff is equal to MPI_BOTTOM, count=1 and all addresses in the type map of datatype are absolute addresses of the form v+i, where v is an absolute address computed by MPI_ADDR, i is an integer displacement, and v+i is in the same sequential storage as v.

Advice to users. Current MPI implementations impose no restrictions on the use of addresses. If Fortran INTEGER's have 32 bits, then the the use of absolute addresses in Fortran programs may be restricted to 4 GB memory. This may require, in the future, to move from INTEGER addresses to INTEGER*8 addresses. (*End of advice to users.*)

3.8   Pack and Unpack

Some existing communication libraries, such as PVM and Parmacs, provide pack and unpack functions for sending noncontiguous data. In these, the application explicitly packs data into a contiguous buffer before sending it, and unpacks it from a contiguous buffer after receiving it. Derived datatypes, described in the previous sections of this chapter, allow one, in most cases, to avoid explicit packing and unpacking. The application specifies the layout of the data to be sent or received, and MPI directly accesses a noncontiguous buffer when derived datatypes are used. The pack/unpack routines are provided for compatibility with previous libraries. Also, they provide some functionality that is not otherwise available in MPI. For instance, a message can be received in several parts, where the receive operation done on a later part may depend on the content of a former part. Another use is that the availability of pack and unpack operations facilitates the development of additional communication libraries layered on top of MPI.

MPI_PACK(inbuf, incount, datatype, outbuf, outsize, position, comm)

IN	inbuf	input buffer
IN	incount	number of input components
IN	datatype	datatype of each input component
OUT	outbuf	output buffer
IN	outsize	output buffer size, in bytes
INOUT	position	current position in buffer, in bytes
IN	comm	communicator for packed message

```
int MPI_Pack(void* inbuf, int incount, MPI_Datatype datatype,
        void *outbuf, int outsize, int *position,
        MPI_Comm comm)
```

```
MPI_PACK(INBUF, INCOUNT, DATATYPE, OUTBUF, OUTSIZE, POSITION, COMM,
        IERROR)
    <type> INBUF(*), OUTBUF(*)
    INTEGER INCOUNT, DATATYPE, OUTSIZE, POSITION, COMM, IERROR
```

MPI_PACK packs a message specified by inbuf, incount, datatype, comm into the buffer space specified by outbuf and outsize. The input buffer can be any communication buffer allowed in MPI_SEND. The output buffer is a contiguous storage area containing outsize bytes, starting at the address outbuf.

The input value of position is the first position in the output buffer to be used for packing. The argument position is incremented by the size of the packed message so that it can be used as input to a subsequent call to MPI_PACK. The comm argument is the communicator that will be subsequently used for sending the packed message.

MPI_UNPACK(inbuf, insize, position, outbuf, outcount, datatype, comm)

IN	inbuf	input buffer
IN	insize	size of input buffer, in bytes
INOUT	position	current position in bytes
OUT	outbuf	output buffer
IN	outcount	number of components to be unpacked
IN	datatype	datatype of each output component
IN	comm	communicator for packed message

```
int MPI_Unpack(void* inbuf, int insize, int *position, void *outbuf,
        int outcount, MPI_Datatype datatype, MPI_Comm comm)
```

```
MPI_UNPACK(INBUF, INSIZE, POSITION, OUTBUF, OUTCOUNT, DATATYPE,
           COMM, IERROR)
   <type> INBUF(*), OUTBUF(*)
   INTEGER INSIZE, POSITION, OUTCOUNT, DATATYPE, COMM, IERROR
```

MPI_UNPACK unpacks a message into the receive buffer specified by outbuf, outcount, datatype from the buffer space specified by inbuf and insize. The output buffer can be any communication buffer allowed in MPI_RECV. The input buffer is a contiguous storage area containing insize bytes, starting at address inbuf. The input value of position is the position in the input buffer where one wishes the unpacking to begin. The output value of position is incremented by the size of the packed message, so that it can be used as input to a subsequent call to MPI_UNPACK. The argument comm was the communicator used to receive the packed message.

Rationale.   The Pack and Unpack calls have a communicator argument in order to facilitate data conversion at the source in a heterogeneous environment. E.g., this will allow for an implementation that uses the XDR format for packed data in a heterogeneous communication domain, and performs no data conversion if the communication domain is homogeneous. If no communicator was provided, the implementation would always use XDR. If the destination was provided, in addition to the communicator, then one would be able to format the pack buffer specifically for that destination. But, then, one loses the ability to pack a buffer once and send it to multiple destinations. (*End of rationale.*)

Advice to users.   Note the difference between MPI_RECV and MPI_UNPACK: in MPI_RECV, the count argument specifies the maximum number of components that can be received. In MPI_UNPACK, the count argument specifies the actual number of components that are unpacked; The reason for that change is that, for a regular receive, the incoming message size determines the number of components that will be received. With MPI_UNPACK, it is up to the user to specify how many components he or she wants to unpack, since one may want to unpack only part of the message. (*End of advice to users.*)

The MPI_PACK/MPI_UNPACK calls relate to message passing as the sprintf/sscanf calls in C relate to file I/O, or internal Fortran files relate to external units. Basically, the MPI_PACK function allows one to "send" a message into a memory buffer; the MPI_UNPACK function allows one to "receive" a message from a memory buffer.

Several communication buffers can be successively packed into one **packing unit**. This is effected by several, successive **related** calls to MPI_PACK, where the first call provides position = 0, and each successive call inputs the value of position that was output by the previous call, and the same values for outbuf, outcount and comm. This packing unit now contains the equivalent information that would have been stored in a message by one send call with a send buffer that is the "concatenation" of the individual send buffers.

A packing unit must be sent using type MPI_PACKED. Any point-to-point or collective communication function can be used. The message sent is identical to the message that would be sent by a send operation with a datatype argument describing the concatenation of the send buffer(s) used in the Pack calls. The message can be received with any datatype that matches this send datatype.

Example 3.25 The following two programs generate identical messages.
Derived datatype is used:
```
int i;
char c[100];

int disp[2];
int blocklen[2] = {1, 100}
MPI_Datatype type[2] = {MPI_INT, MPI_CHAR};
MPI_Datatype Type;

/* create datatype */
MPI_Address(&i, &disp[0]);
MPI_Address(c, &disp[1]);
MPI_Type_struct(2, blocklen, disp, type, &Type);
MPI_Type_commit(&Type);

/* send */
MPI_Send(MPI_BOTTOM, 1, Type, 1, 0, MPI_COMM_WORLD);
```
   Packing is used:
```
int i;
char c[100];

char buffer[110];
int position = 0;

/* pack */
MPI_Pack(&i, 1, MPI_INT, buffer, 110,&position, MPI_COMM_WORLD);
```

```
MPI_Pack(c, 100, MPI_CHAR, buffer, 110, &position, MPI_COMM_WORLD);

/* send */
MPI_Send(buffer, position, MPI_PACKED, 1, 0, MPI_COMM_WORLD);
```

Any message can be received in a point-to-point or collective communication using the type MPI_PACKED. Such a message can then be unpacked by calls to MPI_UNPACK. The message can be unpacked by several, successive calls to MPI_UNPACK, where the first call provides position = 0, and each successive call inputs the value of position that was output by the previous call, and the same values for inbuf, insize and comm.

Example 3.26 Any of the following two programs can be used to receive the message sent in Example 3.25. The outcome will be identical.

Derived datatype is used:

```
int i;
char c[100];

MPI_status status;

int disp[2];
int blocklen[2] = {1, 100}
MPI_Datatype type[2] = {MPI_INT, MPI_CHAR};
MPI_Datatype Type;

/* create datatype */
MPI_Address(&i, &disp[0]);
MPI_Address(c, &disp[1]);
MPI_Type_struct(2, blocklen, disp, type, &Type);
MPI_Type_commit(&Type);

/* receive */
MPI_Recv(MPI_BOTTOM, 1, Type, 0, 0, MPI_COMM_WORLD, &status);
```
   Unpacking is used:
```
int i;
char c[100];
```

```
MPI_Status status;

char buffer[110];
int position = 0;

/* receive */
MPI_Recv(buffer, 110, MPI_PACKED, 1, 0, MPI_COMM_WORLD, &status);

/* unpack */
MPI_Unpack(buffer, 110, &position, &i, 1, MPI_INT, MPI_COMM_WORLD);
MPI_Unpack(buffer, 110, &position, c, 100, MPI_CHAR, MPI_COMM_WORLD);
```

Advice to users. A packing unit may contain, in addition to data, metadata. For example, it may contain in a header, information on the encoding used to represent data; or information on the size of the unit for error checking. Therefore, such a packing unit has to treated as an "atomic" entity which can only be sent using type MPI_PACKED. One cannot concatenate two such packing units and send the result in one send operation (however, a collective communication operation can be used to send multiple packing units in one operations, to the same extent it can be used to send multiple regular messages). Also, one cannot split a packing unit and then unpack the two halves separately (however, a collective communication operation can be used to receive multiple packing units, to the same extent it can be used to receive multiple regular messages). (*End of advice to users.*)

MPI_PACK_SIZE(incount, datatype, comm, size)

IN	incount	count argument to packing call
IN	datatype	datatype argument to packing call
IN	comm	communicator argument to packing call
OUT	size	upper bound on size of packed message, in bytes

```
int MPI_Pack_size(int incount, MPI_Datatype datatype, MPI_Comm comm,
        int *size)
```

```
MPI_PACK_SIZE(INCOUNT, DATATYPE, COMM, SIZE, IERROR)
    INTEGER INCOUNT, DATATYPE, COMM, SIZE, IERROR
```

MPI_PACK_SIZE allows the application to find out how much space is needed to pack a message and, thus, manage space allocation for buffers. The function returns, in size, an upper bound on the increment in position that would occur in a call to MPI_PACK with the same values for incount, datatype, and comm.

Rationale. The MPI_PACK_SIZE call returns an upper bound, rather than an exact bound, since the exact amount of space needed to pack the message may depend on the communication domain (see Chapter 5) (for example, the first message packed in a packing unit may contain additional metadata). (*End of rationale.*)

Example 3.27 We return to the problem of Example 3.15 on page 120. Process zero sends to process one a message containing all class zero particles. Process one receives and stores these structures in contiguous locations. Process zero uses calls to MPI_PACK to gather class zero particles, whereas process one uses a regular receive.

```
struct Partstruct
   {
   char    class;  /* particle class */
   double d[6];    /* particle coordinates */
   char    b[7];   /* some additional information */
   };
struct Partstruct    particle[1000];
int          i, size, position, myrank;
int          count; /* number of class zero particles */
char         *buffer; /* pack buffer */
MPI_Status   status;

/* variables used to create datatype for particle */

MPI_Datatype Particletype;
MPI_Datatype type[3] = {MPI_CHAR, MPI_DOUBLE, MPI_CHAR};
int          blocklen[3] = {1, 6, 7};
MPI_Aint     disp[3] = {0, sizeof(double), 7*sizeof(double)};

/* define datatype for one particle */

MPI_Type_struct( 3, blocklen, disp, type, &Particletype);
MPI_Type_commit( &Particletype);
MPI_Comm_rank(comm, &myrank);
```

```
if (myrank == 0) {

/* send message that consists of class zero particles */

   /* allocate pack buffer */

   MPI_Pack_size(1000, Particletype, comm, &size);
   buffer = (char*)malloc(size);

   /* pack class zero particles */

   position  = 0;
   for(i=0; i < 1000; i++)
      if (particle[i].class == 0)
         MPI_Pack(&particle[i], 1, Particletype, buffer,
                        size, &position, comm);

   /* send */
   MPI_Send(buffer, position, MPI_PACKED, 1, 0, comm);
   }

else if (myrank == 1) {

/* receive class zero particles in contiguous locations in
   array particle */

   MPI_Recv(particle, 1000, Particletype, 0, 0, comm, &status);
   }
```

Example 3.28 This is a variant on the previous example, where the class zero particles have to be received by process one in array **particle** at the same locations where they are in the array of process zero. Process zero packs the entry index with each entry it sends. Process one uses this information to move incoming data to the right locations. As a further optimization, we avoid the transfer of the **class** field, which is known to be zero. (We have ignored in this example the computation of a tight bound on the size of the pack/unpack buffer. One could be rigorous and define an additional derived datatype for the purpose of computing such an estimate. Or one can use an approximate estimate.)

```
struct Partstruct
   {
   char    class;  /* particle class */
   double d[6];    /* particle coordinates */
   char    b[7];   /* some additional information */
   };
struct Partstruct    particle[1000];
int          i, size, myrank;
int          position = 0;
MPI_Status   status;
char         buffer[BUFSIZE]; /* pack-unpack buffer */

/* variables used to create datatype for particle,
   not including class field */

MPI_Datatype Particletype;
MPI_Datatype type[2] = {MPI_DOUBLE, MPI_CHAR};
int          blocklen[2] = {6, 7};
MPI_Aint     disp[2] = {0, 6*sizeof(double)};

/* define datatype */

MPI_Type_struct(2, blocklen, disp, type, &Particletype);
MPI_Type_commit(&Particletype);

MPI_Comm_rank(MPI_COMM_WORLD, &myrank);

if (myrank == 0) {

/* send message that consists of class zero particles */

   /* pack class zero particles and their index */

   for(i=0; i < 1000; i++)
      if (particle[i].class == 0) {
         MPI_Pack(&i, 1, MPI_INT, buffer, BUFSIZE,
                  &position, MPI_COMM_WORLD); /* pack index */
```

```
        MPI_Pack(particle[i].d, 1, Particletype, buffer,
                BUFSIZE, &position, MPI_COMM_WORLD); /* pack struct */
        }
    /* pack negative index as end of list marker */

    i = -1;
    MPI_Pack(&i, 1, MPI_INT, buffer, BUFSIZE,
            &position, MPI_COMM_WORLD);

    /* send */
    MPI_Send(buffer, position, MPI_PACKED, 1, 0, MPI_COMM_WORLD);
    }

else if (myrank == 1) {

/* receive class zero particles at original locations */

    /* receive */
    MPI_Recv(buffer, BUFSIZE, MPI_PACKED, 0, 0, MPI_COMM_WORLD, &status);

    /* unpack */
    while ((MPI_Unpack(buffer, BUFSIZE, &position, &i, 1,
                MPI_INT, MPI_COMM_WORLD); i) >= 0) {  /* unpack index */
        MPI_Unpack(buffer, BUFSIZE, &position, particle[i].d,
                1, Particletype, MPI_COMM_WORLD);     /* unpack struct */
        particle[i].class = 0;
        }
    }
```

3.8.1 Derived Datatypes vs Pack/Unpack

A comparison between Example 3.15 on page 120 and Example 3.27 in the previous section is instructive.

First, programming convenience. It is somewhat less tedious to pack the class zero particles in the loop that locates them, rather then defining in this loop the datatype that will later collect them. On the other hand, it would be very tedious (and inefficient) to pack separately the components of each structure entry in the array. Defining a datatype is more convenient when this definition depends only on declarations; packing may be more convenient when the communication buffer layout is data dependent.

Second, storage use. The packing code uses at least 56,000 bytes for the pack buffer, e.g., up to 1000 copies of the structure (1 char, 6 doubles, and 7 char is $1 + 8 \times 6 + 7 = 56$ bytes). The derived datatype code uses 12,000 bytes for the three, 1,000 long, integer arrays used to define the derived datatype. It also probably uses a similar amount of storage for the internal datatype representation. The difference is likely to be larger in realistic codes. The use of packing requires additional storage for a *copy* of the data, whereas the use of derived datatypes requires additional storage for a *description* of the data layout.

Finally, compute time. The packing code executes a function call for each packed item whereas the derived datatype code executes only a fixed number of function calls. The packing code is likely to require one additional memory to memory copy of the data, as compared to the derived-datatype code. One may expect, on most implementations, to achieve better performance with the derived datatype code.

Both codes send the same size message, so that there is no difference in communication time. However, if the buffer described by the derived datatype is not contiguous in memory, it may take longer to access.

Example 3.28 above illustrates another advantage of pack/unpack; namely the receiving process may use information in part of an incoming message in order to decide how to handle subsequent data in the message. In order to achieve the same outcome without pack/unpack, one would have to send two messages: the first with the list of indices, to be used to construct a derived datatype that is then used to receive the particle entries sent in a second message.

The use of derived datatypes will often lead to improved performance: data copying can be avoided, and information on data layout can be reused, when the same communication buffer is reused. On the other hand, the definition of derived datatypes for complex layouts can be more tedious than explicit packing. Derived datatypes should be used whenever data layout is defined by program declarations (e.g., structures), or is regular (e.g., array sections). Packing might be considered for complex, dynamic, data-dependent layouts. Packing may result in more efficient code in situations where the sender has to communicate to the receiver information that affects the layout of the receive buffer.

4 Collective Communications

4.1 Introduction and Overview

Collective communications transmit data among all processes in a group specified by an intracommunicator object. One function, the barrier, serves to synchronize processes without passing data. MPI provides the following collective communication functions.

- Barrier synchronization across all group members (Section 4.4).
- Global communication functions, which are illustrated in Figure 4.1. They include.
  −Broadcast from one member to all members of a group (Section 4.5).

  −Gather data from all group members to one member (Section 4.6).

  −Scatter data from one member to all members of a group (Section 4.7).

  −A variation on Gather where all members of the group receive the result (Section 4.8). This is shown as "allgather" in Figure 4.1.

  −Scatter/Gather data from all members to all members of a group (also called complete exchange or all-to-all) (Section 4.9). This is shown as "alltoall" in Figure 4.1.
- Global reduction operations such as sum, max, min, or user-defined functions. This includes
  −Reduction where the result is returned to all group members and a variation where the result is returned to only one member (Section 4.10).

  −A combined reduction and scatter operation (Section 4.10.5).

  −Scan across all members of a group (also called prefix) (Section 4.11).

Figure 4.1 gives a pictorial representation of the global communication functions. All these functions (broadcast excepted) come in two variants: the simple variant, where all communicated items are messages of the same size, and the "vector" variant, where each item can be of a different size. In addition, in the simple variant, multiple items originating from the same process or received at the same process, are contiguous in memory; the vector variant allows to pick the distinct items from non-contiguous locations.

Some of these functions, such as broadcast or gather, have a single origin or a single receiving process. Such a process is called the **root**. Global communication functions basically comes in three patterns:

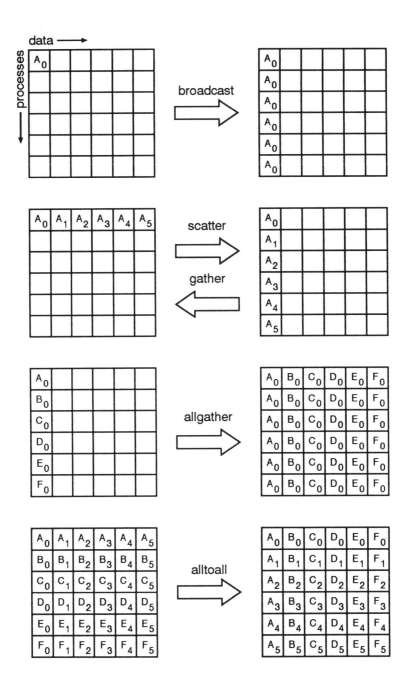

Figure 4.1
Collective move functions illustrated for a group of six processes. In each case, each row of boxes represents data locations in one process. Thus, in the broadcast, initially just the first process contains the item A_0, but after the broadcast all processes contain it.

- Root sends data to all processes (itself included): broadcast and scatter.

- Root receives data from all processes (itself included): gather.

- Each process communicates with each process (itself included): allgather and all-toall.

The syntax and semantics of the MPI collective functions was designed to be consistent with point-to-point communications. However, to keep the number of functions and their argument lists to a reasonable level of complexity, the MPI committee made collective functions more restrictive than the point-to-point functions, in several ways. One restriction is that, in contrast to point-to-point communication, the amount of data sent must exactly match the amount of data specified by the receiver.

A major simplification is that collective functions come in blocking versions only. Though a standing joke at committee meetings concerned the "non-blocking barrier," such functions can be quite useful[1] and may be included in a future version of MPI.

Collective functions do not use a tag argument. Thus, within each intragroup communication domain, collective calls are matched strictly according to the order of execution.

A final simplification of collective functions concerns modes. Collective functions come in only one mode, and this mode may be regarded as analogous to the standard mode of point-to-point. Specifically, the semantics are as follows. A collective function (on a given process) can return as soon as its participation in the overall communication is complete. As usual, the completion indicates that the caller is now free to access and modify locations in the communication buffer(s). It does not indicate that other processes have completed, or even started, the operation. Thus, a collective communication may, or may not, have the effect of synchronizing all calling processes. The barrier, of course, is the exception to this statement.

This choice of semantics was made so as to allow a variety of implementations.

The user of MPI must keep these issues in mind. For example, even though a particular implementation of MPI may provide a broadcast with the side-effect of synchronization (the standard allows this), the standard does not *require* this, and hence, any program that relies on the synchronization will be non-portable. On the other hand, a correct and portable program must allow a collective function to be synchronizing. Though one should not rely on synchronization side-effects, one must program so as to allow for it.

---

[1] Of course the non-blocking barrier would block at the test-for-completion call.

Though these issues and statements may seem unusually obscure, they are merely a consequence of the desire of MPI to:

- allow efficient implementations on a variety of architectures; and,
- be clear about exactly what is, and what is not, guaranteed by the standard.

4.2   Operational Details

A collective operation is executed by having all processes in the group call the communication routine, with matching arguments. The syntax and semantics of the collective operations are defined to be consistent with the syntax and semantics of the point-to-point operations. Thus, user-defined datatypes are allowed and must match between sending and receiving processes as specified in Chapter 3. One of the key arguments is an intracommunicator that defines the group of participating processes and provides a communication domain for the operation. In calls where a root process is defined, some arguments are specified as "significant only at root," and are ignored for all participants except the root. The reader is referred to Chapter 2 for information concerning communication buffers and type matching rules, to Chapter 3 for user-defined datatypes, and to Chapter 5 for information on how to define groups and create communicators.

The type-matching conditions for the collective operations are more strict than the corresponding conditions between sender and receiver in point-to-point. Namely, for collective operations, the amount of data sent must exactly match the amount of data specified by the receiver. Distinct type maps (the layout in memory, see Section 3.2) between sender and receiver are still allowed.

Collective communication calls may use the same communicators as point-to-point communication; MPI guarantees that messages generated on behalf of collective communication calls will not be confused with messages generated by point-to-point communication. A more detailed discussion of correct use of collective routines is found in Section 4.13.

Rationale.   The equal-data restriction (on type matching) was made so as to avoid the complexity of providing a facility analogous to the status argument of MPI_RECV for discovering the amount of data sent. Some of the collective routines would require an array of status values. This restriction also simplifies implementation. (*End of rationale.*)

Advice to users.   As described in Section 4.1, it is dangerous to rely on synchronization side-effects of the collective operations for program correctness. These issues are discussed further in Section 4.13. (*End of advice to users.*)

Advice to implementors. While vendors may write optimized collective routines matched to their architectures, a complete library of the collective communication routines can be written entirely using the MPI point-to-point communication functions and a few auxiliary functions. If implementing on top of point-to-point, a hidden, special communicator must be created for the collective operation so as to avoid interference with any on-going point-to-point communication at the time of the collective call. This is discussed further in Section 4.13.

Although collective communications are described in terms of messages sent directly from sender(s) to receiver(s), implementations may use a communication pattern where data is forwarded through intermediate nodes. Thus, one could use a logarithmic depth tree to implement broadcast, rather then sending data directly from the root to each other process. Messages can be forwarded to intermediate nodes and split (for scatter) or concatenated (for gather). An optimal implementation of collective communication will take advantage of the specifics of the underlying communication network (such as support for multicast, which can be used for MPI broadcast), and will use different algorithms, according to the number of participating processes and the amounts of data communicated. See, e.g. [4]. (*End of advice to implementors.*)

4.3   Communicator Argument

The key concept of the collective functions is to have a "group" of participating processes. The routines do not have a group identifier as an explicit argument. Instead, there is a communicator argument. For the purposes of this chapter, a communicator can be thought of as a group identifier linked with a communication domain. An intercommunicator, that is, a communicator that spans two groups, is *not* allowed as an argument to a collective function.

4.4 Barrier Synchronization

MPI_BARRIER(comm)

    IN   comm   communicator

```
int MPI_Barrier(MPI_Comm comm)
```

```
MPI_BARRIER(COMM, IERROR)
    INTEGER COMM, IERROR
```

MPI_BARRIER blocks the caller until all group members have called it. The call
returns at any process only after all group members have entered the call.

4.5 Broadcast

MPI_BCAST(buffer, count, datatype, root, comm)

INOUT	buffer	starting address of buffer
IN	count	number of entries in buffer
IN	datatype	data type of buffer
IN	root	rank of broadcast root
IN	comm	communicator

```
int MPI_Bcast(void* buffer, int count, MPI_Datatype datatype,
              int root, MPI_Comm comm )
```

```
MPI_BCAST(BUFFER, COUNT, DATATYPE, ROOT, COMM, IERROR)
    <type> BUFFER(*)
    INTEGER COUNT, DATATYPE, ROOT, COMM, IERROR
```

MPI_BCAST broadcasts a message from the process with rank root to all processes
of the group. The argument root must have identical values on all processes, and
comm must represent the same intragroup communication domain. On return, the
contents of root's communication buffer has been copied to all processes.

General, derived datatypes are allowed for datatype. The type signature of count
and datatype on any process must be equal to the type signature of count and
datatype at the root. This implies that the amount of data sent must be equal to

the amount received, pairwise between each process and the root. MPI_BCAST and all other data-movement collective routines make this restriction. Distinct type maps between sender and receiver are still allowed.

4.5.1 Example Using MPI_BCAST

Example 4.1 Broadcast 100 ints from process 0 to every process in the group.

```
MPI_Comm comm;
int array[100];
int root=0;
...
MPI_Bcast( array, 100, MPI_INT, root, comm);
```

Rationale. MPI does not support a *multicast* function, where a broadcast executed by a root can be matched by regular receives at the remaining processes. Such a function is easy to implement if the root directly sends data to each receiving process. But, then, there is little to be gained, as compared to executing multiple send operations. An implementation where processes are used as intermediate nodes in a broadcast tree is hard, since only the root executes a call that identifies the operation as a broadcast. In contrast, in a collective call to MPI_BCAST all processes are aware that they participate in a broadcast. (*End of rationale.*)

4.6   Gather

MPI_GATHER(sendbuf, sendcount, sendtype, recvbuf, recvcount, recvtype, root, comm)

IN	sendbuf	starting address of send buffer
IN	sendcount	number of elements in send buffer
IN	sendtype	data type of send buffer elements
OUT	recvbuf	address of receive buffer
IN	recvcount	number of elements for any single receive
IN	recvtype	data type of recv buffer elements
IN	root	rank of receiving process
IN	comm	communicator

```
int MPI_Gather(void* sendbuf, int sendcount, MPI_Datatype sendtype,
          void* recvbuf, int recvcount, MPI_Datatype recvtype,
          int root, MPI_Comm comm)
```

```
MPI_GATHER(SENDBUF, SENDCOUNT, SENDTYPE, RECVBUF, RECVCOUNT,
          RECVTYPE, ROOT, COMM, IERROR)
   <type> SENDBUF(*), RECVBUF(*)
   INTEGER SENDCOUNT, SENDTYPE, RECVCOUNT, RECVTYPE, ROOT, COMM,
   IERROR
```

Each process (root process included) sends the contents of its send buffer to the root process. The root process receives the messages and stores them in rank order. The outcome is *as if* each of the n processes in the group (including the root process) had executed a call to MPI_Send(sendbuf, sendcount, sendtype, root, ...), and the root had executed n calls to MPI_Recv(recvbuf+i·recvcount·extent(recvtype), recvcount, recvtype, i ,...), where extent(recvtype) is the type extent obtained from a call to MPI_Type_extent().

An alternative description is that the n messages sent by the processes in the group are concatenated in rank order, and the resulting message is received by the root as if by a call to MPI_RECV(recvbuf, recvcount·n, recvtype, ...).

The receive buffer is ignored for all non-root processes.

General, derived datatypes are allowed for both sendtype and recvtype. The type signature of sendcount and sendtype on process i must be equal to the type signature of recvcount and recvtype at the root. This implies that the amount of data sent must be equal to the amount of data received, pairwise between each process and the root. Distinct type maps between sender and receiver are still allowed.

All arguments to the function are significant on process root, while on other processes, only arguments sendbuf, sendcount, sendtype, root, and comm are significant. The argument root must have identical values on all processes and comm must represent the same intragroup communication domain.

The specification of counts and types should not cause any location on the root to be written more than once. Such a call is erroneous.

Note that the recvcount argument at the root indicates the number of items it receives from *each* process, not the total number of items it receives.

4.6.1 Examples Using MPI_GATHER

Example 4.2 Gather 100 ints from every process in group to root. See Figure 4.2.

```
MPI_Comm comm;
int gsize,sendarray[100];
int root, *rbuf;
...
MPI_Comm_size( comm, &gsize);
rbuf = (int *)malloc(gsize*100*sizeof(int));
MPI_Gather( sendarray, 100, MPI_INT, rbuf, 100, MPI_INT, root, comm);
```

Example 4.3 Previous example modified – only the root allocates memory for the receive buffer.

```
MPI_Comm comm;
int gsize,sendarray[100];
int root, myrank, *rbuf;
...
MPI_Comm_rank( comm, myrank);
if ( myrank == root) {
   MPI_Comm_size( comm, &gsize);
   rbuf = (int *)malloc(gsize*100*sizeof(int));
   }
MPI_Gather( sendarray, 100, MPI_INT, rbuf, 100, MPI_INT, root, comm);
```

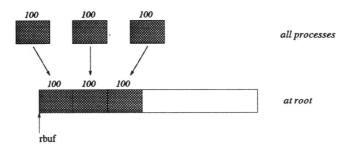

Figure 4.2
The root process gathers 100 ints from each process in the group.

Example 4.4 Do the same as the previous example, but use a derived datatype. Note that the type cannot be the entire set of **gsize*100 ints** since type matching is defined pairwise between the root and each process in the gather.

```
MPI_Comm comm;
int gsize,sendarray[100];
int root, *rbuf;
MPI_Datatype rtype;
...
MPI_Comm_size( comm, &gsize);
MPI_Type_contiguous( 100, MPI_INT, &rtype );
MPI_Type_commit( &rtype );
rbuf = (int *)malloc(gsize*100*sizeof(int));
MPI_Gather( sendarray, 100, MPI_INT, rbuf, 1, rtype, root, comm);
```

4.6.2   Gather, Vector Variant

MPI_GATHERV(sendbuf, sendcount, sendtype, recvbuf, recvcounts, displs, recvtype, root, comm)

IN	sendbuf	starting address of send buffer
IN	sendcount	number of elements in send buffer
IN	sendtype	data type of send buffer elements
OUT	recvbuf	address of receive buffer
IN	recvcounts	integer array
IN	displs	integer array of displacements
IN	recvtype	data type of recv buffer elements
IN	root	rank of receiving process
IN	comm	communicator

```
int MPI_Gatherv(void* sendbuf, int sendcount, MPI_Datatype sendtype,
            void* recvbuf, int *recvcounts, int *displs,
            MPI_Datatype recvtype, int root, MPI_Comm comm)
```

```
MPI_GATHERV(SENDBUF, SENDCOUNT, SENDTYPE, RECVBUF, RECVCOUNTS,
            DISPLS, RECVTYPE, ROOT, COMM, IERROR)
    <type> SENDBUF(*), RECVBUF(*)
    INTEGER SENDCOUNT, SENDTYPE, RECVCOUNTS(*), DISPLS(*), RECVTYPE,
    ROOT, COMM, IERROR
```

MPI_GATHERV extends the functionality of MPI_GATHER by allowing a varying count of data from each process, since recvcounts is now an array. It also allows more flexibility as to where the data is placed on the root, by providing the new argument, displs.

The outcome is *as if* each process, including the root process, sends a message to the root, MPI_Send(sendbuf, sendcount, sendtype, root, ...) and the root executes n receives, MPI_Recv(recvbuf+displs[i]·extent(recvtype), recvcounts[i], recvtype, i, ...).

The data sent from process j is placed in the jth portion of the receive buffer recvbuf on process root. The jth portion of recvbuf begins at offset displs[j] elements (in terms of recvtype) into recvbuf.

The receive buffer is ignored for all non-root processes.

The type signature implied by sendcount and sendtype on process i must be equal to the type signature implied by recvcounts[i] and recvtype at the root. This implies that the amount of data sent must be equal to the amount of data received, pairwise between each process and the root. Distinct type maps between sender and receiver are still allowed, as illustrated in Example 4.6.

All arguments to the function are significant on process root, while on other processes, only arguments sendbuf, sendcount, sendtype, root, and comm are significant. The argument root must have identical values on all processes, and comm must represent the same intragroup communication domain.

The specification of counts, types, and displacements should not cause any location on the root to be written more than once. Such a call is erroneous. On the other hand, the successive displacements in the array displs need not be a monotonic sequence.

4.6.3   Examples Using MPI_GATHERV

Example 4.5 Have each process send 100 ints to root, but place each set (of 100) *stride* ints apart at receiving end. Use MPI_GATHERV and the displs argument to achieve this effect. Assume *stride* $\geq$ 100. See Figure 4.3.

```
MPI_Comm comm;
int gsize,sendarray[100];
int root, *rbuf, stride;
int *displs,i,*rcounts;

...

MPI_Comm_size( comm, &gsize);
rbuf = (int *)malloc(gsize*stride*sizeof(int));
displs = (int *)malloc(gsize*sizeof(int));
rcounts = (int *)malloc(gsize*sizeof(int));
for (i=0; i<gsize; ++i) {
    displs[i] = i*stride;
    rcounts[i] = 100;
}
MPI_Gatherv( sendarray, 100, MPI_INT, rbuf, rcounts, displs, MPI_INT,
                                                         root, comm);
```

Note that the program is erroneous if $-100 < stride < 100$.

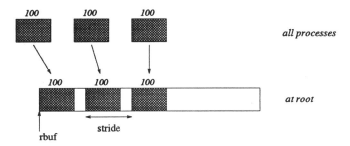

Figure 4.3
The root process gathers 100 ints from each process in the group, each set is placed `stride` ints apart.

Example 4.6 Same as Example 4.5 on the receiving side, but send the 100 ints from the 0th column of a 100×150 int array, in C. See Figure 4.4.

```
MPI_Comm comm;
int gsize,sendarray[100][150];
int root, *rbuf, stride;
MPI_Datatype stype;
int *displs,i,*rcounts;

...

MPI_Comm_size( comm, &gsize);
rbuf = (int *)malloc(gsize*stride*sizeof(int));
displs = (int *)malloc(gsize*sizeof(int));
rcounts = (int *)malloc(gsize*sizeof(int));
for (i=0; i<gsize; ++i) {
    displs[i] = i*stride;
    rcounts[i] = 100;
}
/* Create datatype for 1 column of array
 */
MPI_Type_vector( 100, 1, 150, MPI_INT, &stype);
MPI_Type_commit( &stype );
MPI_Gatherv( sendarray, 1, stype, rbuf, rcounts, displs, MPI_INT,
                                                root, comm);
```

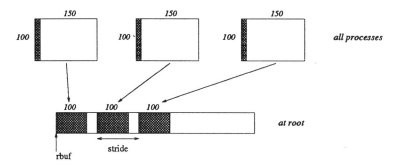

Figure 4.4
The root process gathers column 0 of a 100×150 C array, and each set is placed **stride** ints apart.

Example 4.7 Process i sends (100-i) ints from the ith column of a 100×150 int array, in C. It is received into a buffer with stride, as in the previous two examples. See Figure 4.5.

```
MPI_Comm comm;
int gsize,sendarray[100][150],*sptr;
int root, *rbuf, stride, myrank;
MPI_Datatype stype;
int *displs,i,*rcounts;

    ...

MPI_Comm_size( comm, &gsize);
MPI_Comm_rank( comm, &myrank );
rbuf = (int *)malloc(gsize*stride*sizeof(int));
displs = (int *)malloc(gsize*sizeof(int));
rcounts = (int *)malloc(gsize*sizeof(int));
for (i=0; i<gsize; ++i) {
    displs[i] = i*stride;
    rcounts[i] = 100-i;     /* note change from previous example */
}
/* Create datatype for the column we are sending
 */
MPI_Type_vector( 100-myrank, 1, 150, MPI_INT, &stype);
MPI_Type_commit( &stype );
/* sptr is the address of start of "myrank" column
```

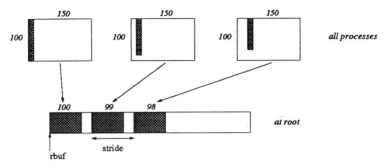

Figure 4.5
The root process gathers 100-i ints from column i of a 100×150 C array, and each set is placed
`stride` ints apart.

```
    */
    sptr = &sendarray[0][myrank];
    MPI_Gatherv( sptr, 1, stype, rbuf, rcounts, displs, MPI_INT,
                                                    root, comm);
```

Note that a different amount of data is received from each process.

Example 4.8 Same as Example 4.7, but done in a different way at the sending
end. We create a datatype that causes the correct striding at the sending end so
that that we read a column of a C array.

```
    MPI_Comm comm;
    int gsize,sendarray[100][150],*sptr;
    int root, *rbuf, stride, myrank, disp[2], blocklen[2];
    MPI_Datatype stype,type[2];
    int *displs,i,*rcounts;

    ...

    MPI_Comm_size( comm, &gsize);
    MPI_Comm_rank( comm, &myrank );
    rbuf = (int *)malloc(gsize*stride*sizeof(int));
    displs = (int *)malloc(gsize*sizeof(int));
    rcounts = (int *)malloc(gsize*sizeof(int));
    for (i=0; i<gsize; ++i) {
        displs[i] = i*stride;
```

```
        rcounts[i] = 100-i;
}
/* Create datatype for one int, with extent of entire row
 */
disp[0] = 0;        disp[1] = 150*sizeof(int);
type[0] = MPI_INT; type[1] = MPI_UB;
blocklen[0] = 1;    blocklen[1] = 1;
MPI_Type_struct( 2, blocklen, disp, type, &stype );
MPI_Type_commit( &stype );
sptr = &sendarray[0][myrank];
MPI_Gatherv( sptr, 100-myrank, stype, rbuf, rcounts, displs, MPI_INT,
                                                    root, comm);
```

Example 4.9 Same as Example 4.7 at sending side, but at receiving side we make the stride between received blocks vary from block to block. See Figure 4.6.

```
MPI_Comm comm;
int gsize,sendarray[100][150],*sptr;
int root, *rbuf, *stride, myrank, bufsize;
MPI_Datatype stype;
int *displs,i,*rcounts,offset;

  ...

MPI_Comm_size( comm, &gsize);
MPI_Comm_rank( comm, &myrank );

stride = (int *)malloc(gsize*sizeof(int));
  ...
/* stride[i] for i = 0 to gsize-1 is set somehow
 */

/* set up displs and rcounts vectors first
 */
displs = (int *)malloc(gsize*sizeof(int));
rcounts = (int *)malloc(gsize*sizeof(int));
offset = 0;
for (i=0; i<gsize; ++i) {
```

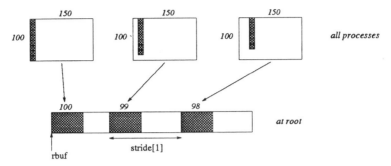

Figure 4.6
The root process gathers 100-i ints from column i of a 100×150 C array, and each set is placed
`stride[i]` ints apart (a varying stride).

```
            displs[i] = offset;
            offset += stride[i];
            rcounts[i] = 100-i;
    }
    /* the required buffer size for rbuf is now easily obtained
     */
    bufsize = displs[gsize-1]+rcounts[gsize-1];
    rbuf = (int *)malloc(bufsize*sizeof(int));
    /* Create datatype for the column we are sending
     */
    MPI_Type_vector( 100-myrank, 1, 150, MPI_INT, &stype);
    MPI_Type_commit( &stype );
    sptr = &sendarray[0][myrank];
    MPI_Gatherv( sptr, 1, stype, rbuf, rcounts, displs, MPI_INT,
                                                    root, comm);
```

Example 4.10 Process i sends **num** ints from the ith column of a 100×150 int
array, in C. The complicating factor is that the various values of **num** are not known
to **root**, so a separate gather must first be run to find these out. The data is placed
contiguously at the receiving end.

```
    MPI_Comm comm;
    int gsize,sendarray[100][150],*sptr;
    int root, *rbuf, stride, myrank, disp[2], blocklen[2];
    MPI_Datatype stype,types[2];
```

```
int *displs,i,*rcounts,num;

...

MPI_Comm_size( comm, &gsize);
MPI_Comm_rank( comm, &myrank );

/* First, gather nums to root
 */
rcounts = (int *)malloc(gsize*sizeof(int));
MPI_Gather( &num, 1, MPI_INT, rcounts, 1, MPI_INT, root, comm);
/* root now has correct rcounts, using these we set displs[] so
 * that data is placed contiguously (or concatenated) at receive end
 */
displs = (int *)malloc(gsize*sizeof(int));
displs[0] = 0;
for (i=1; i<gsize; ++i) {
    displs[i] = displs[i-1]+rcounts[i-1];
}
/* And, create receive buffer
 */
rbuf = (int *)malloc(gsize*(displs[gsize-1]+rcounts[gsize-1])
                                                *sizeof(int));
/* Create datatype for one int, with extent of entire row
 */
disp[0] = 0;      disp[1] = 150*sizeof(int);
type[0] = MPI_INT; type[1] = MPI_UB;
blocklen[0] = 1;   blocklen[1] = 1;
MPI_Type_struct( 2, blocklen, disp, type, &stype );
MPI_Type_commit( &stype );
sptr = &sendarray[0][myrank];
MPI_Gatherv( sptr, num, stype, rbuf, rcounts, displs, MPI_INT,
                                                root, comm);
```

4.7   Scatter

MPI_SCATTER(sendbuf, sendcount, sendtype, recvbuf, recvcount, recvtype, root, comm)

IN	sendbuf	address of send buffer
IN	sendcount	number of elements sent to each process
IN	sendtype	data type of send buffer elements
OUT	recvbuf	address of receive buffer
IN	recvcount	number of elements in receive buffer
IN	recvtype	data type of receive buffer elements
IN	root	rank of sending process
IN	comm	communicator

```
int MPI_Scatter(void* sendbuf, int sendcount, MPI_Datatype sendtype,
          void* recvbuf, int recvcount, MPI_Datatype recvtype,
          int root, MPI_Comm comm)
```

```
MPI_SCATTER(SENDBUF, SENDCOUNT, SENDTYPE, RECVBUF, RECVCOUNT,
          RECVTYPE, ROOT, COMM, IERROR)
   <type> SENDBUF(*), RECVBUF(*)
   INTEGER SENDCOUNT, SENDTYPE, RECVCOUNT, RECVTYPE, ROOT, COMM,
   IERROR
```

MPI_SCATTER is the inverse operation to MPI_GATHER.

The outcome is *as if* the root executed n send operations, MPI_Send(sendbuf+i·sendcount·extent(sendtype), sendcount, sendtype, i,...), i = 0 to n - 1. and each process executed a receive, MPI_Recv(recvbuf, recvcount, recvtype, root,...).

An alternative description is that the root sends a message with MPI_Send(sendbuf, sendcount·n, sendtype, ...). This message is split into n equal segments, the ith segment is sent to the ith process in the group, and each process receives this message as above.

The type signature associated with sendcount and sendtype at the root must be equal to the type signature associated with recvcount and recvtype at all processes. This implies that the amount of data sent must be equal to the amount of data received, pairwise between each process and the root. Distinct type maps between sender and receiver are still allowed.

All arguments to the function are significant on process root, while on other processes, only arguments recvbuf, recvcount, recvtype, root, comm are significant.

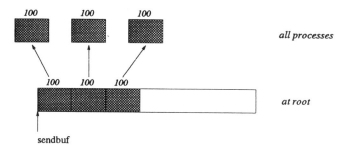

Figure 4.7
The root process scatters sets of 100 ints to each process in the group.

The argument **root** must have identical values on all processes and **comm** must represent the same intragroup communication domain. The send buffer is ignored for all non-root processes.

The specification of counts and types should not cause any location on the root to be read more than once.

Rationale.   Though not essential, the last restriction is imposed so as to achieve symmetry with MPI_GATHER, where the corresponding restriction (a multiple-write restriction) is necessary. (*End of rationale.*)

4.7.1   An Example Using MPI_SCATTER

Example 4.11 The reverse of Example 4.2, page 155. Scatter sets of 100 ints from the root to each process in the group. See Figure 4.7.

```
MPI_Comm comm;
int gsize,*sendbuf;
int root, rbuf[100];
...
MPI_Comm_size( comm, &gsize);
sendbuf = (int *)malloc(gsize*100*sizeof(int));
...
MPI_Scatter( sendbuf, 100, MPI_INT, rbuf, 100, MPI_INT, root, comm);
```

4.7.2   Scatter: Vector Variant

MPI_SCATTERV(sendbuf, sendcounts, displs, sendtype, recvbuf, recvcount, recvtype, root, comm)

IN	sendbuf	address of send buffer
IN	sendcounts	integer array
IN	displs	integer array of displacements
IN	sendtype	data type of send buffer elements
OUT	recvbuf	address of receive buffer
IN	recvcount	number of elements in receive buffer
IN	recvtype	data type of receive buffer elements
IN	root	rank of sending process
IN	comm	communicator

```
int MPI_Scatterv(void* sendbuf, int *sendcounts, int *displs,
          MPI_Datatype sendtype, void* recvbuf, int recvcount,
          MPI_Datatype recvtype, int root, MPI_Comm comm)
```

```
MPI_SCATTERV(SENDBUF, SENDCOUNTS, DISPLS, SENDTYPE, RECVBUF,
          RECVCOUNT, RECVTYPE, ROOT, COMM, IERROR)
   <type> SENDBUF(*), RECVBUF(*)
   INTEGER SENDCOUNTS(*), DISPLS(*), SENDTYPE, RECVCOUNT, RECVTYPE,
   ROOT, COMM, IERROR
```

MPI_SCATTERV is the inverse operation to MPI_GATHERV.

MPI_SCATTERV extends the functionality of MPI_SCATTER by allowing a varying count of data to be sent to each process, since sendcounts is now an array. It also allows more flexibility as to where the data is taken from on the root, by providing the new argument, displs.

The outcome is as if the root executed n send operations, MPI_Send(sendbuf+displs [i]·extent(sendtype), sendcounts[i], sendtype, i,...), i = 0 to n - 1, and each process executed a receive, MPI_Recv(recvbuf, recvcount, recvtype, root,...).

The type signature implied by sendcount[i] and sendtype at the root must be equal to the type signature implied by recvcount and recvtype at process i. This implies that the amount of data sent must be equal to the amount of data received, pairwise between each process and the root. Distinct type maps between sender and receiver are still allowed.

All arguments to the function are significant on process root, while on other processes, only arguments recvbuf, recvcount, recvtype, root, comm are significant. The arguments root must have identical values on all processes, and comm must represent the same intragroup communication domain. The send buffer is ignored for all non-root processes.

The specification of counts, types, and displacements should not cause any location on the root to be read more than once.

4.7.3   Examples Using MPI_SCATTERV

Example 4.12 The reverse of Example 4.5, page 158. The root process scatters sets of 100 ints to the other processes, but the sets of 100 are *stride* ints apart in the sending buffer, where $stride \geq 100$. This requires use of MPI_SCATTERV. See Figure 4.8.

```
MPI_Comm comm;
int gsize,*sendbuf;
int root, rbuf[100], i, *displs, *scounts;

...

MPI_Comm_size( comm, &gsize);
sendbuf = (int *)malloc(gsize*stride*sizeof(int));
...
displs = (int *)malloc(gsize*sizeof(int));
scounts = (int *)malloc(gsize*sizeof(int));
for (i=0; i<gsize; ++i) {
    displs[i] = i*stride;
    scounts[i] = 100;
}
MPI_Scatterv( sendbuf, scounts, displs, MPI_INT, rbuf, 100, MPI_INT,
                                                     root, comm);
```

Example 4.13 The reverse of Example 4.9. We have a varying stride between blocks at sending (root) side, at the receiving side we receive $100 - i$ elements into the ith column of a 100×150 C array at process i. See Figure 4.9.

```
MPI_Comm comm;
int gsize,recvarray[100][150],*rptr;
```

Figure 4.8
The root process scatters sets of 100 ints, moving by stride ints from send to send in the scatter.

```
int root, *sendbuf, myrank, bufsize, *stride;
MPI_Datatype rtype;
int i, *displs, *scounts, offset;
...
MPI_Comm_size( comm, &gsize);
MPI_Comm_rank( comm, &myrank );

stride = (int *)malloc(gsize*sizeof(int));
...
/* stride[i] for i = 0 to gsize-1 is set somehow
 * sendbuf comes from elsewhere */
...
displs = (int *)malloc(gsize*sizeof(int));
scounts = (int *)malloc(gsize*sizeof(int));
offset = 0;
for (i=0; i<gsize; ++i) {
    displs[i] = offset;
    offset += stride[i];
    scounts[i] = 100 - i;
}
/* Create datatype for the column we are receiving */
MPI_Type_vector( 100-myrank, 1, 150, MPI_INT, &rtype);
MPI_Type_commit( &rtype );
rptr = &recvarray[0][myrank];
MPI_Scatterv( sendbuf, scounts, displs, MPI_INT, rptr, 1, rtype,
                                                root, comm);
```

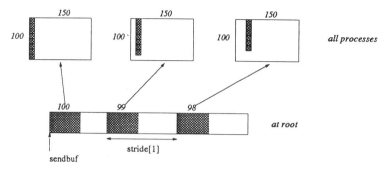

Figure 4.9
The root scatters blocks of 100-i ints into column i of a 100×150 C array. At the sending side, the blocks are `stride[i]` ints apart.

4.8   Gather to All

MPI_ALLGATHER(sendbuf, sendcount, sendtype, recvbuf, recvcount, recvtype, comm)

IN	sendbuf	starting address of send buffer
IN	sendcount	number of elements in send buffer
IN	sendtype	data type of send buffer elements
OUT	recvbuf	address of receive buffer
IN	recvcount	number of elements received from any process
IN	recvtype	data type of receive buffer elements
IN	comm	communicator

```
int MPI_Allgather(void* sendbuf, int sendcount,
          MPI_Datatype sendtype, void* recvbuf, int recvcount,
          MPI_Datatype recvtype, MPI_Comm comm)
```

```
MPI_ALLGATHER(SENDBUF, SENDCOUNT, SENDTYPE, RECVBUF, RECVCOUNT,
          RECVTYPE, COMM, IERROR)
    <type> SENDBUF(*), RECVBUF(*)
    INTEGER SENDCOUNT, SENDTYPE, RECVCOUNT, RECVTYPE, COMM, IERROR
```

MPI_ALLGATHER can be thought of as MPI_GATHER, except all processes receive the result, instead of just the root. The jth block of data sent from each process is received by every process and placed in the jth block of the buffer recvbuf.

The type signature associated with sendcount and sendtype at a process must be equal to the type signature associated with recvcount and recvtype at any other process.

The outcome of a call to MPI_ALLGATHER(...) is as if all processes executed n calls to MPI_GATHER(sendbuf, sendcount, sendtype, recvbuf, recvcount, recvtype, root, comm), for root = 0 , ..., n-1. The rules for correct usage of MPI_ALLGATHER are easily found from the corresponding rules for MPI_GATHER.

4.8.1   An Example Using MPI_ALLGATHER

Example 4.14 The all-gather version of Example 4.2, page 155. Using MPI_ALL-GATHER, we will gather 100 ints from every process in the group to every process.

```
MPI_Comm comm;
int gsize,sendarray[100];
int *rbuf;
...
MPI_Comm_size( comm, &gsize);
rbuf = (int *)malloc(gsize*100*sizeof(int));
MPI_Allgather( sendarray, 100, MPI_INT, rbuf, 100, MPI_INT, comm);
```

After the call, every process has the group-wide concatenation of the sets of data.

4.8.2   Gather to All: Vector Variant

MPI_ALLGATHERV(sendbuf, sendcount, sendtype, recvbuf, recvcounts, displs, recvtype, comm)

IN	sendbuf	starting address of send buffer
IN	sendcount	number of elements in send buffer
IN	sendtype	data type of send buffer elements
OUT	recvbuf	address of receive buffer
IN	recvcounts	integer array
IN	displs	integer array of displacements
IN	recvtype	data type of receive buffer elements
IN	comm	communicator

```
int MPI_Allgatherv(void* sendbuf, int sendcount,
            MPI_Datatype sendtype, void* recvbuf, int *recvcounts,
            int *displs, MPI_Datatype recvtype, MPI_Comm comm)
```

```
MPI_ALLGATHERV(SENDBUF, SENDCOUNT, SENDTYPE, RECVBUF, RECVCOUNTS,
            DISPLS, RECVTYPE, COMM, IERROR)
    <type> SENDBUF(*), RECVBUF(*)
    INTEGER SENDCOUNT, SENDTYPE, RECVCOUNTS(*), DISPLS(*), RECVTYPE,
    COMM, IERROR
```

MPI_ALLGATHERV can be thought of as MPI_GATHERV, except all processes receive the result, instead of just the root. The jth block of data sent from each process is received by every process and placed in the jth block of the buffer recvbuf. These blocks need not all be the same size.

The type signature associated with sendcount and sendtype at process j must be equal to the type signature associated with recvcounts[j] and recvtype at any other process.

The outcome is as if all processes executed calls to MPI_GATHERV(sendbuf, sendcount, sendtype,recvbuf,recvcounts,displs, recvtype,root,comm), for root = 0 , ..., n-1. The rules for correct usage of MPI_ALLGATHERV are easily found from the corresponding rules for MPI_GATHERV.

4.9   All to All Scatter/Gather

MPI_ALLTOALL(sendbuf, sendcount, sendtype, recvbuf, recvcount, recvtype, comm)

IN	sendbuf	starting address of send buffer
IN	sendcount	number of elements sent to each process
IN	sendtype	data type of send buffer elements
OUT	recvbuf	address of receive buffer
IN	recvcount	number of elements received from any process
IN	recvtype	data type of receive buffer elements
IN	comm	communicator

```
int MPI_Alltoall(void* sendbuf, int sendcount, MPI_Datatype sendtype,
          void* recvbuf, int recvcount, MPI_Datatype recvtype,
          MPI_Comm comm)
```

```
MPI_ALLTOALL(SENDBUF, SENDCOUNT, SENDTYPE, RECVBUF, RECVCOUNT,
          RECVTYPE, COMM, IERROR)
   <type> SENDBUF(*), RECVBUF(*)
   INTEGER SENDCOUNT, SENDTYPE, RECVCOUNT, RECVTYPE, COMM, IERROR
```

MPI_ALLTOALL is an extension of MPI_ALLGATHER to the case where each process sends distinct data to each of the receivers. The jth block sent from process i is received by process j and is placed in the ith block of recvbuf.

The type signature associated with sendcount and sendtype at a process must be equal to the type signature associated with recvcount and recvtype at any other process. This implies that the amount of data sent must be equal to the amount of data received, pairwise between every pair of processes. As usual, however, the type maps may be different.

The outcome is as if each process executed a send to each process (itself included) with a call to, MPI_Send(sendbuf+i·sendcount·extent(sendtype), sendcount, sendtype, i, ...), and a receive from every other process with a call to, MPI_Recv(recvbuf+i· recvcount·extent(recvtype), recvcount, i,...), where i = 0, ···, n - 1.

All arguments on all processes are significant. The argument comm must represent the same intragroup communication domain on all processes.

Rationale.   The definition of MPI_ALLTOALL gives as much flexibility as one would achieve by specifying at each process n independent, point-to-point communications, with two exceptions: all messages use the same datatype, and messages are scattered from (or gathered to) sequential storage. (*End of rationale.*)

4.9.1 All to All: Vector Variant

MPI_ALLTOALLV(sendbuf, sendcounts, sdispls, sendtype, recvbuf, recvcounts, rdispls, recvtype, comm)

IN	sendbuf	starting address of send buffer
IN	sendcounts	integer array
IN	sdispls	integer array of send displacements
IN	sendtype	data type of send buffer elements
OUT	recvbuf	address of receive buffer
IN	recvcounts	integer array
IN	rdispls	integer array of receive displacements
IN	recvtype	data type of receive buffer elements
IN	comm	communicator

```
int MPI_Alltoallv(void* sendbuf, int *sendcounts, int *sdispls,
            MPI_Datatype sendtype, void* recvbuf, int *recvcounts,
            int *rdispls, MPI_Datatype recvtype, MPI_Comm comm)
```

```
MPI_ALLTOALLV(SENDBUF, SENDCOUNTS, SDISPLS, SENDTYPE, RECVBUF,
            RECVCOUNTS, RDISPLS, RECVTYPE, COMM, IERROR)
    <type> SENDBUF(*), RECVBUF(*)
    INTEGER SENDCOUNTS(*), SDISPLS(*), SENDTYPE, RECVCOUNTS(*),
    RDISPLS(*), RECVTYPE, COMM, IERROR
```

MPI_ALLTOALLV adds flexibility to MPI_ALLTOALL in that the location of data for the send is specified by sdispls and the location of the placement of the data on the receive side is specified by rdispls.

The jth block sent from process i is received by process j and is placed in the ith block of recvbuf. These blocks need not all have the same size.

The type signature associated with sendcount[j] and sendtype at process i must be equal to the type signature associated with recvcount[i] and recvtype at process j. This implies that the amount of data sent must be equal to the amount of data received, pairwise between every pair of processes. Distinct type maps between sender and receiver are still allowed.

The outcome is as if each process sent a message to process i with MPI_Send(sendbuf + displs[i]·extent(sendtype), sendcounts[i], sendtype, i, ...), and received a message from process i with a call to MPI_Recv(recvbuf + displs[i]·extent(recvtype), recvcounts[i], recvtype, i, ...), where i = 0 ··· n - 1.

All arguments on all processes are significant. The argument comm must specify the same intragroup communication domain on all processes.

Rationale. The definition of MPI_ALLTOALLV gives as much flexibility as one would achieve by specifying at each process n independent, point-to-point communications, with the exception that all messages use the same datatype. (*End of rationale.*)

4.10 Global Reduction Operations

The functions in this section perform a global reduce operation (such as sum, max, logical AND, etc.) across all the members of a group. The reduction operation can be either one of a predefined list of operations, or a user-defined operation. The global reduction functions come in several flavors: a reduce that returns the result of the reduction at one node, an all-reduce that returns this result at all nodes, and a scan (parallel prefix) operation. In addition, a reduce-scatter operation combines the functionality of a reduce and of a scatter operation. In order to improve performance, the functions can be passed an array of values; one call will perform a sequence of element-wise reductions on the arrays of values. Figure 4.10 gives a pictorial representation of these operations.

4.10.1 Reduce

MPI_REDUCE(sendbuf, recvbuf, count, datatype, op, root, comm)

IN	sendbuf	address of send buffer
OUT	recvbuf	address of receive buffer
IN	count	number of elements in send buffer
IN	datatype	data type of elements of send buffer
IN	op	reduce operation
IN	root	rank of root process
IN	comm	communicator

```
int MPI_Reduce(void* sendbuf, void* recvbuf, int count,
            MPI_Datatype datatype, MPI_Op op, int root,
            MPI_Comm comm)
```

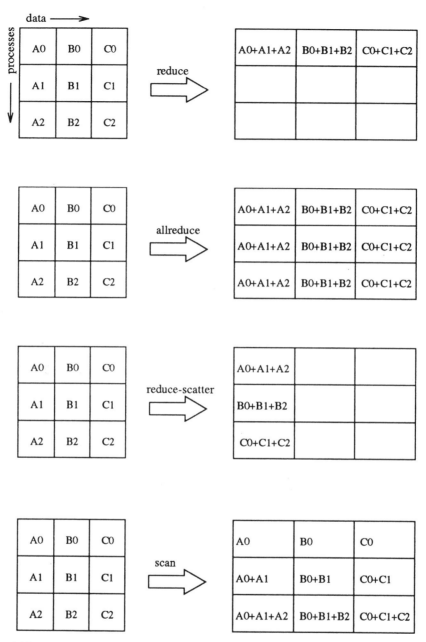

Figure 4.10
Reduce functions illustrated for a group of three processes. In each case, each row of boxes represents data items in one process. Thus, in the reduce, initially each process has three items; after the reduce the root process has three sums.

```
MPI_REDUCE(SENDBUF, RECVBUF, COUNT, DATATYPE, OP, ROOT, COMM,
           IERROR)
  <type> SENDBUF(*), RECVBUF(*)
  INTEGER COUNT, DATATYPE, OP, ROOT, COMM, IERROR
```

MPI_REDUCE combines the elements provided in the input buffer of each process in the group, using the operation op, and returns the combined value in the output buffer of the process with rank root. The input buffer is defined by the arguments sendbuf, count and datatype; the output buffer is defined by the arguments recvbuf, count and datatype; both have the same number of elements, with the same type. The arguments count, op and root must have identical values at all processes, the datatype arguments should match, and comm should represent the same intragroup communication domain. Thus, all processes provide input buffers and output buffers of the same length, with elements of the same type. Each process can provide one element, or a sequence of elements, in which case the combine operation is executed element-wise on each entry of the sequence. For example, if the operation is MPI_MAX and the send buffer contains two elements that are floating point numbers (count = 2 and datatype = MPI_FLOAT), then recvbuf(0) = global max(sendbuf(0)) and recvbuf(1) = global max(sendbuf(1)).

Section 4.10.2 lists the set of predefined operations provided by MPI. That section also enumerates the allowed datatypes for each operation. In addition, users may define their own operations that can be overloaded to operate on several datatypes, either basic or derived. This is further explained in Section 4.12.

The operation op is always assumed to be associative. All predefined operations are also commutative. Users may define operations that are assumed to be associative, but not commutative. The "canonical" evaluation order of a reduction is determined by the ranks of the processes in the group. However, the implementation can take advantage of associativity, or associativity and commutativity in order to change the order of evaluation. This may change the result of the reduction for operations that are not strictly associative and commutative, such as floating point addition.

Advice to implementors. It is strongly recommended that MPI_REDUCE be implemented so that the same result be obtained whenever the function is applied on the same arguments, appearing in the same order. Note that this may prevent optimizations that take advantage of the physical location of processors. (*End of advice to implementors.*)

The datatype argument of MPI_REDUCE must be compatible with op. Predefined operators work only with the MPI types listed in Section 4.10.2 and Section 4.10.3. User-defined operators may operate on general, derived datatypes. In this case, each argument that the reduce operation is applied to is one element described by such a datatype, which may contain several basic values. This is further explained in Section 4.12.

4.10.2 Predefined Reduce Operations

The following predefined operations are supplied for MPI_REDUCE and related functions MPI_ALLREDUCE, MPI_REDUCE_SCATTER, and MPI_SCAN. These operations are invoked by placing the following in op.

Name	Meaning
MPI_MAX	maximum
MPI_MIN	minimum
MPI_SUM	sum
MPI_PROD	product
MPI_LAND	logical and
MPI_BAND	bit-wise and
MPI_LOR	logical or
MPI_BOR	bit-wise or
MPI_LXOR	logical xor
MPI_BXOR	bit-wise xor
MPI_MAXLOC	max value and location
MPI_MINLOC	min value and location

The two operations MPI_MINLOC and MPI_MAXLOC are discussed separately in Section 4.10.3. For the other predefined operations, we enumerate below the allowed combinations of op and datatype arguments. First, define groups of MPI basic datatypes in the following way.

C integer:	MPI_INT, MPI_LONG, MPI_SHORT, MPI_UNSIGNED_SHORT, MPI_UNSIGNED, MPI_UNSIGNED_LONG
Fortran integer:	MPI_INTEGER
Floating point:	MPI_FLOAT, MPI_DOUBLE, MPI_REAL, MPI_DOUBLE_PRECISION, MPI_LONG-_DOUBLE

Logical:	MPI_LOGICAL
Complex:	MPI_COMPLEX
Byte:	MPI_BYTE

Now, the valid datatypes for each option is specified below.

Op	Allowed Types
MPI_MAX, MPI_MIN	C integer, Fortran integer, Floating point
MPI_SUM, MPI_PROD	C integer, Fortran integer, Floating point, Complex
MPI_LAND, MPI_LOR, MPI_LXOR	C integer, Logical
MPI_BAND, MPI_BOR, MPI_BXOR	C integer, Fortran integer, Byte

Example 4.15 A routine that computes the dot product of two vectors that are distributed across a group of processes and returns the answer at node zero.

```
SUBROUTINE PAR_BLAS1(m, a, b, c, comm)
REAL a(m), b(m)        ! local slice of array
REAL c                 ! result (at node zero)
REAL sum
INTEGER m, comm, i, ierr

! local sum
sum = 0.0
DO i = 1, m
   sum = sum + a(i)*b(i)
END DO

! global sum
CALL MPI_REDUCE(sum, c, 1, MPI_REAL, MPI_SUM, 0, comm, ierr)
RETURN
```

Example 4.16 A routine that computes the product of a vector and an array that are distributed across a group of processes and returns the answer at node zero. The distribution of vector a and matrix b is illustrated in Figure 4.11.

```
SUBROUTINE PAR_BLAS2(m, n, a, b, c, comm)
REAL a(m), b(m,n)      ! local slice of array
REAL c(n)                ! result
```

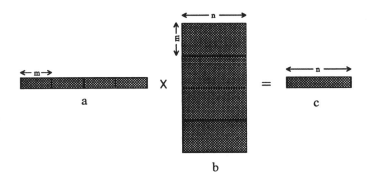

Figure 4.11
vector-matrix product. Vector a and matrix b are distributed in one dimension. The distribution
is illustrated for four processes. The slices need not be all of the same size: each process may
have a different value for m.

```
REAL sum(n)
INTEGER m, n, comm, i, j, ierr

! local sum
DO j= 1, n
  sum(j) = 0.0
  DO i = 1, m
    sum(j) = sum(j) + a(i)*b(i,j)
  END DO
END DO

! global sum
CALL MPI_REDUCE(sum, c, n, MPI_REAL, MPI_SUM, 0, comm, ierr)

! return result at node zero (and garbage at the other nodes)
RETURN
```

4.10.3   MINLOC and MAXLOC

The operator MPI_MINLOC is used to compute a global minimum and also an
index attached to the minimum value. MPI_MAXLOC similarly computes a global
maximum and index. One application of these is to compute a global minimum
(maximum) and the rank of the process containing this value.

The operation that defines MPI_MAXLOC is:

$$\left(\begin{array}{c} u \\ i \end{array}\right) \circ \left(\begin{array}{c} v \\ j \end{array}\right) = \left(\begin{array}{c} w \\ k \end{array}\right) \text{ where } w = \max(u,v) \text{ and } k = \left\{ \begin{array}{ll} i & \text{if } u > v \\ \min(i,j) & \text{if } u = v \\ j & \text{if } u < v \end{array} \right.$$

MPI_MINLOC is defined similarly:

$$\left(\begin{array}{c} u \\ i \end{array}\right) \circ \left(\begin{array}{c} v \\ j \end{array}\right) = \left(\begin{array}{c} w \\ k \end{array}\right) \text{ where } w = \min(u,v) \text{ and } k = \left\{ \begin{array}{ll} i & \text{if } u < v \\ \min(i,j) & \text{if } u = v \\ j & \text{if } u > v \end{array} \right.$$

Both operations are associative and commutative. Note that if MPI_MAXLOC is applied to reduce a sequence of pairs $(u_0, 0), (u_1, 1), \ldots, (u_{n-1}, n-1)$, then the value returned is (u, r), where $u = \max_i u_i$ and r is the index of the first global maximum in the sequence. Thus, if each process supplies a value and its rank within the group, then a reduce operation with op = MPI_MAXLOC will return the maximum value and the rank of the first process with that value. Similarly, MPI_MINLOC can be used to return a minimum and its index. More generally, MPI_MINLOC computes a *lexicographic minimum*, where elements are ordered according to the first component of each pair, and ties are resolved according to the second component.

The reduce operation is defined to operate on arguments that consist of a pair: value and index. In order to use MPI_MINLOC and MPI_MAXLOC in a reduce operation, one must provide a datatype argument that represents a pair (value and index). MPI provides nine such predefined datatypes. In C, the index is an int and the value can be a short or long int, a float, or a double. The potentially mixed-type nature of such arguments is a problem in Fortran. The problem is circumvented, for Fortran, by having the MPI-provided type consist of a pair of the same type as value, and coercing the index to this type also.

The operations MPI_MAXLOC and MPI_MINLOC can be used with each of the following datatypes.

Fortran:

Name	Description
MPI_2REAL	pair of REALs
MPI_2DOUBLE_PRECISION	pair of DOUBLE PRECISION variables
MPI_2INTEGER	pair of INTEGERs

C:

Name	Description
MPI_FLOAT_INT	float and int
MPI_DOUBLE_INT	double and int

MPI_LONG_INT   long and int
MPI_2INT   pair of int
MPI_SHORT_INT   short and int
MPI_LONG_DOUBLE_INT   long double and int

The datatype MPI_2REAL is *as if* defined by the following (see Section 3.3).

```
MPI_TYPE_CONTIGUOUS(2, MPI_REAL, MPI_2REAL)
```

Similar statements apply for MPI_2INTEGER, MPI_2DOUBLE_PRECISION, and MPI-_2INT.

The datatype MPI_FLOAT_INT is *as if* defined by the following sequence of instructions.

```
type[0] = MPI_FLOAT
type[1] = MPI_INT
disp[0] = 0
disp[1] = sizeof(float)
block[0] = 1
block[1] = 1
MPI_TYPE_STRUCT(2, block, disp, type, MPI_FLOAT_INT)
```

Similar statements apply for the other mixed types in C.

Example 4.17 Each process has an array of 30 doubles, in C. For each of the 30 locations, compute the value and rank of the process containing the largest value.

```
    ...
    /* each process has an array of 30 doubles: ain[30]
     */
    double ain[30], aout[30];
    int   ind[30];
    struct {
        double val;
        int    rank;
    } in[30], out[30];
    int i, myrank, root;

    MPI_Comm_rank(MPI_COMM_WORLD, &myrank);
    for (i=0; i<30; ++i) {
        in[i].val = ain[i];
```

```
        in[i].rank = myrank;
    }
    MPI_Reduce( in, out, 30, MPI_DOUBLE_INT, MPI_MAXLOC, root, comm );
    /* At this point, the answer resides on process root
     */
    if (myrank == root) {
        /* read ranks out
         */
        for (i=0; i<30; ++i) {
            aout[i] = out[i].val;
            ind[i] = out[i].rank;
        }
    }
}
```

Example 4.18 Same example, in Fortran.

```
    ...
    ! each process has an array of 30 doubles: ain(30)

    DOUBLE PRECISION ain(30), aout(30)
    INTEGER ind(30);
    DOUBLE PRECISION in(2,30), out(2,30)
    INTEGER i, myrank, root, ierr;

    MPI_COMM_RANK(MPI_COMM_WORLD, myrank);
    DO i=1, 30
        in(1,i) = ain(i)
        in(2,i) = myrank     ! myrank is coerced to a double
    END DO

    MPI_REDUCE( in, out, 30, MPI_2DOUBLE_PRECISION, MPI_MAXLOC, root,
                                                    comm, ierr );
    ! At this point, the answer resides on process root

    IF (myrank .EQ. root) THEN
        ! read ranks out
        DO I= 1, 30
            aout(i) = out(1,i)
```

```
            ind(i) = out(2,i)  ! rank is coerced back to an integer
        END DO
    END IF
```

Example 4.19 Each process has a non-empty array of values. Find the minimum global value, the rank of the process that holds it and its index on this process.

```
#define  LEN    1000

float val[LEN];        /* local array of values */
int count;             /* local number of values */
int myrank, minrank, minindex;
float minval;

struct {
    float value;
    int   index;
} in, out;

    /* local minloc */
in.value = val[0];
in.index = 0;
for (i=1; i < count; i++)
    if (in.value > val[i]) {
        in.value = val[i];
        in.index = i;
    }

    /* global minloc */
MPI_Comm_rank(MPI_COMM_WORLD, &myrank);
in.index = myrank*LEN + in.index;
MPI_Reduce( in, out, 1, MPI_FLOAT_INT, MPI_MINLOC, root, comm );
    /* At this point, the answer resides on process root
     */
if (myrank == root) {
    /* read answer out
     */
    minval = out.value;
```

```
    minrank = out.index / LEN;
    minindex = out.index % LEN;
}
```

Rationale. The definition of MPI_MINLOC and MPI_MAXLOC given here has the advantage that it does not require any special-case handling of these two operations: they are handled like any other reduce operation. A programmer can provide his or her own definition of MPI_MAXLOC and MPI_MINLOC, if so desired. The disadvantage is that values and indices have to be first interleaved, and that indices and values have to be coerced to the same type, in Fortran. (*End of rationale.*)

4.10.4 All Reduce

MPI includes variants of each of the reduce operations where the result is returned to all processes in the group. MPI requires that all processes participating in these operations receive identical results.

MPI_ALLREDUCE(sendbuf, recvbuf, count, datatype, op, comm)

IN	sendbuf	starting address of send buffer
OUT	recvbuf	starting address of receive buffer
IN	count	number of elements in send buffer
IN	datatype	data type of elements of send buffer
IN	op	operation
IN	comm	communicator

```
int MPI_Allreduce(void* sendbuf, void* recvbuf, int count,
            MPI_Datatype datatype, MPI_Op op, MPI_Comm comm)
```

```
MPI_ALLREDUCE(SENDBUF, RECVBUF, COUNT, DATATYPE, OP, COMM, IERROR)
    <type> SENDBUF(*), RECVBUF(*)
    INTEGER COUNT, DATATYPE, OP, COMM, IERROR
```

Same as MPI_REDUCE except that the result appears in the receive buffer of all the group members.

Advice to implementors.   The all-reduce operations can be implemented as a reduce, followed by a broadcast. However, a direct implementation can lead to better performance. In this case care must be taken to make sure that all processes receive the same result. (*End of advice to implementors.*)

Example 4.20 A routine that computes the product of a vector and an array that are distributed across a group of processes and returns the answer at all nodes (see also Example 4.16, page 179).

```
SUBROUTINE PAR_BLAS2(m, n, a, b, c, comm)
REAL a(m), b(m,n)      ! local slice of array
REAL c(n)              ! result
REAL sum(n)
INTEGER m, n, comm, i, j, ierr

! local sum
DO j= 1, n
  sum(j) = 0.0
  DO i = 1, m
    sum(j) = sum(j) + a(i)*b(i,j)
  END DO
END DO

! global sum
CALL MPI_ALLREDUCE(sum, c, n, MPI_REAL, MPI_SUM, comm, ierr)

! return result at all nodes
RETURN
```

4.10.5 Reduce-Scatter

MPI includes variants of each of the reduce operations where the result is scattered to all processes in the group on return.

MPI_REDUCE_SCATTER(sendbuf, recvbuf, recvcounts, datatype, op, comm)

IN	sendbuf	starting address of send buffer
OUT	recvbuf	starting address of receive buffer
IN	recvcounts	integer array
IN	datatype	data type of elements of input buffer
IN	op	operation
IN	comm	communicator

```
int MPI_Reduce_scatter(void* sendbuf, void* recvbuf, int *recvcounts,
        MPI_Datatype datatype, MPI_Op op, MPI_Comm comm)
```

```
MPI_REDUCE_SCATTER(SENDBUF, RECVBUF, RECVCOUNTS, DATATYPE, OP, COMM,
              IERROR)
  <type> SENDBUF(*), RECVBUF(*)
  INTEGER RECVCOUNTS(*), DATATYPE, OP, COMM, IERROR
```

MPI_REDUCE_SCATTER acts as if it first does an element-wise reduction on vector of count $= \sum_i$ recvcounts[i] elements in the send buffer defined by sendbuf, count and datatype. Next, the resulting vector of results is split into n disjoint segments, where n is the number of processes in the group of comm. Segment i contains recvcounts[i] elements. The ith segment is sent to process i and stored in the receive buffer defined by recvbuf, recvcounts[i] and datatype.

Example 4.21 A routine that computes the product of a vector and an array that are distributed across a group of processes and returns the answer in a distributed array. The distribution of vectors a and c and matrix b is illustrated in Figure 4.12.

```
SUBROUTINE PAR_BLAS2(m, n, k, a, b, c, comm)
REAL a(m), b(m,n), c(k)     ! local slice of array
REAL sum(n)
INTEGER m, n, k, comm, i, j, gsize, ierr
INTEGER, ALLOCATABLE recvcounts(:)

! distribute to all processes the sizes of the slices of
! array c (in real life, this would be precomputed)
CALL MPI_COMM_SIZE(comm, gsize, ierr)
ALLOCATE recvcounts(gsize)
CALL MPI_ALLGATHER(k, 1, MPI_INTEGER, recvcounts, 1,
                     MPI_INTEGER, comm, ierr)

! local sum
DO j= 1, n
  sum(j) = 0.0
  DO i = 1, m
    sum(j) = sum(j) + a(i)*b(i,j)
  END DO
END DO

! global sum and distribution of vector c
CALL MPI_REDUCE_SCATTER(sum, c, recvcounts, MPI_REAL,
                     MPI_SUM, comm, ierr)
```

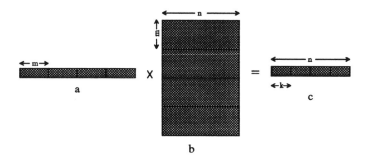

Figure 4.12
vector-matrix product. All vectors and matrices are distributed. The distribution is illustrated
for four processes. Each process may have a different value for **m** and **k**.

```
! return result in distributed vector
RETURN
```

Advice to implementors.   The MPI_REDUCE_SCATTER routine is functionally
equivalent to: A MPI_REDUCE operation function with count equal to the sum
of recvcounts[i] followed by MPI_SCATTERV with sendcounts equal to recvcounts.
However, a direct implementation may run faster. (*End of advice to implementors.*)

4.11   Scan

MPI_SCAN(sendbuf, recvbuf, count, datatype, op, comm)

IN	sendbuf	starting address of send buffer
OUT	recvbuf	starting address of receive buffer
IN	count	number of elements in input buffer
IN	datatype	data type of elements of input buffer
IN	op	operation
IN	comm	communicator

```
int MPI_Scan(void* sendbuf, void* recvbuf, int count,
             MPI_Datatype datatype, MPI_Op op, MPI_Comm comm )
```

```
MPI_SCAN(SENDBUF, RECVBUF, COUNT, DATATYPE, OP, COMM, IERROR)
```

```
<type> SENDBUF(*), RECVBUF(*)
INTEGER COUNT, DATATYPE, OP, COMM, IERROR
```

MPI_SCAN is used to perform a prefix reduction on data distributed across the group. The operation returns, in the receive buffer of the process with rank i, the reduction of the values in the send buffers of processes with ranks 0,...,i (inclusive). The type of operations supported, their semantics, and the constraints on send and receive buffers are as for MPI_REDUCE.

Rationale. The MPI Forum defined an inclusive scan, that is, the prefix reduction on process i includes the data from process i. An alternative is to define scan in an exclusive manner, where the result on i only includes data up to i-1. Both definitions are useful. The latter has some advantages: the inclusive scan can always be computed from the exclusive scan with no additional communication; for non-invertible operations such as max and min, communication is required to compute the exclusive scan from the inclusive scan. There is, however, a complication with exclusive scan since one must define the "unit" element for the reduction in this case. That is, one must explicitly say what occurs for process 0. This was thought to be complex for user-defined operations and hence, the exclusive scan was dropped. (*End of rationale.*)

4.12   User-Defined Operations for Reduce and Scan

MPI_OP_CREATE(function, commute, op)

IN	function	user defined function
IN	commute	true if commutative; false otherwise.
OUT	op	operation

```
int MPI_Op_create(MPI_User_function *function, int commute,
        MPI_Op *op)
```

```
MPI_OP_CREATE( FUNCTION, COMMUTE, OP, IERROR)
    EXTERNAL FUNCTION
    LOGICAL COMMUTE
    INTEGER OP, IERROR
```

MPI_OP_CREATE binds a user-defined global operation to an op handle that can subsequently be used in MPI_REDUCE, MPI_ALLREDUCE, MPI_REDUCE_SCATTER, and MPI_SCAN. The user-defined operation is assumed to be associative. If commute = **true**, then the operation should be both commutative and associative. If commute = **false**, then the order of operations is fixed and is defined to be in ascending, process rank order, beginning with process zero. The order of evaluation can be changed, taking advantage of the associativity of the operation. If commute = **true** then the order of evaluation can be changed, taking advantage of commutativity and associativity.

function is the user-defined function, which must have the following four arguments: invec, inoutvec, len and datatype.

The ANSI-C prototype for the function is the following.

```
typedef void MPI_User_function( void *invec, void *inoutvec, int *len,
                                MPI_Datatype *datatype)
```

The Fortran declaration of the user-defined function appears below.

```
FUNCTION USER_FUNCTION( INVEC(*), INOUTVEC(*), LEN, TYPE)
<type> INVEC(LEN), INOUTVEC(LEN)
INTEGER LEN, TYPE
```

The datatype argument is a handle to the data type that was passed into the call to MPI_REDUCE. The user reduce function should be written such that the following holds: Let u[0], ... , u[len-1] be the len elements in the communication buffer described by the arguments invec, len and datatype when the function is invoked; let v[0], ... , v[len-1] be len elements in the communication buffer described by the arguments inoutvec, len and datatype when the function is invoked; let w[0], ... , w[len-1] be len elements in the communication buffer described by the arguments inoutvec, len and datatype when the function returns; then $w[i] = u[i] o v[i]$, for i=0 , ... , len-1, where o is the reduce operation that the function computes.

Informally, we can think of invec and inoutvec as arrays of len elements that function is combining. The result of the reduction over-writes values in inoutvec, hence the name. Each invocation of the function results in the pointwise evaluation of the reduce operator on len elements: i.e, the function returns in inoutvec[i] the value invec[i] o inoutvec[i], for $i = 0, \ldots, count-1$, where o is the combining operation computed by the function.

Rationale.   The len argument allows MPI_REDUCE to avoid calling the function for each element in the input buffer. Rather, the system can choose to apply the function to chunks of input. In C, it is passed in as a reference for reasons of compatibility with Fortran.

By internally comparing the value of the **datatype** argument to known, global handles, it is possible to overload the use of a single user-defined function for several, different data types. (*End of rationale.*)

General datatypes may be passed to the user function. However, use of datatypes that are not contiguous is likely to lead to inefficiencies.

No MPI communication function may be called inside the user function. MPI_ABORT may be called inside the function in case of an error.

Advice to users. Suppose one defines a library of user-defined reduce functions that are overloaded: the **datatype** argument is used to select the right execution path at each invocation, according to the types of the operands. The user-defined reduce function cannot "decode" the **datatype** argument that it is passed, and cannot identify, by itself, the correspondence between the datatype handles and the datatype they represent. This correspondence was established when the datatypes were created. Before the library is used, a library initialization preamble must be executed. This preamble code will define the datatypes that are used by the library, and store handles to these datatypes in global, static variables that are shared by the user code and the library code.

The Fortran version of MPI_REDUCE will invoke a user-defined reduce function using the Fortran calling conventions and will pass a Fortran-type datatype argument; the C version will use C calling convention and the C representation of a datatype handle. Users who plan to mix languages should define their reduction functions accordingly. (*End of advice to users.*)

Advice to implementors. We outline below a naive and inefficient implementation of MPI_REDUCE.

```
if (rank > 0) {
    MPI_RECV(tempbuf, count, datatype, rank-1,...)
    User_reduce( tempbuf, sendbuf, count, datatype)
}
if (rank < groupsize-1) {
    MPI_SEND( sendbuf, count, datatype, rank+1, ...)
}
/* answer now resides in process groupsize-1 ... now send to root
 */
if (rank == groupsize-1) {
    MPI_SEND( sendbuf, count, datatype, root, ...)
```

```
}
if (rank == root) {
    MPI_RECV(recvbuf, count, datatype, groupsize-1,...)
}
```

The reduction computation proceeds, sequentially, from process 0 to process
`groupsize-1`. This order is chosen so as to respect the order of a possibly non-
commutative operator defined by the function `User_reduce()`. A more efficient
implementation is achieved by taking advantage of associativity and using a logarithmic tree reduction. Commutativity can be used to advantage, for those cases
in which the commute argument to MPI_OP_CREATE is true. Also, the amount
of temporary buffer required can be reduced, and communication can be pipelined
with computation, by transferring and reducing the elements in chunks of size `len`
<`count`.

The predefined reduce operations can be implemented as a library of user-defined
operations. However, better performance might be achieved if MPI_REDUCE handles these functions as a special case. (*End of advice to implementors.*)

MPI_OP_FREE(op)

>   IN   op   operation

```
int MPI_op_free( MPI_Op *op)
```

```
MPI_OP_FREE( OP, IERROR)
    INTEGER OP, IERROR
```

Marks a user-defined reduction operation for deallocation and sets op to MPI_OP-
_NULL.

The following two examples illustrate usage of user-defined reduction.

Example 4.22 Compute the product of an array of complex numbers, in C.
```
typedef struct {
    double real,imag;
} Complex;
```

```
/* the user-defined function
 */
```

```
void myProd( Complex *in, Complex *inout, int *len, MPI_Datatype *dptr )
{
    int i;
    Complex c;

    for (i=0; i< *len; ++i) {
        c.real = inout->real*in->real -
                    inout->imag*in->imag;
        c.imag = inout->real*in->imag +
                    inout->imag*in->real;
        *inout = c;
        in++; inout++;
    }
}

/* and, to call it...
 */
...

    /* each process has an array of 100 Complexes
     */
    Complex a[100], answer[100];
    MPI_Op myOp;
    MPI_Datatype ctype;

    /* explain to MPI how type Complex is defined
     */
    MPI_Type_contiguous( 2, MPI_DOUBLE, &ctype );
    MPI_Type_commit( &ctype );
    /* create the complex-product user-op
     */
    MPI_Op_create( myProd, True, &myOp );

    MPI_Reduce( a, answer, 100, ctype, myOp, root, comm );

    /* At this point, the answer, which consists of 100 Complexes,
     * resides on process root
     */
```

Example 4.23 This example uses a user-defined operation to produce a *segmented scan*. A segmented scan takes, as input, a set of values and a set of logicals, and the logicals delineate the various segments of the scan. For example:

$values$	v_1	v_2	v_3	v_4	v_5	v_6	v_7	v_8
$logicals$	0	0	1	1	1	0	0	1
$result$	v_1	v_1+v_2	v_3	v_3+v_4	$v_3+v_4+v_5$	v_6	v_6+v_7	v_8

The operator that produces this effect is,

$$\begin{pmatrix} u \\ i \end{pmatrix} \circ \begin{pmatrix} v \\ j \end{pmatrix} = \begin{pmatrix} w \\ j \end{pmatrix},$$

where,

$$w = \begin{cases} u+v & \text{if } i=j \\ v & \text{if } i \neq j \end{cases}.$$

Note that this is a non-commutative operator. C code that implements it is given below.

```c
typedef struct {
    double val;
    int log;
} SegScanPair;

/* the user-defined function
 */
void segScan( SegScanPair *in, SegScanPair *inout, int *len,
                                        MPI_Datatype *dptr )
{
    int i;
    SegScanPair c;

    for (i=0; i< *len; ++i) {
        if ( in->log == inout->log )
            c.val = in->val + inout->val;
        else
            c.val = inout->val;
        c.log = inout->log;
        *inout = c;
        in++; inout++;
    }
}
```

```
/* Note that the inout argument to the user-defined
 * function corresponds to the right-hand operand of the
 * operator.  When using this operator, we must be careful
 * to specify that it is non-commutative, as in the following.
 */

int i,base;
SeqScanPair  a, answer;
MPI_Op       myOp;
MPI_Datatype type[2] = {MPI_DOUBLE, MPI_INT};
MPI_Aint     disp[2];
int          blocklen[2] = { 1, 1};
MPI_Datatype sspair;

/* explain to MPI how type SegScanPair is defined
 */
MPI_Address( a, disp);
MPI_Address( a.log, disp+1);
base = disp[0];
for (i=0; i<2; ++i) disp[i] -= base;
MPI_Type_struct( 2, blocklen, disp, type, &sspair );
MPI_Type_commit( &sspair );
/* create the segmented-scan user-op
 */
MPI_Op_create( segScan, False, &myOp );
...
MPI_Scan( a, answer, 1, sspair, myOp, root, comm );
```

4.13   The Semantics of Collective Communications

A correct, portable program must invoke collective communications so that dead-lock will not occur, whether collective communications are synchronizing or not. The following examples illustrate dangerous use of collective routines.

Example 4.24 The following is erroneous.

```
switch(rank) {
    case 0:
        MPI_Bcast(buf1, count, type, 0, comm);
        MPI_Bcast(buf2, count, type, 1, comm);
        break;
    case 1:
        MPI_Bcast(buf2, count, type, 1, comm);
        MPI_Bcast(buf1, count, type, 0, comm);
        break;
}
```

We assume that the group of comm is {0,1}. Two processes execute two broadcast operations in reverse order. MPI may match the first broadcast call of each process, resulting in an error, since the calls do not specify the same root. Alternatively, if MPI matches the calls correctly, then a deadlock will occur if the the operation is synchronizing.

Collective operations must be executed in the same order at all members of the communication group.

Example 4.25 The following is erroneous.

```
switch(rank) {
    case 0:
        MPI_Bcast(buf1, count, type, 0, comm0);
        MPI_Bcast(buf2, count, type, 2, comm2);
        break;
    case 1:
        MPI_Bcast(buf1, count, type, 1, comm1);
        MPI_Bcast(buf2, count, type, 0, comm0);
        break;
    case 2:
        MPI_Bcast(buf1, count, type, 2, comm2);
        MPI_Bcast(buf2, count, type, 1, comm1);
        break;
}
```

Assume that the group of comm0 is {0,1}, of comm1 is {1, 2} and of comm2 is {2,0}. If the broadcast is a synchronizing operation, then there is a cyclic dependency: the broadcast in comm2 completes only after the broadcast in comm0; the broadcast in comm0 completes only after the broadcast in comm1; and the broadcast in comm1 completes only after the broadcast in comm2. Thus, the code will deadlock.

Collective operations must be executed in an order so that no cyclic dependencies occur.

Example 4.26 The following is erroneous.
```
switch(rank) {
    case 0:
        MPI_Bcast(buf1, count, type, 0, comm);
        MPI_Send(buf2, count, type, 1, tag, comm);
        break;
    case 1:
        MPI_Recv(buf2, count, type, 0, tag, comm);
        MPI_Bcast(buf1, count, type, 0, comm);
        break;
}
```

Process zero executes a broadcast, followed by a blocking send operation. Process one first executes a blocking receive that matches the send, followed by broadcast call that matches the broadcast of process zero. This program may deadlock. The broadcast call on process zero *may* block until process one executes the matching broadcast call, so that the send is not executed. Process one will definitely block on the receive and so, in this case, never executes the broadcast.

The relative order of execution of collective operations and point-to-point operations should be such, so that even if the collective operations and the point-to-point operations are synchronizing, no deadlock will occur.

Example 4.27 A correct, but non-deterministic program.
```
switch(rank) {
    case 0:
        MPI_Bcast(buf1, count, type, 0, comm);
        MPI_Send(buf2, count, type, 1, tag, comm);
        break;
    case 1:
        MPI_Recv(buf2, count, type, MPI_ANY_SOURCE, tag, comm);
        MPI_Bcast(buf1, count, type, 0, comm);
        MPI_Recv(buf2, count, type, MPI_ANY_SOURCE, tag, comm);
```

```
        break;
    case 2:
        MPI_Send(buf2, count, type, 1, tag, comm);
        MPI_Bcast(buf1, count, type, 0, comm);
        break;
}
```

All three processes participate in a broadcast. Process 0 sends a message to process 1 after the broadcast, and process 2 sends a message to process 1 before the broadcast. Process 1 receives before and after the broadcast, with a wildcard source argument.

Two possible executions of this program, with different matchings of sends and receives, are illustrated in Figure 4.13. Note that the second execution has the peculiar effect that a send executed after the broadcast is received at another node before the broadcast. This example illustrates the fact that one should not rely on collective communication functions to have particular synchronization effects. A program that works correctly only when the first execution occurs (only when broadcast is synchronizing) is erroneous.

Finally, in multithreaded implementations, one can have more than one, concurrently executing, collective communication calls at a process. In these situations, it is the user's responsibility to ensure that the same communicator is not used concurrently by two different collective communication calls at the same process.

Advice to implementors. Assume that broadcast is implemented using point-to-point MPI communication. Suppose the following two rules are followed.

1. All receives specify their source explicitly (no wildcards).

2. Each process sends all messages that pertain to one collective call before sending any message that pertain to a subsequent collective call.

Then, messages belonging to successive broadcasts cannot be confused, as the order of point-to-point messages is preserved.

It is the implementor's responsibility to ensure that point-to-point messages are not confused with collective messages. One way to accomplish this is, whenever a communicator is created, to also create a "hidden communicator" for collective communication. One could achieve a similar effect more cheaply, for example, by using a hidden tag or context bit to indicate whether the communicator is used for point-to-point or collective communication. (*End of advice to implementors.*)

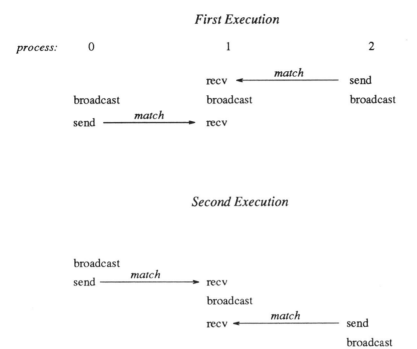

Figure 4.13
A race condition causes non-deterministic matching of sends and receives. One cannot rely on synchronization from a broadcast to make the program deterministic.

5 Communicators

5.1 Introduction

It was the intent of the creators of the MPI standard to address several issues that augment the power and usefulness of point-to-point and collective communications. These issues are mainly concerned with the the creation of portable, efficient and safe libraries and codes with MPI, and will be discussed in this chapter. This effort was driven by the need to overcome several limitations in many message passing systems. The next few sections describe these limitations.

5.1.1 Division of Processes

In some applications it is desirable to divide up the processes to allow different groups of processes to perform independent work. For example, we might want an application to utilize $\frac{2}{3}$ of its processes to predict the weather based on data already processed, while the other $\frac{1}{3}$ of the processes initially process new data. This would allow the application to regularly complete a weather forecast. However, if no new data is available for processing we might want the same application to use all of its processes to make a weather forecast.

Being able to do this efficiently and easily requires the application to be able to logically divide the processes into independent subsets. It is important that these subsets are logically the same as the initial set of processes. For example, the module to predict the weather might use process 0 as the master process to dole out work. If subsets of processes are not numbered in a consistent manner with the initial set of processes, then there may be no process 0 in one of the two subsets. This would cause the weather prediction model to fail.

Applications also need to have collective operations work on a subset of processes. If collective operations only work on the initial set of processes then it is impossible to create independent subsets that perform collective operations. Even if the application does not need independent subsets, having collective operations work on subsets is desirable. Since the time to complete most collective operations increases with the number of processes, limiting a collective operation to only the processes that need to be involved yields much better scaling behavior. For example, if a matrix computation needs to broadcast information along the diagonal of a matrix, only the processes containing diagonal elements should be involved.

5.1.2 Avoiding Message Conflicts Between Modules

Library routines have historically had difficulty in isolating their own message passing calls from those in other libraries or in the user's code. For example, suppose
the user's code posts a non-blocking receive with both tag and source wildcarded
before it enters a library routine. The first send in the library may be received
by the user's posted receive instead of the one posted by the library. This will
undoubtedly cause the library to fail.

The solution to this difficulty is to allow a module to isolate its message passing
calls from the other modules. Some applications may only determine at run time
which modules will run so it can be impossible to statically isolate all modules in
advance. This necessitates a run time callable system to perform this function.

5.1.3 Extensibility by Users

Writers of libraries often want to expand the functionality of the message passing
system. For example, the library may want to create its own special and unique
collective operation. Such a collective operation may be called many times if the
library is called repetitively or if multiple libraries use the same collective routine.
To perform the collective operation efficiently may require a moderately expensive
calculation up front such as determining the best communication pattern. It is
most efficient to reuse the up front calculations if the same the set of processes are
involved. This is most easily done by attaching the results of the up front calculation
to the set of processes involved. These types of optimization are routinely done
internally in message passing systems. The desire is to allow others to perform
similar optimizations in the same way.

5.1.4 Safety

There are two philosophies used to provide mechanisms for creating subgroups,
isolating messages, etc. One point of view is to allow the user total control over the
process. This allows maximum flexibility to the user and can, in some cases, lead
to fast implementations. The other point of view is to have the message passing
system control these functions. This adds a degree of safety while limiting the
mechanisms to those provided by the system. MPI chose to use the latter approach.
The added safety was deemed to be very important for writing portable message
passing codes. Since the MPI system controls these functions, modules that are
written independently can safely perform these operations without worrying about
conflicts. As in other areas, MPI also decided to provide a rich set of functions so
that users would have the functionality they are likely to need.

5.2   Overview

The above features and several more are provided in MPI through communicators. The concepts behind communicators encompass several central and fundamental ideas in MPI. The importance of communicators can be seen by the fact that they are present in most calls in MPI. There are several reasons that these features are encapsulated into a single MPI object. One reason is that it simplifies calls to MPI functions. Grouping logically related items into communicators substantially reduces the number of calling arguments. A second reason is it allows for easier extensibility. Both the MPI system and the user can add information onto communicators that will be passed in calls without changing the calling arguments. This is consistent with the use of opaque objects throughout MPI.

5.2.1   Groups

A **group** is an ordered set of process identifiers (henceforth processes); processes are implementation-dependent objects. Each process in a group is associated with an integer **rank**. Ranks are contiguous and start from zero. Groups are represented by opaque **group objects**, and hence cannot be directly transferred from one process to another.

There is a special pre-defined group: MPI_GROUP_EMPTY, which is a group with no members. The predefined constant MPI_GROUP_NULL is the value used for invalid group handles. MPI_GROUP_EMPTY, which is a valid handle to an empty group, should not be confused with MPI_GROUP_NULL, which is an invalid handle. The former may be used as an argument to group operations; the latter, which is returned when a group is freed, in not a valid argument.

Group operations are discussed in Section 5.3.

5.2.2   Communicator

A communicator is an opaque object with a number of attributes, together with simple rules that govern its creation, use and destruction. The communicator specifies a **communication domain** which can be used for point-to-point communications. An **intracommunicator** is used for communicating within a single group of processes; we call such communication *intra-group communication*. An intracommunicator has two fixed attributes. These are the process group and the topology describing the logical layout of the processes in the group. Process topologies are the subject of chapter 6. Intracommunicators are also used for collective operations within a group of processes.

An **intercommunicator** is used for point-to-point communication between two disjoint groups of processes. We call such communication *inter-group communication*. The fixed attributes of an intercommunicator are the two groups. No topology is associated with an intercommunicator. In addition to fixed attributes a communicator may also have user-defined attributes which are associated with the communicator using MPI's caching mechanism, as described in Section 5.6. The table below summarizes the differences between intracommunicators and intercommunicators.

Functionality	Intracommunicator	Intercommunicator
# of groups	1	2
Communication Safety	Yes	Yes
Collective Operations	Yes	No
Topologies	Yes	No
Caching	Yes	Yes

Intracommunicator operations are described in Section 5.4, and intercommunicator operations are discussed in Section 5.7.

5.2.3   Communication Domains

Any point-to-point or collective communication occurs in MPI within a **communication domain**. Such a communication domain is represented by a set of communicators with consistent values, one at each of the participating processes; each communicator is the local representation of the global communication domain. If this domain is for intra-group communication then all the communicators are intracommunicators, and all have the same group attribute. Each communicator identifies all the other corresponding communicators.

One can think of a communicator as an array of links to other communicators. An intra-group communication domain is specified by a set of communicators such that

- their links form a complete graph: each communicator is linked to all communicators in the set, including itself; and

- links have consistent indices: at each communicator, the i-th link points to the communicator for process i.

This distributed data structure is illustrated in Figure 5.1, for the case of a three member group.

We discuss inter-group communication domains in Section 5.7.

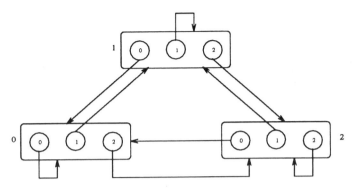

Figure 5.1
Distributed data structure for intra-communication domain.

In point-to-point communication, matching send and receive calls should have communicator arguments that represent the same communication domains. The rank of the processes is interpreted relative to the group, or groups, associated with the communicator. Thus, in an intra-group communication domain, process ranks are relative to the group associated with the communicator.

Similarly, a collective communication call involves all processes in the group of an intra-group communication domain, and all processes should use a communicator argument that represents this domain. Intercommunicators may not be used in collective communication operations.

We shall sometimes say, for simplicity, that two communicators are the same, if they represent the same communication domain. One should not be misled by this abuse of language: Each communicator is really a distinct object, local to a process. Furthermore, communicators that represent the same communication domain may have different attribute values attached to them at different processes.

Advice to implementors. An often-used design is that each communicator is associated with an id which is process-unique, and which is identical at all communicators that define one intra-group communication domain. This id is referred as the communication *context*. Thus, each message is tagged with the context of the send communicator argument, and that context identifies the matching communicator at the receiving process.

In more detail: a group can be represented by an array **group** such that **group[i]** is the address of the process with rank i in **group**. An intracommunicator can be represented by a structure with components **group**, **myrank** and **context**.

When a process posts a send with arguments **dest**, **tag** and **comm**, then the address of the destination is computed as comm.group[dest]. The message sent carries a header with the tuple (comm.myrank, tag, comm.context).

If a process posts a receive with argument source, tag and comm, then headers of incoming messages are matched to the tuple (source, tag, comm.context) (first two may be dontcare).

Another design is to use ids which are process-unique, but not necessarily identical at all processes. In such case, the context component of the communicator structure is an array, where comm.context[i] is the id chosen by the process with rank i for that communication domain. A message is sent with header comm.myrank, tag, comm.context[dest]; a receive call causes incoming messages to be matched against the tuple (source, tag, comm.context[myrank]).

The later design uses more storage for the communicator object, but simplifies the creation of new communicators, since ids can be selected locally (they still need to be broadcast to all other group members).

It is important to remember that MPI does not require a unique context to be associated with each communicator. "Context" is a possible implementation structure, not an MPI object.

With both designs we assumed a "flat" representation for groups, where each process holds a complete list of group members. This requires, at each process, storage of size proportional to the size of the group. While this presents no problem with groups of practical size (100's or 1000's of processes) it is not a scalable design. Other representations will be needed for MPI computations that spawn the Internet. The group information may be distributed and managed hierarchically, as are Internet addresses, at the expense of additional communication. (*End of advice to implementors.*)

MPI is designed to ensure that communicator constructors always generate consistent communicators that are a valid representation of the newly created communication domain. This is done by requiring that a new intracommunicator be constructed out of an existing parent communicator, and that this be a collective operation over all processes in the group associated with the parent communicator. The group associated with a new intracommunicator must be a subgroup of that associated with the parent intracommunicator. Thus, all the intracommunicator constructor routines described in Section 5.4.2 have an existing communicator as an input argument, and the newly created intracommunicator as an output argument. This leads to a chicken-and-egg situation since we must have an existing communicator to create a new communicator. This problem is solved by the provision of a predefined intracommunicator, MPI_COMM_WORLD, which is available for use once the routine MPI_INIT has been called. MPI_COMM_WORLD, which has as its group attribute all processes with which the local process can communicate, can be used as the parent communicator in constructing new communicators. A second pre-defined communicator, MPI_COMM_SELF, is also available for use after calling MPI_INIT and has as its associated group just the process itself. MPI_COMM_SELF is provided as a convenience since it could easily be created out of MPI_COMM_WORLD.

5.2.4 Compatibility with Current Practice

The current practice in many codes is that there is a unique, predefined communication universe that includes all processes available when the parallel program is initiated; the processes are assigned consecutive ranks. Participants in a point-to-point communication are identified by their rank; a collective communication (such as broadcast) always involves all processes. As such, most current message passing libraries have no equivalent argument to the communicator. It is implicitly all the processes as ranked by the system.

This practice can be followed in MPI by using the predefined communicator MPI_COMM_WORLD wherever a communicator argument is required. Thus, using current practice in MPI is very easy. Users that are content with it can ignore most of the information in this chapter. However, everyone should seriously consider understanding the potential risks in using MPI_COMM_WORLD to avoid unexpected behavior of their programs.

5.3 Group Management

This section describes the manipulation of process groups in MPI. These operations are local and their execution do not require interprocess communication. MPI allows manipulation of groups outside of communicators but groups can only be used for message passing inside of a communicator.

5.3.1 Group Accessors

MPI_GROUP_SIZE(group, size)

IN	group	group
OUT	size	number of processes in group

```
int MPI_Group_size(MPI_Group group, int *size)
```

```
MPI_GROUP_SIZE(GROUP, SIZE, IERROR)
    INTEGER GROUP, SIZE, IERROR
```

MPI_GROUP_SIZE returns the number of processes in the group. Thus, if group = MPI_GROUP_EMPTY then the call will return size = 0. (On the other hand, a call with group = MPI_GROUP_NULL is erroneous.)

MPI_GROUP_RANK(group, rank)

IN	group	group
OUT	rank	rank of the calling process in group

```
int MPI_Group_rank(MPI_Group group, int *rank)
```

```
MPI_GROUP_RANK(GROUP, RANK, IERROR)
    INTEGER GROUP, RANK, IERROR
```

MPI_GROUP_RANK returns the rank of the calling process in group. If the process is not a member of group then MPI_UNDEFINED is returned.

MPI_GROUP_TRANSLATE_RANKS (group1, n, ranks1, group2, ranks2)

IN	group1	group1
IN	n	number of ranks in ranks1 and ranks2 arrays
IN	ranks1	array of zero or more valid ranks in group1
IN	group2	group2
OUT	ranks2	array of corresponding ranks in group2

```
int MPI_Group_translate_ranks (MPI_Group group1, int n, int *ranks1,
        MPI_Group group2, int *ranks2)
```

```
MPI_GROUP_TRANSLATE_RANKS(GROUP1, N, RANKS1, GROUP2, RANKS2, IERROR)
    INTEGER GROUP1, N, RANKS1(*), GROUP2, RANKS2(*), IERROR
```

MPI_GROUP_TRANSLATE_RANKS maps the ranks of a set of processes in group1
to their ranks in group2. Upon return, the array ranks2 contains the ranks in group2
for the processes in group1 with ranks listed in ranks1. If a process in group1 found
in ranks1 does not belong to group2 then MPI_UNDEFINED is returned in ranks2.

This function is important for determining the relative numbering of the same
processes in two different groups. For instance, if one knows the ranks of certain
processes in the group of MPI_COMM_WORLD, one might want to know their ranks
in a subset of that group.

Example 5.1 Let group1 be a handle to the group {a,b,c,d,e,f} and let group2
be a handle to the group {d,e,a,c}. Let ranks1 = (0,5,0,2). Then, a call to
MPI_GROUP_TRANSLATE_RANKS will return the ranks of the processes {a,f,a,c}
in group2, namely ranks2 = (2,⊥,2,3). (⊥ denotes the value MPI_UNDEFINED.)

MPI_GROUP_COMPARE(group1, group2, result)

IN	group1	first group
IN	group2	second group
OUT	result	result

```
int MPI_Group_compare(MPI_Group group1,MPI_Group group2, int *result)
```

```
MPI_GROUP_COMPARE(GROUP1, GROUP2, RESULT, IERROR)
    INTEGER GROUP1, GROUP2, RESULT, IERROR
```

MPI_GROUP_COMPARE returns the relationship between two groups. MPI_IDENT
results if the group members and group order is exactly the same in both groups.
This happens, for instance, if group1 and group2 are handles to the same object.
MPI_SIMILAR results if the group members are the same but the order is different.
MPI_UNEQUAL results otherwise.

5.3.2 Group Constructors

Group constructors are used to construct new groups from existing groups, using
various set operations. These are local operations, and distinct groups may be
defined on different processes; a process may also define a group that does not

include itself. Consistent definitions are required when groups are used as arguments in communicator-building functions. MPI does not provide a mechanism to build a group from scratch, but only from other, previously defined groups. The base group, upon which all other groups are defined, is the group associated with the initial communicator MPI_COMM_WORLD (accessible through the function MPI_COMM_GROUP).

Local group creation functions are useful since some applications have the needed information distributed on all nodes. Thus, new groups can be created locally without communication. This can significantly reduce the necessary communication in creating a new communicator to use this group.

In Section 5.4.2, communicator creation functions are described which also create new groups. These are more general group creation functions where the information does not have to be local to each node. They are part of communicator creation since they will normally require communication for group creation. Since communicator creation may also require communication, it is logical to group these two functions together for this case.

Rationale. In what follows, there is no group duplication function analogous to MPI_COMM_DUP, defined later in this chapter. There is no need for a group duplicator. A group, once created, can have several references to it by making copies of the handle. However, care should be taken when "aliasing" groups in this way since a call to free a group using MPI_GROUP_FREE may leave dangling references. (*End of rationale.*)

Advice to implementors. Each group constructor behaves as if it returned a new group object. When this new group is a copy of an existing group, then one can avoid creating such new objects, using a reference-count mechanism. (*End of advice to implementors.*)

MPI_COMM_GROUP(comm, group)

IN	comm	communicator
OUT	group	group corresponding to comm

```
int MPI_Comm_group(MPI_Comm comm, MPI_Group *group)
```

```
MPI_COMM_GROUP(COMM, GROUP, IERROR)
    INTEGER COMM, GROUP, IERROR
```

MPI_COMM_GROUP returns in group a handle to the group of comm.

The following three functions do standard set type operations. The only difference is that ordering is important so that ranks are consistently defined.

MPI_GROUP_UNION(group1, group2, newgroup)

IN	group1	first group
IN	group2	second group
OUT	newgroup	union group

```
int MPI_Group_union(MPI_Group group1, MPI_Group group2,
        MPI_Group *newgroup)
```

```
MPI_GROUP_UNION(GROUP1, GROUP2, NEWGROUP, IERROR)
    INTEGER GROUP1, GROUP2, NEWGROUP, IERROR
```

MPI_GROUP_INTERSECTION(group1, group2, newgroup)

IN	group1	first group
IN	group2	second group
OUT	newgroup	intersection group

```
int MPI_Group_intersection(MPI_Group group1, MPI_Group group2,
        MPI_Group *newgroup)
```

```
MPI_GROUP_INTERSECTION(GROUP1, GROUP2, NEWGROUP, IERROR)
    INTEGER GROUP1, GROUP2, NEWGROUP, IERROR
```

MPI_GROUP_DIFFERENCE(group1, group2, newgroup)

IN	group1	first group
IN	group2	second group
OUT	newgroup	difference group

```
int MPI_Group_difference(MPI_Group group1, MPI_Group group2,
        MPI_Group *newgroup)
```

```
MPI_GROUP_DIFFERENCE(GROUP1, GROUP2, NEWGROUP, IERROR)
    INTEGER GROUP1, GROUP2, NEWGROUP, IERROR
```

The operations are defined as follows:

union All elements of the first group (group1), followed by all elements of second group (group2) not in first.

intersection All elements of the first group that are also in the second group, ordered as in first group.

difference All elements of the first group that are not in the second group, ordered as in the first group.

Note that for these operations the order of processes in the output group is determined primarily by order in the first group (if possible) and then, if necessary, by order in the second group. Neither union nor intersection are commutative, but both are associative.

The new group can be empty, that is, equal to MPI_GROUP_EMPTY.

Example 5.2 Let group1 $= \{a, b, c, d\}$ and group2 $= \{d, a, e\}$. Then

group1 $\bigcup$ group2 $= \{a, b, c, d, e\}$ (union);

group1 $\bigcap$ group2 $= \{a, d\}$ (intersection);

and

group1 $\setminus$ group2 $= \{b, c\}$ (difference).

MPI_GROUP_INCL(group, n, ranks, newgroup)

IN	group	group
IN	n	number of elements in array ranks (and size of newgroup)
IN	ranks	ranks of processes in group to appear in newgroup
OUT	newgroup	new group derived from above, in the order defined by ranks

```
int MPI_Group_incl(MPI_Group group, int n, int *ranks,
          MPI_Group *newgroup)
```

```
MPI_GROUP_INCL(GROUP, N, RANKS, NEWGROUP, IERROR)
```

```
INTEGER GROUP, N, RANKS(*), NEWGROUP, IERROR
```

The function **MPI_GROUP_INCL** creates a group **newgroup** that consists of the n processes in **group** with ranks rank[0],..., rank[n-1]; the process with rank i in **newgroup** is the process with rank ranks[i] in **group**. Each of the n elements of **ranks** must be a valid rank in **group** and all elements must be distinct, or else the call is erroneous. If n = 0, then **newgroup** is **MPI_GROUP_EMPTY**. This function can, for instance, be used to reorder the elements of a group.

Example 5.3 Let **group** be a handle to the group {a,b,c,d,e,f} and let ranks = (3,1,2). Then, a handle to the group {d,b,c} is returned in **newgroup**.

Assume that **newgroup** was created by a call to MPI_GROUP_INCL(group, n, ranks, newgroup). Then, a subsequent call to MPI_GROUP_TRANSLATE_RANKS(group, n, ranks, newgroup, newranks) will return $\texttt{newranks}[i] = i$, $i = 0,\ldots,n-1$ (in C) or $\texttt{newranks}(i+1) = i$, $i = 0,\ldots,n-1$ (in Fortran).

MPI_GROUP_EXCL(group, n, ranks, newgroup)

IN	group	group
IN	n	number of elements in array ranks
IN	ranks	array of integer ranks in group not to appear in newgroup
OUT	newgroup	new group derived from above, preserving the order defined by group

```
int MPI_Group_excl(MPI_Group group, int n, int *ranks,
          MPI_Group *newgroup)
```

```
MPI_GROUP_EXCL(GROUP, N, RANKS, NEWGROUP, IERROR)
    INTEGER GROUP, N, RANKS(*), NEWGROUP, IERROR
```

The function **MPI_GROUP_EXCL** creates a group of processes **newgroup** that is obtained by deleting from **group** those processes with ranks ranks[0],..., ranks[n-1] in C or ranks[1],..., ranks[n] in Fortran. The ordering of processes in **newgroup** is identical to the ordering in **group**. Each of the n elements of **ranks** must be a valid rank in **group** and all elements must be distinct; otherwise, the call is erroneous. If n = 0, then **newgroup** is identical to **group**.

Example 5.4 Let **group** be a handle to the group {a,b,c,d,e,f} and let ranks = (3,1,2). Then, a handle to the group {a,e,f} is returned in **newgroup**.

Suppose one calls MPI_GROUP_INCL(group, n, ranks, newgroupi) and MPI_GROUP-_EXCL(group, n, ranks, newgroupe). The call MPI_GROUP_UNION(newgroupi, new-groupe, newgroup) would return in newgroup a group with the same members as group but possibly in a different order. The call MPI_GROUP_INTERSECTION(groupi, groupe, newgroup) would return MPI_GROUP_EMPTY.

MPI_GROUP_RANGE_INCL(group, n, ranges, newgroup)

IN	group	group
IN	n	number of triplets in array ranges
IN	ranges	an array of integer triplets, of the form (first rank, last rank, stride) indicating ranks in group of processes to be included in newgroup
OUT	newgroup	new group derived from above, in the order defined by ranges

```
int MPI_Group_range_incl(MPI_Group group, int n, int ranges[][3],
        MPI_Group *newgroup)
```

```
MPI_GROUP_RANGE_INCL(GROUP, N, RANGES, NEWGROUP, IERROR)
    INTEGER GROUP, N, RANGES(3,*), NEWGROUP, IERROR
```

Each triplet in ranges specifies a sequence of ranks for processes to be included in the newly created group. The newly created group contains the processes specified by the first triplet, followed by the processes specified by the second triplet, etc.

Example 5.5 Let group be a handle to the group {a,b,c,d,e,f,g,h,i,j} and let ranges = ((6,7,1),(1,6,2),(0,9,4)). The first triplet (6,7,1)} specifies the processes {g,h}, with ranks (6,7); the second triplet (1,6,2) specifies the processes {b,d,f}, with ranks (1,3,5); and the third triplet (0,9,4) specifies the processes {a,e,i}, with ranks (0,4,8). The call creates the new group {g,h,b,d,f,a,e,i}.

Generally, if ranges consist of the triplets

$$(first_1, last_1, stride_1), \ldots, (first_n, last_n, stride_n)$$

then newgroup consists of the sequence of processes in group with ranks

$$first_1, first_1 + stride_1, \ldots, first_1 + \left\lfloor \frac{last_1 - first_1}{stride_1} \right\rfloor \cdot stride_1, \ldots$$

$$first_n, first_n + stride_n, \ldots, first_n + \left\lfloor \frac{last_n - first_n}{stride_n} \right\rfloor \cdot stride_n.$$

Each computed rank must be a valid rank in **group** and all computed ranks must be distinct, or else the call is erroneous. Note that a call may have $first_i > last_i$, and $stride_i$ may be negative, but cannot be zero.

The functionality of this routine is specified to be equivalent to expanding the array of ranges to an array of the included ranks and passing the resulting array of ranks and other arguments to MPI_GROUP_INCL. A call to MPI_GROUP_INCL is equivalent to a call to MPI_GROUP_RANGE_INCL with each rank i in **ranks** replaced by the triplet (i,i,1) in the argument **ranges**.

MPI_GROUP_RANGE_EXCL(group, n, ranges, newgroup)

IN	group	group
IN	n	number of elements in array ranks
IN	ranges	an array of integer triplets of the form (first rank, last rank, stride), indicating the ranks in group of processes to be excluded from the output group newgroup.
OUT	newgroup	new group derived from above, preserving the order in group

```
int MPI_Group_range_excl(MPI_Group group, int n, int ranges[][3],
          MPI_Group *newgroup)
```

```
MPI_GROUP_RANGE_EXCL(GROUP, N, RANGES, NEWGROUP, IERROR)
     INTEGER GROUP, N, RANGES(3,*), NEWGROUP, IERROR
```

Each triplet in **ranges** specifies a sequence of ranks for processes to be excluded from the newly created group. The newly created group contains the remaining processes, ordered as in **group**.

Example 5.6 Let, as in Example 5.5, **group** be a handle to the group {a,b,c,d,e,f,g,-h,i,j} and let **ranges** = ((6,7,1),(1,6,2),(0,9,4)). The call creates the new group {c,j}, consisting of all processes in the old group omitted by the list of triplets.

Each computed rank must be a valid rank in **group** and all computed ranks must be distinct, or else the call is erroneous.

The functionality of this routine is specified to be equivalent to expanding the array of ranges to an array of the excluded ranks and passing the resulting array of ranks and other arguments to MPI_GROUP_EXCL. A call to MPI_GROUP_EXCL is equivalent to a call to MPI_GROUP_RANGE_EXCL with each rank i in ranks replaced by the triplet (i,i,1) in the argument ranges.

Advice to users.   The range operations do not explicitly enumerate ranks, and therefore are more scalable if implemented efficiently. Hence, it is recommend that MPI programmers use them whenever possible, as high-quality implementations may take advantage of this fact. (*End of advice to users.*)

Advice to implementors.   The range operations should be implemented, if possible, without enumerating the group members, in order to obtain better scalability (time and space). (*End of advice to implementors.*)

5.3.3   Group Destructors

MPI_GROUP_FREE(group)

INOUT	group	group

```
int MPI_Group_free(MPI_Group *group)
```

```
MPI_GROUP_FREE(GROUP, IERROR)
    INTEGER GROUP, IERROR
```

This operation marks a group object for deallocation. The handle group is set to MPI_GROUP_NULL by the call. Any ongoing operation using this group will complete normally.

Advice to implementors.   One can keep a reference count that is incremented for each call to MPI_COMM_CREATE and MPI_COMM_DUP, and decremented for each call to MPI_GROUP_FREE or MPI_COMM_FREE; the group object is ultimately deallocated when the reference count drops to zero. (*End of advice to implementors.*)

5.4   Communicator Management

This section describes the manipulation of communicators in MPI. Operations that access communicators are local and their execution does not require interprocess communication. Operations that create communicators are collective and may require interprocess communication. We describe the behavior of these functions, assuming that their comm argument is an intracommunicator; we describe later in Section 5.7 their semantics for intercommunicator arguments.

5.4.1 Communicator Accessors

The following are all local operations.

MPI_COMM_SIZE(comm, size)

IN	comm	communicator
OUT	size	number of processes in the group of comm

```
int MPI_Comm_size(MPI_Comm comm, int *size)
```

```
MPI_COMM_SIZE(COMM, SIZE, IERROR)
    INTEGER COMM, SIZE, IERROR
```

MPI_COMM_SIZE returns the size of the group associated with comm.

This function indicates the number of processes involved in an intracommunicator. For MPI_COMM_WORLD, it indicates the total number of processes available at initialization time. (For this version of MPI, this is also the total number of processes available throughout the computation).

Rationale. This function is equivalent to accessing the communicator's group with MPI_COMM_GROUP (see above), computing the size using MPI_GROUP_SIZE, and then freeing the group temporary via MPI_GROUP_FREE. However, this function is so commonly used, that this shortcut was introduced. (*End of rationale.*)

MPI_COMM_RANK(comm, rank)

IN	comm	communicator
OUT	rank	rank of the calling process in group of comm

```
int MPI_Comm_rank(MPI_Comm comm, int *rank)
```

```
MPI_COMM_RANK(COMM, RANK, IERROR)
    INTEGER COMM, RANK, IERROR
```

MPI_COMM_RANK indicates the rank of the process that calls it, in the range from 0...size−1, where size is the return value of MPI_COMM_SIZE. This rank is relative to the group associated with the intracommunicator comm. Thus, MPI-_COMM_RANK(MPI_COMM_WORLD, rank) returns in rank the "absolute" rank of the calling process in the global communication group of MPI_COMM_WORLD; MPI_COMM_RANK(MPI_COMM_SELF, rank) returns rank = 0.

Rationale. This function is equivalent to accessing the communicator's group with MPI_COMM_GROUP (see above), computing the rank using MPI_GROUP_RANK, and then freeing the group temporary via MPI_GROUP_FREE. However, this function is so commonly used, that this shortcut was introduced. (*End of rationale.*)

Advice to users. Many programs will be written with the master-slave model, where one process (such as the rank-zero process) will play a supervisory role, and the other processes will serve as compute nodes. In this framework, the two preceding calls are useful for determining the roles of the various processes of a communicator. (*End of advice to users.*)

MPI_COMM_COMPARE(comm1, comm2, result)

IN	comm1	first communicator
IN	comm2	second communicator
OUT	result	result

```
int MPI_Comm_compare(MPI_Comm comm1,MPI_Comm comm2, int *result)
```

```
MPI_COMM_COMPARE(COMM1, COMM2, RESULT, IERROR)
    INTEGER COMM1, COMM2, RESULT, IERROR
```

MPI_COMM_COMPARE is used to find the relationship between two intra-communicators. MPI_IDENT results if and only if comm1 and comm2 are handles for the same object (representing the same communication domain). MPI_CONGRUENT results if the underlying groups are identical in constituents and rank order (the communicators represent two distinct communication domains with the same group attribute). MPI_SIMILAR results if the group members of both communicators are the same but the rank order differs. MPI_UNEQUAL results otherwise. The groups associated with two *different* communicators could be gotten via MPI_COMM_GROUP and then used in a call to MPI_GROUP_COMPARE. If MPI_COMM_COMPARE gives MPI_CONGRUENT then MPI_GROUP_COMPARE will give MPI_IDENT. If MPI-

_COMM_COMPARE gives MPI_SIMILAR then MPI_GROUP_COMPARE will give MPI-
_SIMILAR.

5.4.2 Communicator Constructors

The following are collective functions that are invoked by all processes in the group
associated with comm.

MPI_COMM_DUP(comm, newcomm)

IN	comm	communicator
OUT	newcomm	copy of comm

```
int MPI_Comm_dup(MPI_Comm comm, MPI_Comm *newcomm)
```

```
MPI_COMM_DUP(COMM, NEWCOMM, IERROR)
    INTEGER COMM, NEWCOMM, IERROR
```

MPI_COMM_DUP creates a new intracommunicator, newcomm, with the same
fixed attributes (group, or groups, and topology) as the input intracommunicator,
comm. The newly created communicators at the processes in the group of comm
define a new, distinct communication domain, with the same group as the old
communicators. The function can also be used to replicate intercommunicators.

The association of user-defined (or cached) attributes with newcomm is controlled
by the copy callback function specified when the attribute was attached to comm.
For each key value, the respective copy callback function determines the attribute
value associated with this key in the new communicator. User-defined attributes
are discussed in Section 5.6.

Advice to users.   This operation can be used to provide a parallel library call
with a duplicate communication space that has the same properties as the original
communicator. This includes any user-defined attributes (see below), and topologies (see chapter 6). This call is valid even if there are pending point-to-point
communications involving the communicator comm. A typical call might involve a
MPI_COMM_DUP at the beginning of the parallel call, and an MPI_COMM_FREE
of that duplicated communicator at the end of the call – see Example 5.11. Other
models of communicator management are also possible. (*End of advice to users.*)

Advice to implementors.   Assume that communicators are implemented as described on page 205. If a unique context is used per communication domain, then
the generation of a new communicator requires a collective call where processes

agree on a new context value. E.g., this could be $1 + \max\{$already_used_contexts$\}$, computed using an MPI_ALLREDUCE call (assuming there is no need to garbage collect contexts). If a different context is used by each process, then a collective call is needed where each process exchange with all other processes the value of the context it selected, using an MPI_ALLGATHER call.

It is theoretically possible to agree on a group-wide unique context with no communication: e.g. one could use as context a unique encoding of the group, followed by a sequence number for intracommunicators with this group. Since all processes in the group execute the same sequence of calls to MPI_COMM_DUP with this group argument, all processes will locally compute the same id. This design is not be practical because it generates large context ids. Implementations may strike various compromises between communication overhead for communicator creation and context size.

Important: If new communicators are created without synchronizing the processes involved then the communication system should be able to cope with messages arriving for a communicator that has not yet been created at the receiving process.

When a communicator is duplicated, one need not actually copy the group information, but only add a new reference and increment the reference count. (*End of advice to implementors.*)

MPI_COMM_CREATE(comm, group, newcomm)

IN	comm	communicator
IN	group	Group, which is a subset of the group of comm
OUT	newcomm	new communicator

```
int MPI_Comm_create(MPI_Comm comm, MPI_Group group,
          MPI_Comm *newcomm)
```

```
MPI_COMM_CREATE(COMM, GROUP, NEWCOMM, IERROR)
    INTEGER COMM, GROUP, NEWCOMM, IERROR
```

This function creates a new intracommunicator newcomm with communication group defined by group. No attributes propagates from comm to newcomm. The function returns MPI_COMM_NULL to processes that are not in group. The communicators returned at the processes in group define a new intra-group communication domain.

The call is erroneous if not all **group** arguments have the same value on different processes, or if **group** is not·a subset of the group associated with **comm** (but it does not have to be a proper subset). Note that the call is to be executed by all processes in **comm**, even if they do not belong to the new group.

Rationale. The requirement that the entire group of **comm** participate in the call stems from the following considerations:

- It allows the implementation to layer MPI_COMM_CREATE on top of regular collective communications.

- It provides additional safety, in particular in the case where partially overlapping groups are used to create new communicators.

- It permits implementations sometimes to avoid communication related to the creation of communicators.

(*End of rationale.*)

Advice to users. MPI_COMM_CREATE provides a means to subset a group of processes for the purpose of separate MIMD computation, with a separate communication space. newcomm, which emerges from MPI_COMM_CREATE can be used in subsequent calls to MPI_COMM_CREATE (or other communicator constructors) further to subdivide a computation into parallel sub-computations. A more general service is provided by MPI_COMM_SPLIT, below. (*End of advice to users.*)

MPI_COMM_SPLIT(comm, color, key, newcomm)

IN	comm	communicator
IN	color	control of subset assignment
IN	key	control of rank assignment
OUT	newcomm	new communicator

```
int MPI_Comm_split(MPI_Comm comm, int color, int key,
          MPI_Comm *newcomm)
```

```
MPI_COMM_SPLIT(COMM, COLOR, KEY, NEWCOMM, IERROR)
    INTEGER COMM, COLOR, KEY, NEWCOMM, IERROR
```

This function partitions the group associated with **comm** into disjoint subgroups, one for each value of **color**. Each subgroup contains all processes of the same color. Within each subgroup, the processes are ranked in the order defined by the value of the argument key, with ties broken according to their rank in the old group. A new communication domain is created for each subgroup and a handle to the representative communicator is returned in newcomm. A process may supply the color value MPI_UNDEFINED to not be a member of any new group, in which case newcomm returns MPI_COMM_NULL. This is a collective call, but each process is permitted to provide different values for color and key. The value of color must be nonnegative.

Example 5.7 Assume that a collective call to MPI_COMM_SPLIT is executed in a 10 element group, with the arguments listed in the table below.

rank	0	1	2	3	4	5	6	7	8	9
process	a	b	c	d	e	f	g	h	i	j
color	0	⊥	3	0	3	0	0	5	3	⊥
key	3	1	2	5	1	1	1	2	1	0

The call generates three new communication domains: the first with group {f,g,a,d}, the second with group {e,i,c}, and the third with singleton group {h}. The processes b and j do not participate in any of the newly created communication domains, and are returned a null communicator handle.

A call to MPI_COMM_CREATE(comm, group, newcomm) is equivalent to a call to MPI_COMM_SPLIT(comm, color, key, newcomm), where all members of group provide color = 0 and key = rank in group, and all processes that are not members of group provide color = MPI_UNDEFINED. The function MPI_COMM_SPLIT allows more general partitioning of a group into one or more subgroups with optional reordering.

Advice to users. This is an extremely powerful mechanism for dividing a single communicating group of processes into k subgroups, with k chosen implicitly by the user (by the number of colors asserted over all the processes). Each resulting communication domain will be unique and their associated groups are non-overlapping. Such a division could be useful for defining a hierarchy of computations, such as for multigrid, or linear algebra.

Multiple calls to MPI_COMM_SPLIT can be used to overcome the requirement that any call have no overlap of the resulting communicators (each process is of only one color per call). In this way, multiple overlapping communication structures can be created.

Note that, for a fixed color, the keys need not be unique. It is MPI_COMM_SPLIT's responsibility to sort processes in ascending order according to this key, and to break ties according to old rank. If all the keys are specified with the same value, then all the processes in a given color will have the same relative rank order as they did in their parent group. (*End of advice to users.*)

5.4.3 Communicator Destructor

MPI_COMM_FREE(comm)

      INOUT   comm   communicator to be destroyed

```
int MPI_Comm_free(MPI_Comm *comm)
```

```
MPI_COMM_FREE(COMM, IERROR)
    INTEGER COMM, IERROR
```

This collective operation marks the communication object for deallocation. The handle is set to MPI_COMM_NULL. Any pending operations that use this communicator will complete normally; the object is actually deallocated only if there are no other active references to it. This call applies to intra- and intercommunicators. The delete callback functions for all cached attributes (see Section 5.6) are called in arbitrary order. It is erroneous to attempt to free MPI_COMM_NULL.

Advice to implementors. Though collective, it is anticipated that this operation will normally be implemented with no communication, though the debugging version of an MPI library might choose to synchronize. (*End of advice to implementors.*)

Advice to users. Aliasing of communicators (e.g., comma = commb) is possible, but is not generally advised. After calling MPI_COMM_FREE any aliased communicator handle will be left in an undefined state. (*End of advice to users.*)

5.5 Safe Parallel Libraries

This section illustrates the design of parallel libraries, and the use of communicators to ensure the safety of internal library communications.

Assume that a new parallel library function is needed that is similar to the MPI broadcast function, except that it is not required that all processes provide the rank of the root process. Instead of the root argument of MPI_BCAST, the function takes a Boolean flag input that is true if the calling process is the root, false, otherwise. To simplify the example we make another assumption: namely that the datatype

of the send buffer is identical to the datatype of the receive buffer, so that only
one datatype argument is needed. A possible code for such a modified broadcast
function is shown below.

Example 5.8 Code for modified broadcast function mcast(). The algorithm uses a
broadcast tree that is built dynamically. The root divides the sequence of processes
that follows the root into two segments. It sends a message to the first process
in the second segment, which becomes the root for this segment. The process is
repeated, recursively, within each subsegment.

In this example, we use blocking communication. Also, we select the two segments
to be of equal size; performance can be improved by using a biased tree, and by
using nonblocking communication.

```
void mcast( void *buff,        /* address of output buffer at   */
                               /* root; address of input buffer */
                               /* at other processes.           */
            int count,         /* number of items to broadcast  */
            MPI_Datatype type, /* types of items to broadcast   */
            int isroot,        /* =1 if calling process is root */
                               /* =0, otherwise                 */
            MPI_Comm comm)     /* communicator for broadcast    */

{
int size,       /* group size                                  */
    rank,       /* rank in group                               */
    numleaves,  /* number of leaves in broadcast tree          */
    child,      /* rank of current child in broadcast tree     */
    childleaves; /* number of leaves in child's broadcast tree */
MPI_Status status;

MPI_Comm_size(comm, &size);
MPI_Comm_rank(comm, &rank);

if (isroot) {
   numleaves = size-1;
   }
else {
```

```
        /* receive from parent leaf count and message */
        MPI_Recv(&numleaves, 1, MPI_INT, MPI_ANY_SOURCE, 0, comm, &status);
        MPI_Recv(buff, count, type, MPI_ANY_SOURCE, 0, comm, &status);
        }
while (numleaves > 0) {
        /* pick child in middle of current leaf processes */
        child = (rank + (numleaves+1)/2)%size;
        childleaves = numleaves/2;
        /* send to child leaf count and message */
        MPI_Send(&childleaves, 1, MPI_INT, child, 0, comm);
        MPI_Send(buff, count, type, child, 0, comm);
        /* compute remaining number of leaves */
        numleaves -= (childleaves+1);
        }
}
```

Consider a collective invocation to the broadcast function just defined, in the context of the program segment shown in the example below, for a group of three processes.

Example 5.9 Before the collective invocation to mcast(), process 2 sends a message to process 1; process 1 posts a receive with a dontcare source. mcast is invoked, with process 0 as the root.

```
. . .
MPI_Comm_rank(comm, &myrank);
if (myrank == 2)
   MPI_Send(&i, 1, MPI_INT, 1, 0, comm);
else if (myrank == 1)
   MPI_Recv(&i, 1, MPI_INT, MPI_ANY_SOURCE, 0, comm, &status);

mcast(&i, 1, MPI_INT, (myrank ==0), comm);
. . .
```

A (correct) execution of this code is illustrated in Figure 5.2, with arrows used to indicate communications.

Since the invocation of mcast at the three processes is not simultaneous, it may actually happen that mcast is invoked at process 0 before process 1 executed the

Figure 5.2
Correct invocation of mcast

Figure 5.3
Erroneous invocation of mcast

receive in the caller code. This receive, rather than being matched by the caller code send at process 2, might be matched by the first send of process 0 within mcast. The erroneous execution illustrated in Figure 5.3 results.

How can such erroneous execution be prevented? One option is to enforce synchronization at the entry to mcast, and, for symmetric reasons, at the exit from mcast. E.g., the first and last executable statements within the code of mcast would be a call to MPI_Barrier(comm). This, however, introduces two superfluous synchronizations that will slow down execution. Furthermore, this synchronization works only if the caller code obeys the convention that messages sent before a collective invocation should also be received at their destination before the matching invocation. Consider an invocation to mcast() in a context that does not obey this restriction, as shown in the example below.

Example 5.10 Before the collective invocation to mcast(), process 2 sends a message to process 1; process 1 posts a matching receive with a dontcare source after the invocation to mcast.

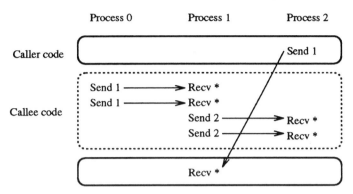

Figure 5.4
Correct invocation of mcast

```
...
MPI_Comm_rank(comm, &myrank);
if (myrank == 2)
   MPI_Send(&i, 1, MPI_INT, 1, 0, comm);

mcast(&i, 1, MPI_INT, (myrank ==0), comm);

if (myrank == 1)
   MPI_Recv(&i, 1, MPI_INT, MPI_ANY_SOURCE, 0, comm, &status);
```

The desired execution of the code in this example is illustrated in Figure 5.4.

However, a more likely matching of sends with receives will lead to the erroneous execution is illustrated in Figure 5.5. Erroneous results may also occur if a process that is not in the group of comm and does not participate in the collective invocation of mcast sends a message to processes one or two in the group of comm.

A more robust solution to this problem is to use a distinct communication domain for communication within the library, which is not used by the caller code. This will ensure that messages sent by the library are not received outside the library, and vice-versa. The modified code of the function mcast is shown below.

Example 5.11 Code for modified broadcast function mcast() that uses a private communicator. The code is identical to the one in Example 5.8, with the following exceptions: Upon entry, a duplicate pcomm of the input communicator comm is created. This private communicator is used for communication within the library

Figure 5.5
Erroneous invocation of mcast

code. It is freed before exit.

```
void mcast( void *buff, int count, MPI_Datatype type,
                          int isroot, MPI_Comm comm)
{
int size, rank, numleaves, child, childleaves;
MPI_Status status;
MPI_Comm pcomm;  /* private communicator, for internal communication */

MPI_Comm_dup(comm, &pcomm);

MPI_Comm_size(pcomm, &size);
MPI_Comm_rank(pcomm, &rank);

if (isroot) {
   numleaves = size-1;
   }
else {
    /* receive from parent leaf count and message */
   MPI_Recv(&numleaves, 1, MPI_INT, MPI_ANY_SOURCE, 0, pcomm, &status);
   MPI_Recv(buff, count, type, MPI_ANY_SOURCE, 0, pcomm, &status);
   }
while (numleaves > 0) {
    /* pick child in middle of current leaf processes */
```

```
    child = (rank + (numleaves+1)/2)%size;
    childleaves = numleaves/2;
    /* send to child leaf count and message */
    MPI_Send(&childleaves, 1, MPI_INT, child, 0, pcomm);
    MPI_Send(buff, count, type, child, 0, pcomm);
    /* compute remaining number of leaves */
    numleaves -= (childleaves+1);
    }

MPI_Comm_free(&pcomm);
}
```

This code suffers the penalty of one communicator allocation and deallocation at each invocation. We show in the next section, in Example 5.12, how to avoid this overhead, by using a preallocated communicator.

5.6 Caching

5.6.1 Introduction

As the previous examples showed, a communicator provides a "scope" for collective invocations. The communicator, which is passed as parameter to the call, specifies the group of processes that participate in the call and provide a private communication domain for communications within the callee body. In addition, it may carry information about the logical topology of the executing processes. It is often useful to attach additional persistent values to this scope; e.g., initialization parameters for a library, or additional communicators to provide a separate, private communication domain.

MPI provides a caching facility that allows an application to attach arbitrary pieces of information, called **attributes**, to both intra- and intercommunicators. More precisely, the caching facility allows a portable library to do the following:

- pass information between calls by associating it with an MPI intra- or inter-communicator,
- quickly retrieve that information, and
- be guaranteed that out-of-date information is never retrieved, even if the communicator is freed and its handle subsequently reused by MPI.

Each attribute is associated with a **key**.   To provide safety, MPI internally generates key values. MPI functions are provided which allow the user to allocate and deallocate key values (MPI_KEYVAL_CREATE and MPI_KEYVAL_FREE). Once a key is allocated by a process, it can be used to attach one attribute to any communicator defined at that process. Thus, the allocation of a key can be thought of as creating an empty box at each current or future communicator object at that process; this box has a lock that matches the allocated key. (The box is "virtual": one need not allocate any actual space before an attempt is made to store something in the box.)

Once the key is allocated, the user can set or access attributes associated with this key. The MPI call MPI_ATTR_PUT can be used to set an attribute. This call stores an attribute, or replaces an attribute in one box: the box attached with the specified communicator with a lock that matches the specified key.

The call MPI_ATTR_GET can be used to access the attribute value associated with a given key and communicator. I.e., it allows one to access the content of the box attached with the specified communicator, that has a lock that matches the specified key. This call is valid even if the box is empty, e.g., if the attribute was never set. In such case, a special "empty" value is returned.

Finally, the call MPI_ATTR_DELETE allows one to delete an attribute. I.e., it allows one to empty the box attached with the specified communicator with a lock that matches the specified key.

To be general, the attribute mechanism must be able to store arbitrary user information. On the other hand, attributes must be of a fixed, predefined type, both in Fortran and C — the type specified by the MPI functions that access or update attributes. Attributes are defined in C to be of type void *. Generally, such an attribute will be a pointer to a user-defined data structure or a handle to an MPI opaque object. In Fortran, attributes are of type INTEGER. These can be handles to opaque MPI objects or indices to user-defined tables.

An attribute, from the MPI viewpoint, is a pointer or an integer. An attribute, from the application viewpoint, may contain arbitrary information that is attached to the "MPI attribute". User-defined attributes are "copied" when a new communicator is created by a call to MPI_COMM_DUP; they are "deleted" when a communicator is deallocated by a call to MPI_COMM_FREE. Because of the arbitrary nature of the information that is copied or deleted, the user has to specify the semantics of attribute copying or deletion. The user does so by providing copy and delete callback functions when the attribute key is allocated (by a call to MPI_KEYVAL_CREATE). Predefined, default copy and delete callback functions are available.

All attribute manipulation functions are local and require no communication. Two communicator objects at two different processes that represent the same communication domain may have a different set of attribute keys and different attribute values associated with them.

MPI reserves a set of predefined key values in order to associate with MPI_COMM_WORLD information about the execution environment, at MPI initialization time. These attribute keys are discussed in Chapter 7. These keys cannot be deallocated and the associated attributes cannot be updated by the user. Otherwise, they behave like user-defined attributes.

Rationale. A much smaller interface, consisting of just a callback facility, would allow the entire caching facility to be implemented by portable code. However, such a minimal interface does not provide good protection when different libraries try to attach attributes to the same communicator. Some convention will be needed to avoid them using the same key values. With the current design, the initialization code for each library can allocate a separate key value for that library; the code written for one library is independent of the code used by another library. Furthermore the more complete interface defined here allows high-quality implementations of MPI to implement fast attribute access algorithms (e.g., using an incrementable dictionary data structure).

Attribute keys are allocated process-wide, rather then specifically for one communicator. This often simplifies usage, since a particular type of attribute may be associated with many communicators; and simplifies implementation.

The use of callback functions for attribute copying and deletion allows one to define different behaviors for these operations. For example, copying may involve the allocation of a new data structure, if the attribute is modifiable; or, it may involve only the increment of a reference count if the attribute is not modifiable. With the current design, the implementation of attribute copying and deletion is defined when the attribute key is allocated, and need not be visible to all program modules that use this key. (*End of rationale.*)

Advice to users. The communicator MPI_COMM_SELF can be used to store process-local attributes, via this attribute caching mechanism. (*End of advice to users.*)

Advice to implementors. C Attributes are scalar values, equal in size to, or larger than a C-language pointer. Fortran attributes are of type **INTEGER**. Attributes can always hold an MPI handle. It is very desirable to have identical attribute types, both for Fortran and C, in order to facilitate mixed language programming. E.g., on systems with 64 bit C pointers but 32 bit Fortran **INTEGER**, one could use 64 bit attribute values. Fortran calls will convert from **INTEGER(4)** to **INTEGER(8)**, and vice versa.

Caching and callback functions are only called synchronously, in response to explicit application requests. This avoid problems that result from repeated crossings between user and system space. (This synchronous calling rule is a general property of MPI.) (*End of advice to implementors.*)

5.6.2 Caching Functions

MPI provides the following services related to caching. They are all process local.

MPI_KEYVAL_CREATE(copy_fn, delete_fn, keyval, extra_state)

IN	copy_fn	Copy callback function for keyval
IN	delete_fn	Delete callback function for keyval
OUT	keyval	key value for future access
IN	extra_state	Extra state for callback functions

```
int MPI_Keyval_create(MPI_Copy_function *copy_fn, MPI_Delete_function
       *delete_fn, int *keyval, void* extra_state)
```

```
MPI_KEYVAL_CREATE(COPY_FN, DELETE_FN, KEYVAL, EXTRA_STATE, IERROR)
    EXTERNAL COPY_FN, DELETE_FN
    INTEGER KEYVAL, EXTRA_STATE, IERROR
```

MPI_KEYVAL_CREATE allocates a new attribute key value. Key values are unique in a process. Once allocated, the key value can be used to associate attributes and access them on any locally defined communicator. The special key value MPI_KEYVAL_INVALID is never returned by MPI_KEYVAL_CREATE. Therefore, it can be used for static initialization of key variables, to indicate an "unallocated" key.

The copy_fn function is invoked when a communicator is duplicated by MPI-_COMM_DUP. copy_fn should be of type MPI_Copy_function, which is defined as follows:

```
typedef int MPI_Copy_function(MPI_Comm oldcomm, int keyval,
                     void *extra_state, void *attribute_val_in,
                     void *attribute_val_out, int *flag)
```

A Fortran declaration for such a function is as follows:

```
SUBROUTINE COPY_FUNCTION(OLDCOMM, KEYVAL, EXTRA_STATE,
             ATTRIBUTE_VAL_IN, ATTRIBUTE_VAL_OUT, FLAG, IERR)
   INTEGER OLDCOMM, KEYVAL, EXTRA_STATE, ATTRIBUTE_VAL_IN,
   ATTRIBUTE_VAL_OUT, IERR
   LOGICAL FLAG
```

Whenever a communicator is replicated using the function MPI_COMM_DUP, all callback copy functions for attributes that are currently set are invoked (in arbitrary order). Each call to the copy callback is passed as input parameters the old communicator oldcomm, the key value keyval, the additional state extra_state that was provided to MPI_KEYVAL_CREATE when the key value was created, and the current attribute value attribute_val_in. If it returns flag = false, then the attribute is deleted in the duplicated communicator. Otherwise, when flag = true, the new attribute value is set to the value returned in attribute_val_out. The function returns MPI_SUCCESS on success and an error code on failure (in which case MPI_COMM_DUP will fail).

copy_fn may be specified as MPI_NULL_COPY_FN or MPI_DUP_FN from either C or FORTRAN. MPI_NULL_COPY_FN is a function that does nothing other than returning flag = 0 and MPI_SUCCESS; I.e., the attribute is not copied. MPI_DUP_FN sets flag = 1, returns the value of attribute_val_in in attribute_val_out and returns MPI_SUCCESS. I.e., the attribute value is copied, with no side-effects.

Rationale. The use of the extra_state argument allows one to specialize the behavior of a generic copy callback function to a particular attribute. E.g., one might have a generic copy function that allocates m bytes of storage, copy m bytes from address attribute_val_in into the newly allocated space, and returns the address of the allocated space in attribute_val_out; the value of m, i.e., the size of the data structure for a specific attribute, can be specified via extra_state. (*End of rationale.*)

Advice to users. Even though both formal arguments attribute_val_in and attribute_val_out are of type void *, their usage differs. The C copy function is passed by MPI in attribute_val_in the *value* of the attribute, and in attribute_val_out the *address* of the attribute, so as to allow the function to return the (new) attribute value. The use of type void * for both is to avoid messy type casts.

A valid copy function is one that completely duplicates the information by making a full duplicate copy of the data structures implied by an attribute; another might just make another reference to that data structure, while using a reference-count mechanism. Other types of attributes might not copy at all (they might be specific to oldcomm only). (*End of advice to users.*)

Advice to implementors. A C interface should be assumed for copy and delete functions associated with key values created in C; a Fortran calling interface should be assumed for key values created in Fortran. (*End of advice to implementors.*)

Analogous to copy_fn is a callback deletion function, defined as follows. The delete_fn function is invoked when a communicator is deleted by MPI_COMM_FREE or by a call to MPI_ATTR_DELETE or MPI_ATTR_PUT. delete_fn should be of type MPI_Delete_function, which is defined as follows:

```
typedef int MPI_Delete_function(MPI_Comm comm, int keyval,
                        void *attribute_val, void *extra_state);
```

A Fortran declaration for such a function is as follows:
```
SUBROUTINE DELETE_FUNCTION(COMM, KEYVAL, ATTRIBUTE_VAL, EXTRA_STATE,
              IERR)
   INTEGER COMM, KEYVAL, ATTRIBUTE_VAL, EXTRA_STATE, IERR
```

Whenever a communicator is deleted using the function MPI_COMM_FREE, all callback delete functions for attributes that are currently set are invoked (in arbitrary order). In addition the callback delete function for the deleted attribute is invoked by MPI_ATTR_DELETE and MPI_ATTR_PUT. The function is passed as input parameters the communicator comm, the key value keyval, the current attribute value attribute_val, and the additional state extra_state that was passed to MPI_KEYVAL_CREATE when the key value was allocated. The function returns MPI_SUCCESS on success and an error code on failure (in which case MPI_COMM-_FREE will fail).

delete_fn may be specified as MPI_NULL_DELETE_FN from either C or FORTRAN; MPI_NULL_DELETE_FN is a function that does nothing, other than returning MPI_SUCCESS.

Advice to users. The delete callback function may be invoked by MPI asynchronously, after the call to MPI_COMM_FREE returned, when MPI actually deletes the communicator object. (*End of advice to users.*)

MPI_KEYVAL_FREE(keyval)

    INOUT   keyval   Frees the integer key value

```
int MPI_Keyval_free(int *keyval)
```

```
MPI_KEYVAL_FREE(KEYVAL, IERROR)
    INTEGER KEYVAL, IERROR
```

MPI_KEYVAL_FREE deallocates an attribute key value. This function sets the value of keyval to MPI_KEYVAL_INVALID. Note that it is not erroneous to free an attribute key that is in use (i.e., has attached values for some communicators); the key value is not actually deallocated until after no attribute values are locally attached to this key. All such attribute values need to be explicitly deallocated by the program, either via calls to MPI_ATTR_DELETE that free one attribute instance, or by calls to MPI_COMM_FREE that free all attribute instances associated with the freed communicator.

MPI_ATTR_PUT(comm, keyval, attribute_val)

IN	comm	communicator to which attribute will be attached
IN	keyval	key value, as returned by MPI_KEYVAL_CREATE
IN	attribute_val	attribute value

```
int MPI_Attr_put(MPI_Comm comm, int keyval, void* attribute_val)
```

```
MPI_ATTR_PUT(COMM, KEYVAL, ATTRIBUTE_VAL, IERROR)
    INTEGER COMM, KEYVAL, ATTRIBUTE_VAL, IERROR
```

MPI_ATTR_PUT associates the value attribute_val with the key keyval on communicator comm. If a value is already associated with this key on the communicator, then the outcome is as if MPI_ATTR_DELETE was first called to delete the previous value (and the callback function delete_fn was executed), and a new value was next stored. The call is erroneous if there is no key with value keyval; in particular MPI_KEYVAL_INVALID is an erroneous value for keyval.

MPI_ATTR_GET(comm, keyval, attribute_val, flag)

IN	comm	communicator to which attribute is attached
IN	keyval	key value
OUT	attribute_val	attribute value, unless flag = false
OUT	flag	true if an attribute value was extracted; false if no attribute is associated with the key

```
int MPI_Attr_get(MPI_Comm comm, int keyval, void *attribute_val,
        int *flag)
```

```
MPI_ATTR_GET(COMM, KEYVAL, ATTRIBUTE_VAL, FLAG, IERROR)
    INTEGER COMM, KEYVAL, ATTRIBUTE_VAL, IERROR
    LOGICAL FLAG
```

MPI_ATTR_GET retrieves an attribute value by key. The call is erroneous if there is no key with value keyval. In particular MPI_KEYVAL_INVALID is an erroneous value for keyval. On the other hand, the call is correct if the key value exists, but no attribute is attached on comm for that key; in such a case, the call returns flag = false. If an attribute is attached on comm to keyval, then the call returns flag = true, and returns the attribute value in attribute_val.

Advice to users. The call to MPI_Attr_put passes in attribute_val the *value* of the attribute; the call to MPI_Attr_get passes in attribute_val the *address* of the the location where the attribute value is to be returned. Thus, if the attribute value itself is a pointer of type void*, then the actual attribute_val parameter to MPI_Attr_put will be of type void* and the actual attribute_val parameter to MPI_Attr_get will be of type void**. (*End of advice to users.*)

Rationale. The use of a formal parameter attribute_val of type void* (rather than void**) in MPI_Attr_get avoids the messy type casting that would be needed if the attribute is declared with a type other than void*. (*End of rationale.*)

MPI_ATTR_DELETE(comm, keyval)

| IN | comm | communicator to which attribute is at-tached |
| IN | keyval | The key value of the deleted attribute |

```
int MPI_Attr_delete(MPI_Comm comm, int keyval)
```

```
MPI_ATTR_DELETE(COMM, KEYVAL, IERROR)
    INTEGER COMM, KEYVAL, IERROR
```

MPI_ATTR_DELETE deletes the attribute attached to key keyval on comm. This function invokes the attribute delete function delete_fn specified when the keyval was created. The call will fail if there is no key with value keyval or if the delete_fn function returns an error code other than MPI_SUCCESS. On the other hand, the call is correct even if no attribute is currently attached to keyval on comm.

Example 5.12 We come back to the code in Example 5.11. Rather than duplicating the communicator comm at each invocation, we desire to do it once, and store the duplicate communicator. It would be inconvenient to require initialization code that duplicates all communicators to be used later with mcast. Fortunately, this is not needed. Instead, we shall use an initialization code that allocates an attribute key for the exclusive use of mcast(). This key can then be used to store, with each communicator comm, a private copy of comm which is used by mcast. This copy is created once at the first invocation of mcast with argument comm.

```
static int *extra_state;        /* not used */
static void *mcast_key = MPI_KEYVAL_INVALID;
                /* attribute key for mcast                 */
int mcast_delete_fn(MPI_Comm comm, int keyval, void *attr_val,
                void *extra_state)
                /* delete function to be used for mcast_key */
                /* attribute.  The callback function frees  */
                /* the private communicator attached to     */
                /* this key                                 */
{
return MPI_Comm_free((MPI_Comm *)&attr_val);
}

void mcast_init()   /* initialization function for mcast.  It  */
```

```
                          /* should be invoked once by each process  */
                          /* before it invokes mcast                 */
{
MPI_Keyval_create( MPI_NULL_COPY_FN, mcast_delete_fn,
                   &mcast_key, extra_state);
}


void mcast(void *buff, int count, MPI_Datatype type,
                           int isroot, MPI_Comm comm)
{
int size, rank, numleaves, child, childleaves, flag;
MPI_Comm pcomm;
void *attr_val;
MPI_Status status;

MPI_Attr_get(comm, mcast_key, &attr_val, &flag);
if (flag)          /* private communicator cached              */
   pcomm = (MPI_Comm)attr_val;
else {             /* first invocation; no cached communicator */
                   /* create private communicator              */
  MPI_Comm_dup(comm, &pcomm);
                   /* and cache it                             */
  MPI_Attr_put(comm, mcast_key, pcomm);
  }

/* continue now as before */

MPI_Comm_size(pcomm, &size);
MPI_Comm_rank(pcomm, &rank);

if (isroot) {
  numleaves = size-1;
  }
else {
    /* receive from parent leaf count and message */
  MPI_RECV(&numleaves, 1, MPI_INT, MPI_ANY_SOURCE, 0, pcomm, &status);
  MPI_RECV(buff, count, type, MPI_ANY_SOURCE, 0, pcomm, &status);
  }
```

```
while (numleaves > 0) {
    /* pick child in middle of current leaf processes */
    child = mod(rank + (numleaves+1)/2, size);
    childleaves = numleaves/2;
    /* send to child leaf count and message */
    MPI_SEND(&childleaves, 1, MPI_INT, child, 0, pcomm);
    MPI_SEND(buff, count, type, child, 0, pcomm);
    /* compute remaining number of leaves */
    numleaves -= (childleaves+1);
    }
}
```

The code above dedicates a statically allocated private communicator for the use of mcast. This segregates communication within the library from communication outside the library. However, this approach does not provide separation of communications belonging to distinct invocations of the same library function, since they all use the same communication domain. Consider two successive collective invocations of mcast by four processes, where process 0 is the broadcast root in the first one, and process 3 is the root in the second one. The intended execution and communication flow for these two invocations is illustrated in Figure 5.6.

However, there is a race between messages sent by the first invocation of mcast, from process 0 to process 1, and messages sent by the second invocation of mcast, from process 3 to process 1. The erroneous execution illustrated in Figure 5.7 may occur, where messages sent by second invocation overtake messages from the first invocation. This phenomenon is known as *backmasking*.

How can we avoid backmasking? One option is to revert to the approach in Example 5.11, where a separate communication domain is generated for each invocation. Another option is to add a barrier synchronization, either at the entry or at the exit from the library call. Yet another option is to rewrite the library code, so as to prevent the nondeterministic race. The race occurs because receives with dontcare's are used. It is often possible to avoid the use of such constructs. Unfortunately, avoiding dontcares leads to a less efficient implementation of mcast. A possible alternative is to use increasing tag numbers to disambiguate successive invocations of mcast. An "invocation count" can be cached with each communicator, as an additional library attribute. The resulting code is shown below.

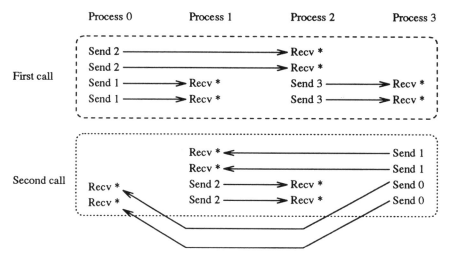

Figure 5.6
Correct execution of two successive invocations of mcast

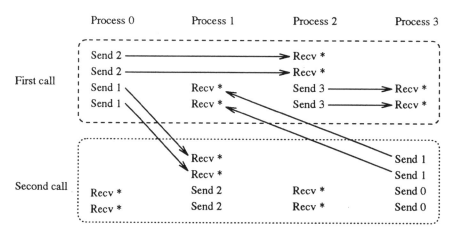

Figure 5.7
Erroneous execution of two successive invocations of mcast

Example 5.13 Code in previous example is modified, to prevent backmasking: successive invocations of mcast with the same communicator use distinct tags.

```
static int *extra_state;           /* not used */
static void *mcast_key = MPI_KEYVAL_INVALID;
typedef  struct {          /* mcast attribute structure */
     MPI_Comm pcomm;      /* private communicator      */
     int invcount;        /* invocation count          */
     } Mcast_attr;

int mcast_delete_fn(MPI_Comm comm, int keyval, void *attr_val,
                    void *extra_state)
{
MPI_Comm_free(&((Mcast_attr *)attr_val)->pcomm);
free(attr_val);
}

void mcast_init()    /* initialization function for mcast.      */
{
MPI_Keyval_create( MPI_NULL_COPY_FN, mcast_delete_fn,
                   &mcast_key, extra_state);
}

void mcast(void *buff, int count, MPI_Datatype type,
                          int isroot, MPI_Comm comm)
{
int size, rank, numleaves, child, childleaves, flag, tag;
MPI_Comm pcomm;
void *attr_val;
Mcast_attr *attr_struct;
MPI_Status status;

MPI_Attr_get(comm, mcast_key, &attr_val, &flag);
if (flag) {        /* attribute  cached                     */
    attr_struct = (Mcast_attr *)attr_val;
    pcomm = attr_struct->pcomm;
    tag = ++attr_struct->invcount;
   }
```

```
  else {                    /* first invocation; no cached communicator  */
                            /* create private communicator               */
     MPI_Comm_dup(comm, &pcomm);
                            /* create attribute structure                */
     attr_struct = (Mcast_attr *)malloc(sizeof(Mcast_attr));
     attr_struct->pcomm = pcomm;
     attr_struct->invcount = 0;
     MPI_Attr_put(comm, mcast_key, attr_struct);
   }

/* broadcast code, using tag     */

MPI_Comm_size(pcomm, &size);
MPI_Comm_rank(pcomm, &rank);

if (isroot) {
   numleaves = size-1;
   }
else {
     /* receive from parent leaf count and message */
   MPI_RECV(&numleaves, 1, MPI_INT, MPI_ANY_SOURCE, tag, pcomm, &status);
   MPI_RECV(buff, count, type, MPI_ANY_SOURCE, tag, pcomm, &status);
   }
while (numleaves > 0) {
   /* pick child in middle of current leaf processes */
   child = mod(rank + (numleaves+1)/2, size);
   childleaves = numleaves/2;
   /* send to child leaf count and message */
   MPI_SEND(&childleaves, 1, MPI_INT, child, 0, pcomm);
   MPI_SEND(buff, count, type, child, 0, pcomm);
   /* compute remaining number of leaves */
   numleaves -= (childleaves+1);
   }
}
```

5.7 Intercommunication

5.7.1 Introduction

This section introduces the concept of inter-communication and describes the portions of MPI that support it.

All point-to-point communication described thus far has involved communication between processes that are members of the same group. In modular and multi-disciplinary applications, different process groups execute distinct modules and processes within different modules communicate with one another in a pipeline or a more general module graph. In these applications, the most natural way for a process to specify a peer process is by the rank of the peer process within the peer group. In applications that contain internal user-level servers, each server may be a process group that provides services to one or more clients, and each client may be a process group that uses the services of one or more servers. It is again most natural to specify the peer process by rank within the peer group in these applications.

An inter-group communication domain is specified by a set of intercommunicators with the pair of disjoint groups (A,B) as their attribute, such that

- their links form a bipartite graph: each communicator at a process in group A is linked to all communicators at processes in group B, and vice-versa; and

- links have consistent indices: at each communicator at a process in group A, the i-th link points to the communicator for process i in group B; and vice-versa.

This distributed data structure is illustrated in Figure 5.8, for the case of a pair of groups (A,B), with two (upper box) and three (lower box) processes, respectively.

The communicator structure distinguishes between a *local* group, namely the group containing the process where the structure reside, and a *remote* group, namely the other group. The structure is symmetric: for processes in group A, then A is the local group and B is the remote group, whereas for processes in group B, then B is the local group and A is the remote group.

An inter-group communication will involve a process in one group executing a send call and another process, in the other group, executing a matching receive call. As in intra-group communication, the matching process (destination of send or source of receive) is specified using a (communicator, rank) pair. Unlike intra-group communication, the rank is relative to the second, remote group. Thus, in the communication domain illustrated in Figure 5.8, process 1 in group A sends a

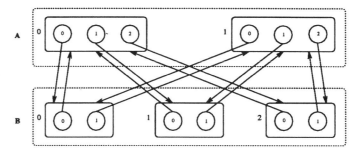

Figure 5.8
Distributed data structure for inter-communication domain.

message to process 2 in group B with a call MPI_SEND(..., 2, tag, comm); process 2 in group B receives this message with a call MPI_RECV(..., 1, tag, comm). Conversely, process 2 in group B sends a message to process 1 in group A with a call to MPI_SEND(..., 1, tag, comm), and the message is received by a call to MPI_RECV(..., 2, tag, comm); a remote process is identified in the same way for the purposes of sending or receiving. All point-to-point communication functions can be used with intercommunicators for inter-group communication.

Here is a summary of the properties of inter-group communication and intercommunicators:

- The syntax of point-to-point communication is the same for both inter- and intra-communication. The same communicator can be used both for send and for receive operations.
- A target process is addressed by its rank in the remote group, both for sends and for receives.
- Communications using an intercommunicator are guaranteed not to conflict with any communications that use a different communicator.
- An intercommunicator cannot be used for collective communication.
- A communicator will provide either intra- or inter-communication, never both.

The routine MPI_COMM_TEST_INTER may be used to determine if a communicator is an inter- or intracommunicator. Intercommunicators can be used as arguments to some of the other communicator access routines. Intercommunicators cannot be used as input to some of the constructor routines for intracommunicators (for instance, MPI_COMM_CREATE).

Rationale. The correspondence between inter- and intracommunicators can be best understood by thinking of an intra-group communication domain as a special case of an inter-group communication domain, where both communication groups happen to be identical. This interpretation can be used to derive a consistent semantics for communicator inquiry functions and for point-to-point communication, or an identical implementation for both types of objects.

This correspondence indicates how collective communication functions could be extended to inter-group communication: Rather than a symmetric design, where processes in the group both send and receive, one would have an asymmetric design, where one group sends (either from a single root or from all processes) and the other group receives (either to a single root or to all processes). Additional syntax is needed to distinguish sender group from receiver group. Such extensions are discussed for MPI-2.

Note, however, that the two groups of an intercommunicator are currently required to be disjoint, for reasons explained later in this section. (*End of rationale.*)

Advice to implementors. An intercommunicator can be implemented with a data structure very similar to that used for an intracommunicator. The intercommunicator can be represented by a structure with components group, myrank, local_context and remote_context. The group array represents the remote group, whereas myrank is the rank of the process in the local group.

When a process posts a send with arguments dest, tag and comm, then the address of the destination is computed as comm.group[dest]. The message sent carries a header with the tuple (comm.myrank, tag, comm.remote_context).

If a process posts a receive with argument source, tag and comm, then headers of incoming messages are matched to the tuple (source, tag, comm.local_context) (first two may be dontcare's).

This design provides a safe inter-group communication domain provided that

- the local_context is process unique and is identical at all processes in the same group; and

- the local_context of one group equals to the remote_context of the other group.

Note that this data structure can be used to represent intracommunicators merely be setting local_context = remote_context. It is then identical to the first representation discussed on page 205.

Another design is to use ids which are process-unique, but not necessarily identical at all processes. In such case, the remote_context component of the communicator structure is an array, where comm.remote_context[i] is the context chosen by process i in remote group to identify that communication domain; local_context is the context chosen by the local process to identify that communication domain. A message is sent with header comm.myrank, tag, comm.remote_context[dest]; a receive call causes incoming messages to be matched against the tuple (source, tag, comm.local_context).

Comparing with the second implementation outlined on page 205, we see again that the same data structure can be used to represent an intra-group communication domain, with no changes. When used for an intracommunicator, then the identity comm.local_context = comm.remote_context[myrank] holds. (*End of advice to implementors.*)

It is often convenient to generate an inter-group communication domain by joining together two intra-group communication domains, i.e., building the pair of communicating groups from the individual groups. This requires that there exists one process in each group that can communicate with each other through a communication domain that serves as a bridge between the two groups. For example, suppose that comm1 has 3 processes and comm2 has 4 processes (see Figure 5.9). In terms of the MPI_COMM_WORLD, the processes in comm1 are 0, 1 and 2 and in comm2 are 3, 4, 5 and 6. Let local process 0 in each intracommunicator form the bridge. They can communicate via MPI_COMM_WORLD where process 0 in comm1 has rank 0 and process 0 in comm2 has rank 3. Once the intercommunicator is formed, the original group for each intracommunicator is the local group in the intercommunicator and the group from the other intracommunicator becomes the remote group. For communication with this intercommunicator, the rank in the remote group is used. For example, if a process in comm1 wants to send to process 2 of comm2 (MPI_COMM_WORLD rank 5) then it uses 2 as the rank in the send.

Intercommunicators are created in this fashion by the call MPI_INTERCOMM-_CREATE. The two joined groups are required to be disjoint. The converse function of building an intracommunicator from an intercommunicator is provided by the call MPI_INTERCOMM_MERGE. This call generates a communication domain with a group which is the union of the two groups of the inter-group communication domain. Both calls are blocking. Both will generally require collective communication within each of the involved groups, as well as communication across the groups.

Rationale. The two groups of an inter-group communication domain are required to be disjoint in order to support the defined intercommunicator creation function. If the groups were not disjoint then a process in the intersection of the two groups would have to make two calls to MPI_INTERCOMM_CREATE, one on behalf of each

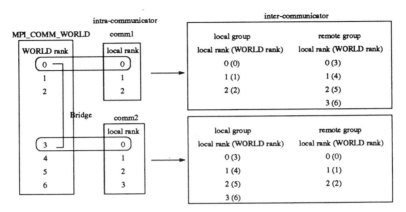

Figure 5.9
Example of two intracommunicators merging to become one intercommunicator.

group it belongs to. This is not feasible with a blocking call. One would need to use a nonblocking call, implemented using nonblocking collective communication, in order to relax the disjointness condition. (*End of rationale.*)

5.7.2   Intercommunicator Accessors

MPI_COMM_TEST_INTER(comm, flag)

IN	comm	communicator
OUT	flag	true if comm is intercommunicator

```
int MPI_Comm_test_inter(MPI_Comm comm, int *flag)
```

```
MPI_COMM_TEST_INTER(COMM, FLAG, IERROR)
    INTEGER COMM, IERROR
    LOGICAL FLAG
```

MPI_COMM_TEST_INTER is a local routine that allows the calling process to determine if a communicator is an intercommunicator or an intracommunicator. It returns true if it is an intercommunicator, otherwise false.

When an intercommunicator is used as an input argument to the communicator accessors described in Section 5.4.1, the following table describes the behavior.

MPI_COMM_* Function Behavior (in Inter-Communication Mode)	
MPI_COMM_SIZE	returns the size of the local group.
MPI_COMM_GROUP	returns the local group.
MPI_COMM_RANK	returns the rank in the local group

Furthermore, the operation MPI_COMM_COMPARE is valid for intercommunicators. Both communicators must be either intra- or intercommunicators, or else MPI_UNEQUAL results. Both corresponding local and remote groups must compare correctly to get the results MPI_CONGRUENT and MPI_SIMILAR. In particular, it is possible for MPI_SIMILAR to result because either the local or remote groups were similar but not identical.

The following accessors provide consistent access to the remote group of an intercommunicator; they are all local operations.

MPI_COMM_REMOTE_SIZE(comm, size)

IN	comm	intercommunicator
OUT	size	number of processes in the remote group of comm

```
int MPI_Comm_remote_size(MPI_Comm comm, int *size)
```

```
MPI_COMM_REMOTE_SIZE(COMM, SIZE, IERROR)
    INTEGER COMM, SIZE, IERROR
```

MPI_COMM_REMOTE_SIZE returns the size of the remote group in the intercommunicator. Note that the size of the local group is given by MPI_COMM_SIZE.

MPI_COMM_REMOTE_GROUP(comm, group)

IN	comm	intercommunicator
OUT	group	remote group corresponding to comm

```
int MPI_Comm_remote_group(MPI_Comm comm, MPI_Group *group)
```

```
MPI_COMM_REMOTE_GROUP(COMM, GROUP, IERROR)
    INTEGER COMM, GROUP, IERROR
```

MPI_COMM_REMOTE_GROUP returns the remote group in the intercommunicator. Note that the local group is give by MPI_COMM_GROUP.

Advice to implementors. It is necessary to expand the representation outlined on page 245, in order to support intercommunicator accessors that return information on the local group: namely, the data structure has to carry information on the local group, in addition to the remote group. This information is also needed in order to support conveniently the call MPI_INTERCOMM_MERGE. (*End of advice to implementors.*)

5.7.3   Intercommunicator Constructors

An intercommunicator can be created by a call to MPI_COMM_DUP, see Section 5.4.2. As for intracommunicators, this call generates a new inter-group communication domain with the same groups as the old one, and also replicates user-defined attributes. An intercommunicator is deallocated by a call to MPI_COMM-_FREE. The other intracommunicator constructor functions of Section 5.4.2 do not apply to intercommunicators. Two new functions are specific to intercommunicators.

MPI_INTERCOMM_CREATE(local_comm, local_leader, bridge_comm, remote_leader, tag, newintercomm)

IN	local_comm	local intracommunicator
IN	local_leader	rank of local group leader in local_comm
IN	bridge_comm	"bridge" communicator; significant only at two local leaders
IN	remote_leader	rank of remote group leader in bridge_comm; significant only at two local leaders
IN	tag	"safe" tag
OUT	newintercomm	new intercommunicator (handle)

```
int MPI_Intercomm_create(MPI_Comm local_comm, int local_leader,
            MPI_Comm bridge_comm, int remote_leader, int tag,
            MPI_Comm *newintercomm)
```

```
MPI_INTERCOMM_CREATE(LOCAL_COMM, LOCAL_LEADER, PEER_COMM,
            REMOTE_LEADER, TAG, NEWINTERCOMM, IERROR)
    INTEGER LOCAL_COMM, LOCAL_LEADER, PEER_COMM, REMOTE_LEADER, TAG,
    NEWINTERCOMM, IERROR
```

MPI_INTERCOMM_CREATE creates an intercommunicator. The call is collective over the union of the two groups. Processes should provide matching local_comm and identical local_leader arguments within each of the two groups. The two leaders specify matching bridge_comm arguments, and each provide in remote_leader the rank of the other leader within the domain of bridge_comm. Both provide identical tag values.

Wildcards are not permitted for remote_leader, local_leader, nor tag.

This call uses point-to-point communication with communicator bridge_comm, and with tag tag between the leaders. Thus, care must be taken that there be no pending communication on bridge_comm that could interfere with this communication.

MPI_INTERCOMM_MERGE(intercomm, high, newintracómm)

IN	intercomm	InterCommunicator
IN	high	see below
OUT	newintracomm	new intracommunicator

```
int MPI_Intercomm_merge(MPI_Comm intercomm, int high,
        MPI_Comm *newintracomm)
```

```
MPI_INTERCOMM_MERGE(INTERCOMM, HIGH, NEWINTRACOMM, IERROR)
    INTEGER INTERCOMM, NEWINTRACOMM, IERROR
    LOGICAL HIGH
```

MPI_INTERCOMM_MERGE creates an intracommunicator from the union of the two groups that are associated with intercomm. All processes should provide the same high value within each of the two groups. If processes in one group provided the value high = false and processes in the other group provided the value high = true then the union orders the "low" group before the "high" group. If all processes provided the same high argument then the order of the union is arbitrary. This call is blocking and collective within the union of the two groups.

Advice to implementors. In order to implement MPI_INTERCOMM_MERGE, MPI_COMM_FREE and MPI_COMM_DUP, it is necessary to support collective communication within the two groups as well as communication between the two groups. One possible mechanism is to create a data structure that will allow one to run code similar to that used for MPI_INTERCOMM_CREATE: A private communication domain for each group, a leader for each group, and a private bridge communication domain for the two leaders. (*End of advice to implementors.*)

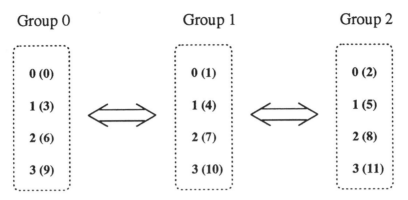

Figure 5.10
Three-group pipeline. The figure shows the local rank and (within brackets) the global rank of
each process.

Example 5.14 In this example, processes are divided in three groups. Groups 0
and 1 communicate. Groups 1 and 2 communicate. Therefore, group 0 requires one
intercommunicator, group 1 requires two intercommunicators, and group 2 requires
1 intercommunicator. See Figure 5.10

```
#include <mpi.h>

main(int argc, char **argv)
{
  MPI_Comm    myComm;       /* intra-communicator of local sub-group */
  MPI_Comm    myFirstComm;  /* inter-communicator */
  MPI_Comm    mySecondComm; /* second inter-communicator (group 1 only) */
  int membershipKey, rank;

  MPI_Init(&argc, &argv);
  MPI_Comm_rank(MPI_COMM_WORLD, &rank);

  /* Generate membershipKey in the range [0, 1, 2] */
  membershipKey = rank % 3;

  /* Build intra-communicator for local sub-group */
  MPI_Comm_split(MPI_COMM_WORLD, membershipKey, rank, &myComm);

  /* Build inter-communicators.  Tags are hard-coded. */
```

```
if (membershipKey == 0) {
  /* Group 0 communicates with group 1. */
  MPI_Intercomm_create( myComm, 0, MPI_COMM_WORLD, 1, 01, &myFirstComm);
}
else if (membershipKey == 1) {
  /* Group 1 communicates with groups 0 and 2. */
  MPI_Intercomm_create( myComm, 0, MPI_COMM_WORLD, 0, 01, &myFirstComm);
  MPI_Intercomm_create( myComm, 0, MPI_COMM_WORLD, 2, 12, &mySecondComm);
}
else if (membershipKey == 2) {
  /* Group 2 communicates with group 1. */
  MPI_Intercomm_create( myComm, 0, MPI_COMM_WORLD, 1, 12, &myFirstComm);
}

/* Do work ... (not shown) */

/* free communicators appropriately */
MPI_Comm_free(&myComm);
MPI_Comm_free(&myFirstComm);
if(membershipkey == 1)
  MPI_Comm_free(&mySecondComm);
MPI_Finalize();
}
```

6 Process Topologies

6.1 Introduction

This chapter discusses the MPI topology mechanism. A topology is an extra, optional attribute that one can give to an intra-communicator; topologies cannot be added to inter-communicators. A topology can provide a convenient naming mechanism for the processes of a group (within a communicator), and additionally, may assist the runtime system in mapping the processes onto hardware.

As stated in Chapter 5, a process group in MPI is a collection of n processes. Each process in the group is assigned a rank between 0 and n-1. In many parallel applications a linear ranking of processes does not adequately reflect the logical communication pattern of the processes (which is usually determined by the underlying problem geometry and the numerical algorithm used). Often the processes are arranged in topological patterns such as two- or three-dimensional grids. More generally, the logical process arrangement is described by a graph. In this chapter we will refer to this logical process arrangement as the "virtual topology."

A clear distinction must be made between the virtual process topology and the topology of the underlying, physical hardware. The virtual topology can be exploited by the system in the assignment of processes to physical processors, if this helps to improve the communication performance on a given machine. How this mapping is done, however, is outside the scope of MPI. The description of the virtual topology, on the other hand, depends only on the application, and is machine-independent. The functions in this chapter deal only with machine-independent mapping.

Rationale. Though physical mapping is not discussed, the existence of the virtual topology information may be used as advice by the runtime system. There are well-known techniques for mapping grid/torus structures to hardware topologies such as hypercubes or grids. For more complicated graph structures good heuristics often yield nearly optimal results [21]. On the other hand, if there is no way for the user to specify the logical process arrangement as a "virtual topology," a random mapping is most likely to result. On some machines, this will lead to unnecessary contention in the interconnection network. Some details about predicted and measured performance improvements that result from good process-to-processor mapping on modern wormhole-routing architectures can be found in [9, 8].

Besides possible performance benefits, the virtual topology can function as a convenient, process-naming structure, with tremendous benefits for program readability and notational power in message-passing programming. (*End of rationale.*)

6.2 Virtual Topologies

The communication pattern of a set of processes can be represented by a graph. The nodes stand for the processes, and the edges connect processes that communicate with each other. Since communication is most often symmetric, communication graphs are assumed to be symmetric: if an edge uv connects node u to node v, then an edge vu connects node v to node u.

MPI provides message-passing between any pair of processes in a group. There is no requirement for opening a channel explicitly. Therefore, a "missing link" in the user-defined process graph does not prevent the corresponding processes from exchanging messages. It means, rather, that this connection is neglected in the virtual topology. This strategy implies that the topology gives no convenient way of naming this pathway of communication. Another possible consequence is that an automatic mapping tool (if one exists for the runtime environment) will not take account of this edge when mapping, and communication on the "missing" link will be less efficient.

Rationale.   As previously stated, the message passing in a program can be represented as a directed graph where the vertices are processes and the edges are messages. On many systems, optimizing communication speeds requires a minimization of the contention for physical wires by messages occurring simultaneously. Performing this optimization requires knowledge of when messages occur and their resource requirements. Not only is this information difficult to represent, it may not be available at topology creation time in complex programs. A simpler alternative is to provide information about "spatial" distribution of communication and ignore "temporal" distribution. Though the former method can lead to greater optimizations and faster programs, the later method is used in MPI to allow a simpler interface that is well understood at the current time. As a result, the programmer tells the MPI system the typical connections, e.g., topology, of their program. This can lead to compromises when a specific topology may over- or under-specify the connectivity that is used at any time in the program. Overall, however, the chosen topology mechanism was seen as a useful compromise between functionality and ease of usage. Experience with similar techniques in PARMACS [3, 7] show that this information is usually sufficient for a good mapping. (*End of rationale.*)

0 (0,0)	1 (0,1)	2 (0,2)	3 (0,3)
4 (1,0)	5 (1,1)	6 (1,2)	7 (1,3)
8 (2,0)	9 (2,1)	10 (2,2)	11 (2,3)

Figure 6.1
Relationship between ranks and Cartesian coordinates for a 3x4 2D topology. The upper number in each box is the rank of the process and the lower value is the (row, column) coordinates.

Specifying the virtual topology in terms of a graph is sufficient for all applications. However, in many applications the graph structure is regular, and the detailed set-up of the graph would be inconvenient for the user and might be less efficient at run time. A large fraction of all parallel applications use process topologies like rings, two- or higher-dimensional grids, or tori. These structures are completely defined by the number of dimensions and the numbers of processes in each coordinate direction. Also, the mapping of grids and tori is generally an easier problem than general graphs. Thus, it is desirable to address these cases explicitly.

Process coordinates in a Cartesian structure begin their numbering at 0. Row-major numbering is always used for the processes in a Cartesian structure. This means that, for example, the relation between group rank and coordinates for twelve processes in a 3×4 grid is as shown in Figure 6.1.

6.3   Overlapping Topologies

In some applications, it is desirable to use different Cartesian topologies at different stages in the computation. For example, in a QR factorization, the ith transformation is determined by the data below the diagonal in the ith column of the matrix. It is often easiest to think of the upper right hand corner of the 2D topology as starting on the process with the ith diagonal element of the matrix for the ith stage of the computation. Since the original matrix was laid out in the original 2D topology, it is necessary to maintain a relationship between it and the shifted 2D topology in the ith stage. For example, the processes forming a row or column in the original 2D topology must also form a row or column in the shifted 2D topology in the ith stage. As stated in Section 6.2 and shown in Figure 6.1, there is a clear correspondence between the rank of a process and its coordinates in a Cartesian topology. This relationship can be used to create multiple Cartesian topologies with the desired relationship. Figure 6.2 shows the relationship of two 2D Cartesian topologies where the second one is shifted by two rows and two columns.

0 / (0,0) 6 / (1,2)	1 / (0,1) 7 / (1,3)	2 / (0,2) 4 / (1,0)	3 / (0,3) 5 / (1,1)
4 / (1,0) 10 / (2,2)	5 / (1,1) 11 / (2,3)	6 / (1,2) 8 / (2,0)	7 / (1,3) 9 / (2,1)
8 / (2,0) 2 / (0,2)	9 / (2,1) 3 / (0,3)	10 / (2,2) 0 / (0,0)	11 / (2,3) 1 / (0,1)

Figure 6.2
The relationship between two overlaid topologies on a 3 × 4 torus. The upper values in each process is the rank / (row,col) in the original 2D topology and the lower values are the same for the shifted 2D topology. Note that rows and columns of processes remain intact.

6.4   Embedding in MPI

The support for virtual topologies as defined in this chapter is consistent with other parts of MPI, and, whenever possible, makes use of functions that are defined elsewhere. Topology information is associated with communicators. It can be implemented using the caching mechanism described in Chapter 5.

Rationale.   As with collective communications, the virtual topology features can be layered on top of point-to-point and communicator functionality. By doing this, a layered implementation is possible, though not required. A consequence of this design is that topology information is not given directly to point-to-point nor collective routines. Instead, the topology interface provides functions to translate between the virtual topology and the ranks used in MPI communication routines. (*End of rationale.*)

6.5   Cartesian Topology Functions

This section describes the MPI functions for creating Cartesian topologies.

6.5.1   Cartesian Constructor Function

MPI_CART_CREATE can be used to describe Cartesian structures of arbitrary dimension. For each coordinate direction one specifies whether the process structure is periodic or not. For a 1D topology, it is linear if it is not periodic and a ring if it is periodic. For a 2D topology, it is a rectangle, cylinder, or torus as it goes from non-periodic to periodic in one dimension to fully periodic. Note that an n-dimensional hypercube is an n-dimensional torus with 2 processes per coordinate direction. Thus, special support for hypercube structures is not necessary.

MPI_CART_CREATE(comm_old, ndims, dims, periods, reorder, comm_cart)

IN	comm_old	input communicator
IN	ndims	number of dimensions of Cartesian grid
IN	dims	integer array of size ndims specifying the number of processes in each dimension
IN	periods	logical array of size ndims specifying whether the grid is periodic (true) or not (false) in each dimension
IN	reorder	ranks may be reordered (true) or not (false)
OUT	comm_cart	communicator with new Cartesian topology

```
int MPI_Cart_create(MPI_Comm comm_old, int ndims, int *dims,
            int *periods, int reorder, MPI_Comm *comm_cart)
```

```
MPI_CART_CREATE(COMM_OLD, NDIMS, DIMS, PERIODS, REORDER, COMM_CART,
            IERROR)
    INTEGER COMM_OLD, NDIMS, DIMS(*), COMM_CART, IERROR
    LOGICAL PERIODS(*), REORDER
```

MPI_CART_CREATE returns a handle to a new communicator to which the Cartesian topology information is attached. In analogy to the function MPI_COMM-_CREATE, no cached information propagates to the new communicator. Also, this function is collective. As with other collective calls, the program must be written to work correctly, whether the call synchronizes or not.

If reorder = false then the rank of each process in the new group is identical to its rank in the old group. Otherwise, the function may reorder the processes (possibly so as to choose a good embedding of the virtual topology onto the physical machine). If the total size of the Cartesian grid is smaller than the size of the group of comm_old, then some processes are returned MPI_COMM_NULL, in analogy to MPI_COMM_SPLIT. The call is erroneous if it specifies a grid that is larger than the group size.

Advice to implementors. MPI_CART_CREATE can be implemented by creating a new communicator, and caching with the new communicator a description of the Cartesian grid, e.g.,

1. ndims (number of dimensions),
2. dims (numbers of processes per coordinate direction),
3. periods (periodicity information),
4. own_position (own position in grid)

(*End of advice to implementors.*)

6.5.2   Cartesian Convenience Function: MPI_DIMS_CREATE

For Cartesian topologies, the function MPI_DIMS_CREATE helps the user select a balanced distribution of processes per coordinate direction, depending on the number of processes in the group to be balanced and optional constraints that can be specified by the user. One possible use of this function is to partition all the processes (the size of MPI_COMM_WORLD's group) into an n-dimensional topology.

MPI_DIMS_CREATE(nnodes, ndims, dims)

IN	nnodes	number of nodes in a grid
IN	ndims	number of Cartesian dimensions
INOUT	dims	integer array of size ndims specifying the number of nodes in each dimension

```
int MPI_Dims_create(int nnodes, int ndims, int *dims)
```

```
MPI_DIMS_CREATE(NNODES, NDIMS, DIMS, IERROR)
    INTEGER NNODES, NDIMS, DIMS(*), IERROR
```

The entries in the array dims are set to describe a Cartesian grid with ndims dimensions and a total of nnodes nodes. The dimensions are set to be as close to each other as possible, using an appropriate divisibility algorithm. The caller may further constrain the operation of this routine by specifying elements of array dims. If dims[i] is set to a positive number, the routine will not modify the number of nodes in dimension i; only those entries where dims[i] = 0 are modified by the call.

Negative input values of dims[i] are erroneous. An error will occur if nnodes is not a multiple of $\prod_{i,dims[i]\neq 0} dims[i]$.

For dims[i] set by the call, dims[i] will be ordered in monotonically decreasing order. Array dims is suitable for use as input to routine MPI_CART_CREATE. MPI_DIMS_CREATE is local. Several sample calls are shown in Example 6.1.

	dims before call	function call	dims on return
Example 6.1	(0,0)	MPI_DIMS_CREATE(6, 2, dims)	(3,2)
	(0,0)	MPI_DIMS_CREATE(7, 2, dims)	(7,1)
	(0,3,0)	MPI_DIMS_CREATE(6, 3, dims)	(2,3,1)
	(0,3,0)	MPI_DIMS_CREATE(7, 3, dims)	erroneous call

6.5.3   Cartesian Inquiry Functions

Once a Cartesian topology is set up, it may be necessary to inquire about the topology. These functions are given below and are all local calls.

MPI_CARTDIM_GET(comm, ndims)

IN	comm	communicator with Cartesian structure
OUT	ndims	number of dimensions of the Cartesian structure

int MPI_Cartdim_get(MPI_Comm comm, int *ndims)

MPI_CARTDIM_GET(COMM, NDIMS, IERROR)
    INTEGER COMM, NDIMS, IERROR

MPI_CARTDIM_GET returns the number of dimensions of the Cartesian structure associated with comm. This can be used to provide the other Cartesian inquiry

functions with the correct size of arrays. The communicator with the topology in
Figure 6.1 would return ndims = 2.

MPI_CART_GET(comm, maxdims, dims, periods, coords)

IN	comm	communicator with Cartesian structure
IN	maxdims	length of vectors dims, periods, and coords in the calling program
OUT	dims	number of processes for each Cartesian dimension
OUT	periods	periodicity (true/false) for each Cartesian dimension
OUT	coords	coordinates of calling process in Cartesian structure

```
int MPI_Cart_get(MPI_Comm comm, int maxdims, int *dims, int *periods,
        int *coords)
```

```
MPI_CART_GET(COMM, MAXDIMS, DIMS, PERIODS, COORDS, IERROR)
    INTEGER COMM, MAXDIMS, DIMS(*), COORDS(*), IERROR
    LOGICAL PERIODS(*)
```

MPI_CART_GET returns information on the Cartesian topology associated with
comm. maxdims must be at least ndims as returned by MPI_CARTDIM_GET. For
the example in Figure 6.1, dims = (3, 4). The coords are as given for the rank of
the calling process as shown, e.g., process 6 returns coords = (1, 2).

6.5.4 Cartesian Translator Functions

The functions in this section translate to/from the rank and the Cartesian topology
coordinates. These calls are local.

MPI_CART_RANK(comm, coords, rank)

IN	comm	communicator with Cartesian structure
IN	coords	integer array specifying the Cartesian coordinates of a process
OUT	rank	rank of specified process

```
int MPI_Cart_rank(MPI_Comm comm, int *coords, int *rank)
```

```
MPI_CART_RANK(COMM, COORDS, RANK, IERROR)
    INTEGER COMM, COORDS(*), RANK, IERROR
```

For a process group with Cartesian structure, the function MPI_CART_RANK translates the logical process coordinates to process ranks as they are used by the point-to-point routines. coords is an array of size ndims as returned by MPI_CART-DIM_GET. For the example in Figure 6.1, coords $= (1,2)$ would return rank $= 6$.

For dimension i with periods(i) = true, if the coordinate, coords(i), is out of range, that is, coords(i) $<$ 0 or coords(i) $\geq$ dims(i), it is shifted back to the interval $0 \leq$ coords(i) $<$ dims(i) automatically. If the topology in Figure 6.1 is periodic in both dimensions (torus), then coords $= (4,6)$ would also return rank $= 6$. Out-of-range coordinates are erroneous for non-periodic dimensions.

MPI_CART_COORDS(comm, rank, maxdims, coords)

IN	comm	communicator with Cartesian structure
IN	rank	rank of a process within group of comm
IN	maxdims	length of vector coord in the calling program
OUT	coords	integer array containing the Cartesian coordinates of specified process

```
int MPI_Cart_coords(MPI_Comm comm, int rank, int maxdims,
            int *coords)
```

```
MPI_CART_COORDS(COMM, RANK, MAXDIMS, COORDS, IERROR)
    INTEGER COMM, RANK, MAXDIMS, COORDS(*), IERROR
```

MPI_CART_COORDS is the rank-to-coordinates translator. It is the inverse mapping of MPI_CART_RANK. maxdims is at least as big as ndims as returned by MPI_CARTDIM_GET. For the example in Figure 6.1, rank $= 6$ would return coords $= (1,2)$.

6.5.5   Cartesian Shift Function

If the process topology is a Cartesian structure, a MPI_SENDRECV operation is likely to be used along a coordinate direction to perform a shift of data. As input, MPI_SENDRECV takes the rank of a source process for the receive, and the rank of a destination process for the send. A Cartesian shift operation is specified by the coordinate of the shift and by the size of the shift step (positive or negative). The

function MPI_CART_SHIFT inputs such specification and returns the information
needed to call MPI_SENDRECV. The function MPI_CART_SHIFT is local.

MPI_CART_SHIFT(comm, direction, disp, rank_source, rank_dest)

IN	comm	communicator with Cartesian structure
IN	direction	coordinate dimension of shift
IN	disp	displacement (> 0: upwards shift, < 0: downwards shift)
OUT	rank_source	rank of source process
OUT	rank_dest	rank of destination process

```
int MPI_Cart_shift(MPI_Comm comm, int direction, int disp,
                   int *rank_source, int *rank_dest)
```

```
MPI_CART_SHIFT(COMM, DIRECTION, DISP, RANK_SOURCE, RANK_DEST, IERROR)
    INTEGER COMM, DIRECTION, DISP, RANK_SOURCE, RANK_DEST, IERROR
```

The direction argument indicates the dimension of the shift, i.e., the coordinate
whose value is modified by the shift. The coordinates are numbered from 0 to
ndims-1, where ndims is the number of dimensions.

Depending on the periodicity of the Cartesian group in the specified coordinate
direction, MPI_CART_SHIFT provides the identifiers for a circular or an end-off
shift. In the case of an end-off shift, the value MPI_PROC_NULL may be returned in
rank_source and/or rank_dest, indicating that the source and/or the destination for
the shift is out of range. This is a valid input to the sendrecv functions.

Neither MPI_CART_SHIFT, nor MPI_SENDRECV are collective functions. It is
not required that all processes in the grid call MPI_CART_SHIFT with the same
direction and disp arguments, but only that sends match receives in the subsequent
calls to MPI_SENDRECV. Example 6.2 shows such use of MPI_CART_SHIFT, where
each column of a 2D grid is shifted by a different amount. Figures 6.3 and 6.4 show
the result on 12 processors.

Example 6.2 The communicator, comm, has a 3×4 periodic, Cartesian topology
associated with it. A two-dimensional array of REALs is stored one element per process, in variable a. One wishes to skew this array, by shifting column i (vertically,
i.e., along the column) by i steps.

```
INTEGER comm_2d, rank, coords(2), ierr, source, dest
INTEGER status(MPI_STATUS_SIZE), dims(2)
LOGICAL reorder, periods(2)
```

```
REAL a, b

CALL MPI_COMM_SIZE(MPI_COMM_WORLD, isize, ierr)
IF (isize.LT.12) CALL MPI_ABORT(MPI_COMM_WORLD, MPI_ERR_OTHER, ierr)
CALL MPI_COMM_RANK(MPI_COMM_WORLD, rank, ierr)

! initialize arrays
a = rank
b = -1

! create topology
! values to run on 12 processes
dims(1) = 3
dims(2) = 4
! change to .FALSE. for non-periodic
periods(1) = .TRUE.
periods(2) = .TRUE.
reorder = .FALSE.
CALL MPI_CART_CREATE(MPI_COMM_WORLD, 2, dims, periods,
                                    reorder, comm_2d, ierr)
! first 12 processes of MPI_COMM_WORLD are in group of comm_2d,
! with same rank as in MPI_COMM_WORLD

! find Cartesian coordinates
CALL MPI_CART_COORDS(comm_2d, rank, 2, coords, ierr)
! compute shift source and destination
CALL MPI_CART_SHIFT(comm_2d, 0, coords(2), source, dest, ierr)

! skew a into b
 CALL MPI_SENDRECV(a, 1, MPI_REAL, dest, 13, b, 1, MPI_REAL,
                            source, 13, comm_2d, status, ierr)
```

Rationale. The effect of returning MPI_PROC_NULL when the source of an end-off shift is out of range is that, in the subsequent shift, the destination buffer stays unchanged. This is different from the behavior of a Fortran 90 EOSHIFT intrinsic function, where the user can provide a fill value for the target of a shift, if the source is out of range, with a default which is zero or blank. To achieve the behavior of the Fortran function, one would need that a receive from MPI_PROC_NULL put a

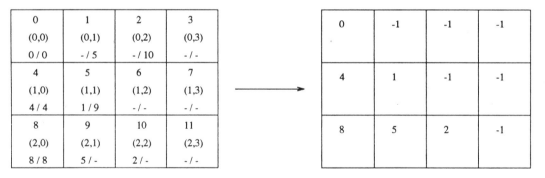

Figure 6.3
Outcome of Example 6.2 when the 2D topology is periodic (a torus) on 12 processes. In the boxes on the left, the upper number in each box represents the process rank, the middle values are the (row, column) coordinate, and the lower values are the source/dest for the sendrecv operation. The value in the boxes on the right are the results in b after the sendrecv has completed.

0 (0,0) 0 / 0	1 (0,1) - / 5	2 (0,2) - / 10	3 (0,3) - / -
4 (1,0) 4 / 4	5 (1,1) 1 / 9	6 (1,2) - / -	7 (1,3) - / -
8 (2,0) 8 / 8	9 (2,1) 5 / -	10 (2,2) 2 / -	11 (2,3) - / -

0	-1	-1	-1
4	1	-1	-1
8	5	2	-1

Figure 6.4
Similar to Figure 6.3 except the 2D Cartesian topology is not periodic (a rectangle). This results when the values of periods(1) and periods(2) are made .FALSE. A "-" in a source or dest value indicates MPI_CART_SHIFT returns MPI_PROC_NULL.

fixed fill value in the receive buffer. A default fill cannot be easily provided, since a different fill value is required for each **datatype** argument used in the sendreceive call. Since the user can mimic the **EOSHIFT** behavior with little additional code, it was felt preferable to choose the simpler interface. (*End of rationale.*)

Advice to users.   In Fortran, the dimension indicated by DIRECTION = i has DIMS(i+1) processes, where DIMS is the array that was used to create the grid. In C, the dimension indicated by direction = i is the dimension specified by dims[i]. (*End of advice to users.*)

6.5.6   Cartesian Partition Function

MPI_CART_SUB(comm, remain_dims, newcomm)

IN	comm	communicator with Cartesian structure
IN	remain_dims	the ith entry of remain_dims specifies whether the ith dimension is kept in the subgrid (true) or is dropped (false)
OUT	newcomm	communicator containing the subgrid that includes the calling process

```
int MPI_Cart_sub(MPI_Comm comm, int *remain_dims, MPI_Comm *newcomm)
```

```
MPI_CART_SUB(COMM, REMAIN_DIMS, NEWCOMM, IERROR)
    INTEGER COMM, NEWCOMM, IERROR
    LOGICAL REMAIN_DIMS(*)
```

If a Cartesian topology has been created with MPI_CART_CREATE, the function MPI_CART_SUB can be used to partition the communicator group into subgroups that form lower-dimensional Cartesian subgrids, and to build for each subgroup a communicator with the associated subgrid Cartesian topology. This call is collective.

Advice to users. The same functionality as MPI_CART_SUB can be achieved with MPI_COMM_SPLIT. However, since MPI_CART_SUB has additional information, it can greatly reduce the communication and work needed by logically working on the topology. As such, MPI_CART_SUB can be easily implemented in a scalable fashion. (*End of advice to users.*)

Advice to implementors. The function MPI_CART_SUB(comm, remain_dims, comm-_new) can be implemented by a call to MPI_COMM_SPLIT(comm, color, key, comm-_new), using a single number encoding of the lost dimensions as color and a single number encoding of the preserved dimensions as key. In addition, the new topology information has to be cached. (*End of advice to implementors.*)

Example 6.3 Assume that MPI_CART_CREATE(..., comm) has defined a $(2 \times 3 \times 4)$ grid. Let remain_dims = (true, false, true). Then a call to,

```
MPI_CART_SUB(comm, remain_dims, comm_new),
```

will create three communicators each with eight processes in a 2×4 Cartesian topology. If remain_dims = `(false, false, true)` then the call to MPI_CART-_SUB(comm, remain_dims, comm_new) will create six non-overlapping communicators, each with four processes, in a one-dimensional Cartesian topology.

6.5.7 Cartesian Low-level Functions

Typically, the functions already presented are used to create and use Cartesian topologies. However, some applications may want more control over the process. MPI_CART_MAP returns the Cartesian map recommended by the MPI system, in order to map well the virtual communication graph of the application on the physical machine topology. This call is collective.

MPI_CART_MAP(comm, ndims, dims, periods, newrank)

IN	comm	input communicator
IN	ndims	number of dimensions of Cartesian structure
IN	dims	integer array of size ndims specifying the number of processes in each coordinate direction
IN	periods	logical array of size ndims specifying the periodicity specification in each coordinate direction
OUT	newrank	reordered rank of the calling process; MPI-_UNDEFINED if calling process does not belong to grid

```
int MPI_Cart_map(MPI_Comm comm, int ndims, int *dims, int *periods,
         int *newrank)
```

```
MPI_CART_MAP(COMM, NDIMS, DIMS, PERIODS, NEWRANK, IERROR)
   INTEGER COMM, NDIMS, DIMS(*), NEWRANK, IERROR
   LOGICAL PERIODS(*)
```

MPI_CART_MAP computes an "optimal" placement for the calling process on the physical machine.

Advice to implementors. The function MPI_CART_CREATE(comm, ndims, dims, periods, reorder, comm_cart), with reorder = true can be implemented by calling

MPI_CART_MAP(comm, ndims, dims, periods, newrank), then calling
MPI_COMM_SPLIT(comm, color, key, comm_cart), with color = 0 if newrank $\neq$
MPI_UNDEFINED, color = MPI_UNDEFINED otherwise, and key = newrank. (*End of
advice to implementors.*)

6.6 Graph Topology Functions

This section describes the MPI functions for creating graph topologies.

6.6.1 Graph Constructor Function

MPI_GRAPH_CREATE(comm_old, nnodes, index, edges, reorder, comm_graph)

IN	comm_old	input communicator
IN	nnodes	number of nodes in graph
IN	index	array of integers describing node degrees (see below)
IN	edges	array of integers describing graph edges (see below)
IN	reorder	ranking may be reordered (true) or not (false)
OUT	comm_graph	communicator with graph topology added

```
int MPI_Graph_create(MPI_Comm comm_old, int nnodes, int *index,
          int *edges, int reorder, MPI_Comm *comm_graph)
```

```
MPI_GRAPH_CREATE(COMM_OLD, NNODES, INDEX, EDGES, REORDER, COMM_GRAPH,
        IERROR)
    INTEGER COMM_OLD, NNODES, INDEX(*), EDGES(*), COMM_GRAPH, IERROR
    LOGICAL REORDER
```

MPI_GRAPH_CREATE returns a new communicator to which the graph topology
information is attached. If reorder = false then the rank of each process in the
new group is identical to its rank in the old group. Otherwise, the function may
reorder the processes. If the size, nnodes, of the graph is smaller than the size
of the group of comm_old, then some processes are returned MPI_COMM_NULL, in
analogy to MPI_COMM_SPLIT. The call is erroneous if it specifies a graph that is
larger than the group size of the input communicator. In analogy to the function
MPI_COMM_CREATE, no cached information propagates to the new communicator.

Also, this function is collective. As with other collective calls, the program must be written to work correctly, whether the call synchronizes or not.

The three parameters nnodes, index and **edges** define the graph structure. nnodes is the number of nodes of the graph. The nodes are numbered from 0 to **nnodes-1**. The ith entry of array index stores the total number of neighbors of the first i graph nodes. The lists of neighbors of nodes 0, 1, ..., nnodes-1 are stored in consecutive locations in array **edges**. The array **edges** is a flattened representation of the edge lists. The total number of entries in index is nnodes and the total number of entries in edges is equal to the number of graph edges.

The definitions of the arguments **nnodes**, **index**, and **edges** are illustrated in Example 6.4.

Example 6.4 Assume there are four processes 0, 1, 2, 3 with the following adjacency matrix:

process	neighbors
0	1, 3
1	0
2	3
3	0, 2

Then, the input arguments are:

```
nnodes =    4
index =     (2, 3, 4, 6)
edges =     (1, 3, 0, 3, 0, 2)
```

Thus, in C, index[0] is the degree of node zero, and index[i] - index[i-1] is the degree of node i, i=1, ..., nnodes-1; the list of neighbors of node zero is stored in edges[j], for $0 \leq j \leq \text{index}[0] - 1$ and the list of neighbors of node i, $i > 0$, is stored in edges[j], $\text{index}[i-1] \leq j \leq \text{index}[i] - 1$.

In Fortran, index(1) is the degree of node zero, and index(i+1) - index(i) is the degree of node i, i=1, ..., nnodes-1; the list of neighbors of node zero is stored in edges(j), for $1 \leq j \leq \text{index}(1)$ and the list of neighbors of node i, $i > 0$, is stored in edges(j), $\text{index}(i) + 1 \leq j \leq \text{index}(i + 1)$.

Rationale.   Since bidirectional communication is assumed, the edges array is symmetric. To allow input checking and to make the graph construction easier for the user, the full graph is given and not just half of the symmetric graph. (*End of rationale.*)

Advice to implementors. A graph topology can be implemented by caching with the communicator the two arrays

1. **index**,

2. **edges**

The number of nodes is equal to the number of processes in the group. An additional zero entry at the start of array index simplifies access to the topology information. (*End of advice to implementors.*)

6.6.2 Graph Inquiry Functions

Once a graph topology is set up, it may be necessary to inquire about the topology. These functions are given below and are all local calls.

MPI_GRAPHDIMS_GET(comm, nnodes, nedges)

IN	comm	communicator for group with graph structure
OUT	nnodes	number of nodes in graph
OUT	nedges	number of edges in graph

```
int MPI_Graphdims_get(MPI_Comm comm, int *nnodes, int *nedges)
```

```
MPI_GRAPHDIMS_GET(COMM, NNODES, NEDGES, IERROR)
    INTEGER COMM, NNODES, NEDGES, IERROR
```

MPI_GRAPHDIMS_GET returns the number of nodes and the number of edges in the graph. The number of nodes is identical to the size of the group associated with comm. nnodes and nedges can be used to supply arrays of correct size for index and edges, respectively, in MPI_GRAPH_GET. MPI_GRAPHDIMS_GET would return nnodes = 4 and nedges = 6 for Example 6.4.

MPI_GRAPH_GET(comm, maxindex, maxedges, index, edges)

IN	comm	communicator with graph structure
IN	maxindex	length of vector index in the calling program
IN	maxedges	length of vector edges in the calling program
OUT	index	array of integers containing the graph structure
OUT	edges	array of integers containing the graph structure

```
int MPI_Graph_get(MPI_Comm comm, int maxindex, int maxedges,
          int *index, int *edges)
```

```
MPI_GRAPH_GET(COMM, MAXINDEX, MAXEDGES, INDEX, EDGES, IERROR)
    INTEGER COMM, MAXINDEX, MAXEDGES, INDEX(*), EDGES(*), IERROR
```

MPI_GRAPH_GET returns index and edges as was supplied to MPI_GRAPH_CRE-ATE. maxindex and maxedges are at least as big as nnodes and nedges, respectively, as returned by MPI_GRAPHDIMS_GET above. Using the comm created in Example 6.4 would return the index and edges given in the example.

6.6.3   Graph Information Functions

The functions in this section provide information about the structure of the graph topology. All calls are local.

MPI_GRAPH_NEIGHBORS_COUNT(comm, rank, nneighbors)

IN	comm	communicator with graph topology
IN	rank	rank of process in group of comm
OUT	nneighbors	number of neighbors of specified process

```
int MPI_Graph_neighbors_count(MPI_Comm comm, int rank,
          int *nneighbors)
```

```
MPI_GRAPH_NEIGHBORS_COUNT(COMM, RANK, NNEIGHBORS, IERROR)
    INTEGER COMM, RANK, NNEIGHBORS, IERROR
```

MPI_GRAPH_NEIGHBORS_COUNT returns the number of neighbors for the process signified by rank. It can be used by MPI_GRAPH_NEIGHBORS to give an array of correct size for neighbors. Using Example 6.4 with rank = 3 would give nneighbors = 2.

MPI_GRAPH_NEIGHBORS(comm, rank, maxneighbors, neighbors)

IN	comm	communicator with graph topology
IN	rank	rank of process in group of comm
IN	maxneighbors	size of array neighbors
OUT	neighbors	array of ranks of processes that are neighbors to specified process

```
int MPI_Graph_neighbors(MPI_Comm comm, int rank, int maxneighbors,
          int *neighbors)
```

```
MPI_GRAPH_NEIGHBORS(COMM, RANK, MAXNEIGHBORS, NEIGHBORS, IERROR)
    INTEGER COMM, RANK, MAXNEIGHBORS, NEIGHBORS(*), IERROR
```

MPI_GRAPH_NEIGHBORS returns the part of the edges array associated with process rank. Using Example 6.4, rank = 3 would return neighbors = 0, 2. Another use is given in Example 6.5.

Example 6.5 Suppose that comm is a communicator with a shuffle-exchange topology. The group has 2^n members. Each process is labeled by $a_1, \ldots, a_n$ with $a_i \in \{0, 1\}$, and has three neighbors: exchange$(a_1, \ldots, a_n) = a_1, \ldots, a_{n-1}, \bar{a}_n$ $(\bar{a} = 1-a)$, unshuffle$(a_1, \ldots, a_n) = a_2, \ldots, a_n, a_1$, and shuffle$(a_1, \ldots, a_n) = a_n, a_1, \ldots, a_{n-1}$. The graph adjacency list is illustrated below for $n = 3$.

node		exchange neighbors(1)	unshuffle neighbors(2)	shuffle neighbors(3)
0	(000)	1	0	0
1	(001)	0	2	4
2	(010)	3	4	1
3	(011)	2	6	5
4	(100)	5	1	2
5	(101)	4	3	6
6	(110)	7	5	3
7	(111)	6	7	7

Suppose that the communicator comm has this topology associated with it. The following code fragment cycles through the three types of neighbors and performs an appropriate permutation for each.

```
! assume: each process has stored a real number A.
! extract neighborhood information
CALL MPI_COMM_RANK(comm, myrank, ierr)
CALL MPI_GRAPH_NEIGHBORS(comm, myrank, 3, neighbors, ierr)
!  perform exchange permutation
CALL MPI_SENDRECV_REPLACE(A, 1, MPI_REAL, neighbors(1), 0,
                          neighbors(1), 0, comm, status, ierr)
!  perform unshuffle permutation
CALL MPI_SENDRECV_REPLACE(A, 1, MPI_REAL, neighbors(2), 0,
                          neighbors(3), 0, comm, status, ierr)
! perform shuffle permutation
CALL MPI_SENDRECV_REPLACE(A, 1, MPI_REAL, neighbors(3), 0,
                          neighbors(2), 0, comm, status, ierr)
```

6.6.4 Low-level Graph Functions

The low-level function for general graph topologies as in the Cartesian topologies given in Section 6.5.7 is as follows. This call is collective.

MPI_GRAPH_MAP(comm, nnodes, index, edges, newrank)

IN	comm	input communicator
IN	nnodes	number of graph nodes
IN	index	integer array specifying the graph structure, see MPI_GRAPH_CREATE
IN	edges	integer array specifying the graph structure
OUT	newrank	reordered rank of the calling process; MPI_UNDEFINED if the calling process does not belong to graph

```
int MPI_Graph_map(MPI_Comm comm, int nnodes, int *index, int *edges,
          int *newrank)
```

```
MPI_GRAPH_MAP(COMM, NNODES, INDEX, EDGES, NEWRANK, IERROR)
    INTEGER COMM, NNODES, INDEX(*), EDGES(*), NEWRANK, IERROR
```

Advice to implementors.   The function MPI_GRAPH_CREATE(comm, nnodes, index, edges, reorder, comm_graph), with reorder = true can be implemented by calling MPI_GRAPH_MAP(comm, nnodes, index, edges, newrank), then calling MPI_COMM_SPLIT(comm, color, key, comm_graph), with color = 0 if newrank $\neq$ MPI_UNDEFINED, color = MPI_UNDEFINED otherwise, and key = newrank. (*End of advice to implementors.*)

6.7   Topology Inquiry Functions

A routine may receive a communicator for which it is unknown what type of topology is associated with it. MPI_TOPO_TEST allows one to answer this question. This is a local call.

MPI_TOPO_TEST(comm, status)

IN	comm	communicator
OUT	status	topology type of communicator comm

```
int MPI_Topo_test(MPI_Comm comm, int *status)
```

```
MPI_TOPO_TEST(COMM, STATUS, IERROR)
    INTEGER COMM, STATUS, IERROR
```

The function MPI_TOPO_TEST returns the type of topology that is assigned to a communicator.

The output value status is one of the following:

MPI_GRAPH	graph topology
MPI_CART	Cartesian topology
MPI_UNDEFINED	no topology

6.8   An Application Example

Example 6.6 We present here two algorithms for parallel matrix product. Both codes compute a product $C = A \times B$, where A is an $n_1 \times n_2$ matrix and B is an $n_2 \times n_3$ matrix (the result matrix C has size $n_1 \times n_3$). The input matrices are initially available on process zero, and the result matrix is returned at process zero.

The first parallel algorithm maps the computation onto a $p_1 \times p_2$ 2-dimensional grid of processes. The matrices are partitioned as shown in Figure 6.5: matrix A is partitioned into p_1 horizontal slices, the matrix B is partitioned into p_2 vertical slices, and matrix C is partitioned into $p_1 \times p_2$ submatrices.

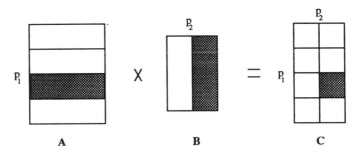

Figure 6.5
Data partition in 2D parallel matrix product algorithm.

Each process (i, j) computes the product of the i-th slice of **A** and the j-th slice of **B**, resulting in submatrix (i, j) of **C**.

The successive phases of the computation are illustrated in Figure 6.6:

1. Matrix **A** is scattered into slices on the $(x, 0)$ line;
2. Matrix **B** is scattered into slices on the $(0, y)$ line.
3. The slices of **A** are replicated in the y dimension.
4. The slices of **B** are replicated in the x dimension.
5. Each process computes one submatrix product.
6. Matrix **C** is gathered from the (x, y) plane.

```
SUBROUTINE PMATMULT( A, B, C, n, p, comm)
      ! subroutine arguments are meaningful only at process 0
INTEGER n(3)
      ! matrix dimensions
REAL    A(n(1),n(2)),
        B(n(2),n(3)),
        C(n(1),n(3))
      ! data
INTEGER p(2)
      ! dimensions of processor grid. p(1) divides n(1), p(2)
      ! divides n(3) and the product of the 2 dimensions
      ! must equal the size of the group of comm
INTEGER comm
      ! communicator for processes that participate in computation

INTEGER nn(2)
```

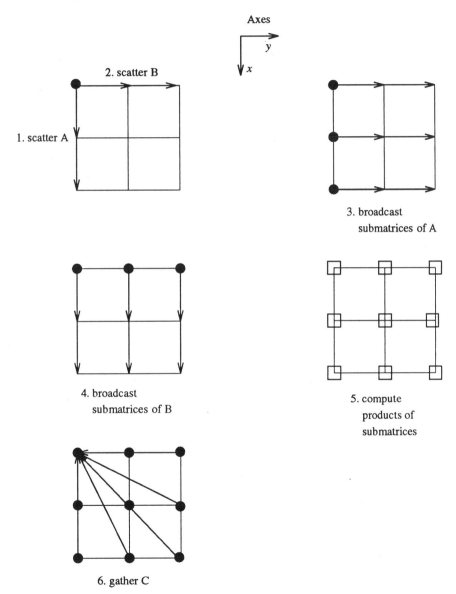

Figure 6.6
Phases in 2D parallel matrix product algorithm.

```
      ! dimensions of local submatrices
REAL, ALLOCATABLE AA(:), BB(:), CC(:,:)
      ! local submatrices
INTEGER  comm_2D, comm_1D(2), pcomm
      ! communicators for 2D grid, for subspaces, and copy of comm
INTEGER coords(2)
      ! Cartesian coordinates
INTEGER rank
      ! process rank
INTEGER, ALLOCATABLE dispc(:), countc(:)
      ! displacement and count array for gather call.
INTEGER typea, typec, types(2), blen(2), disp(2)
      ! datatypes and arrays for datatype creation
INTEGER ierr, i, j, k, sizeofreal
LOGICAL periods(2), remains(2)

CALL MPI_COMM_DUP( comm, pcomm, ierr)

! broadcast parameters n(3) and p(2)
CALL MPI_BCAST( n, 3, MPI_INTEGER, 0, pcomm, ierr)
CALL MPI_BCAST( p, 2, MPI_INTEGER, 0, pcomm, ierr)

! create 2D grid of processes
periods = (/ .FALSE., .FALSE./)
CALL MPI_CART_CREATE( pcomm, 2, p, periods, .FALSE., comm_2D, ierr)

! find rank and Cartesian coordinates
CALL MPI_COMM_RANK( comm_2D, rank, ierr)
CALL MPI_CART_COORDS( comm_2D, rank, 2, coords, ierr)

! compute communicators for subspaces
DO i = 1, 2
   DO j = 1, 2
      remains(j) = (i.EQ.j)
   END DO
   CALL MPI_CART_SUB( comm_2D, remains, comm_1D(i), ierr)
END DO
```

```
! allocate submatrices
nn(1) = n(1)/p(1)
nn(2) = n(3)/p(2)
END DO
ALLOCATE (AA(nn(1),n(2)), BB(n(2),nn(2)), CC(nn(1),nn(2)))

IF (rank.EQ.0) THEN
   ! compute datatype for slice of A
   CALL MPI_TYPE_VECTOR( n(2), nn(1), n(1), MPI_REAL,
                                        types(1), ierr)
   ! and correct extent to size of subcolumn so that
   ! consecutive slices be "contiguous"
   CALL MPI_TYPE_EXTENT( MPI_REAL, sizeofreal, ierr)
   blen = (/ 1, 1 /)
   disp = (/ 0, sizeofreal*nn(1) /)
   types(2) = MPI_UB
   CALL MPI_TYPE_STRUCT( 2, blen, disp, types, typea, ierr)
   CALL MPI_TYPE_COMMIT( typea, ierr)

   ! compute datatype for submatrix of C
   CALL MPI_TYPE_VECTOR( nn(2), nn(1), n(1), MPI_REAL,
                                        types(1), ierr)
   ! and correct extent to size of subcolumn
   CALL MPI_TYPE_STRUCT(2, blen, disp, types, typec, ierr)
   CALL MPI_TYPE_COMMIT(typec, ierr)

   ! compute number of subcolumns preceeding each successive
   ! submatrix of C.  Submatrices are ordered in row-major
   ! order, to fit the order of processes in the grid.
   ALLOCATE (dispc(p(1)*p(2)), countc(p(1)*p(2)))
   DO i = 1, p(1)
      DO j = 1, p(2)
         dispc((i-1)*p(2)+j) = ((j-1)*p(1) + (i-1))*nn(2)
         countc((i-1)*p(2)+j) = 1
      END DO
   END DO
END IF
```

```
! and now, the computation

! 1. scatter row slices of matrix A on x axis
IF (coords(2).EQ.0) THEN
   CALL MPI_SCATTER(A, 1, typea, AA, nn(1)*n(2), MPI_REAL,
                                     0, comm_1D(1), ierr)
END IF

! 2. scatter column slices of matrix B on y axis
IF (coords(1).EQ.0) THEN
   CALL MPI_SCATTER(B, n(2)*nn(2), MPI_REAL, BB,
                 n(2)*nn(2), MPI_REAL, 0, comm_1D(2), ierr)
END IF

! 3. broadcast matrix AA in y dimension
CALL MPI_BCAST(AA, nn(1)*n(2), MPI_REAL, 0, comm_1D(2))

! 4. broadcast matrix BB in x dimension
 CALL MPI_BCAST(BB, n(2)*nn(2), MPI_REAL, 0, comm_1D(1))

! 5. compute submatrix products
DO j = 1, nn(2)
   DO i = 1, nn(1)
      CC(i,j) = 0
      DO k = 1, n(2)
         CC(i,j) = CC(i,j) + AA(i,k)*BB(k,j)
      END DO
   END DO
END DO

! 6. gather results from plane to node 0
CALL MPI_GATHERV( CC, nn(1)*nn(2), MPI_REAL,
              C, countc, dispc, typec, 0, comm_2D, ierr)
! clean up
DEALLOCATE(AA, BB, CC)
MPI_COMM_FREE( pcomm, ierr)
MPI_COMM_FREE( comm_2D, ierr)
DO i = 1, 2
```

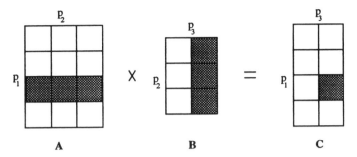

Figure 6.7
Data partition in 3D parallel matrix product algorithm.

```
   MPI_COMM_FREE( comm_1D(i), ierr)
END DO
IF (rank.EQ.0) THEN
   DEALLOCATE(countc, dispc)
   MPI_TYPE_FREE( typea, ierr)
   MPI_TYPE_FREE( typec, ierr)
   MPI_TYPE_FREE( types(1), ierr)
END IF

! returns matrix C at process 0
RETURN
END
```

Example 6.7 For large matrices, performance can be improved by using Strassen's algorithm, rather than the n^3 one. Even if one uses the simple, n^3 algorithm, the amount of communication can be decreased by using an algorithm that maps the computation on a 3-dimensional grid of processes.

The parallel computation maps the $n_1 \times n_2 \times n_3$ volume of basic products onto a three-dimensional grid of dimensions $p_1 \times p_2 \times p_3$. The matrices are partitioned as shown in Figure 6.7: matrix **A** is partitioned into $p_1 \times p_2$ submatrices, matrix **B** is partitioned into $p_2 \times p_3$ submatrices, and matrix **C** is partitioned into $p_1 \times p_3$ submatrices. Process (i, j, k) computes the product of submatrix (i, j) of matrix **A** and submatrix (j, k) of matrix **B**. The submatrix (i, k) of matrix **C** is obtained by summing the subproducts computed at processes (i, j, k), $j = 0, \ldots, p_2 - 1$.

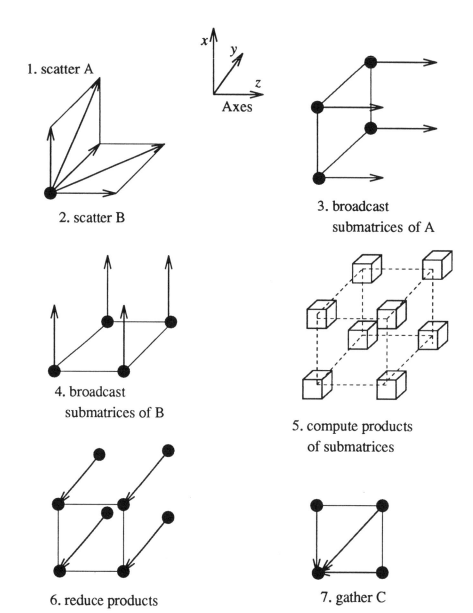

1. scatter A

2. scatter B

3. broadcast
submatrices of A

4. broadcast
submatrices of B

5. compute products
of submatrices

6. reduce products

7. gather C

Figure 6.8
Phases in 3D parallel matrix product algorithm.

The successive phases of the computation are illustrated in Figure 6.8.

1. The submatrices of A are scattered in the $(x, y, 0)$ plane;
2. The submatrices of B are scattered in the $(0, y, z)$ plane.
3. The submatrices of A are replicated in the z dimension.
4. The submatrices of B are replicated in the x dimension.
5. Each process computes one submatrix product.
6. The subproducts are reduced in the y dimension.
7. Matrix C is gathered from the $(x, 0, z)$ plane.

```fortran
SUBROUTINE PMATMULT( A, B, C, n, p, comm)
      ! subroutine arguments are meaningful only at process 0
INTEGER n(3)
      ! matrix dimensions
REAL    A(n(1),n(2)),
        B(n(2),n(3)),
        C(n(1),n(3))
      ! data
INTEGER p(3)
      ! dimensions of processor grid. p(i) must divide
      ! exactly n(i) and the product of the 3 dimensions
      ! must equal the size of the group of comm
INTEGER comm
      ! communicator for processes that participate in computation


INTEGER nn(3)
      ! dimensions of local submatrices
REAL, ALLOCATABLE AA(:,:), BB(:,:), CC(:,:), CC1(:,:)
      ! local submatrices
INTEGER  comm_3D, comm_2D(3), comm_1D(3), pcomm
      ! communicators for 3D grid, for subspaces, and copy of comm
INTEGER coords(3)
      ! Cartesian coordinates
INTEGER rank
      ! process rank
INTEGER, ALLOCATABLE dispa(:), dispb(:), dispc(:),
                     counta(:), countb(:), countc(:)
      ! displacement and count arrays for scatter/gather calls.
INTEGER typea, typeb, typec, types(2), blen(2), disp(2)
```

```fortran
      ! datatypes and arrays for datatype creation
INTEGER ierr, i, j, k, sizeofreal
LOGICAL periods(3), remains(3)

CALL MPI_COMM_DUP( comm, pcomm, ierr)

! broadcast parameters n(3) and p(3)
CALL MPI_BCAST( n, 3, MPI_INTEGER, 0, pcomm, ierr)
CALL MPI_BCAST( p, 3, MPI_INTEGER, 0, pcomm, ierr)

! create 3D grid of processes
periods = (\ .FALSE., .FALSE., .FALSE.\)
CALL MPI_CART_CREATE( pcomm, 3, p, periods, .FALSE., comm_3D, ierr)

! find rank and Cartesian coordinates
CALL MPI_COMM_RANK(comm_3D, rank, ierr)
CALL MPI_CART_COORDS(comm_3D, rank, 3, coords, ierr)

! compute communicators for subspaces

! 2D subspaces
DO i = 1, 3
   DO j = 1, 3
      remains(j) = (i.NE.j)
   END DO
   CALL MPI_CART_SUB( comm_3D, remains, comm_2D(i), ierr)
END DO

! 1D subspaces
DO i = 1, 3
   DO j = 1, 3
      remains(j) = (i.EQ.j)
   END DO
   CALL MPI_CART_SUB( comm_3D, remains, comm_1D(i), ierr)
END DO

! allocate submatrices
DO i = 1, 3
```

```
   nn(i) = n(i)/p(i)
END DO
ALLOCATE (AA(nn(1),nn(2)), BB(nn(2),nn(3)), CC(nn(1),nn(3)))

IF (rank.EQ.0) THEN
   ! compute datatype for submatrix of A
   CALL MPI_TYPE_VECTOR( nn(2), nn(1), n(1), MPI_REAL,
                                             types(1), ierr)
   ! and correct extent to size of subcolumn
   MPI_TYPE_EXTENT( MPI_REAL, sizeofreal, ierr)
   blen = (\ 1, 1 \)
   disp = (\ 0, sizeofreal*nn(1) \)
   types(2) = MPI_UB
   CALL MPI_TYPE_STRUCT( 2, blen, disp, types, typea, ierr)
   CALL MPI_TYPE_COMMIT( typea, ierr)

   ! compute number of subcolumns preceeding each
   ! submatrix of A.  Submatrices are ordered in row-major
   ! order, to fit the order of processes in the grid.
   ALLOCATE (dispa(p(1)*p(2)), counta(p(1)*p(2)))
   DO i = 1, p(1)
      DO j = 1, p(2)
        dispa((i-1)*p(2)+j) = ((j-1)*p(1) + (i-1))*nn(2)
        counta((i-1)*p(2)+j) = 1
      END DO
   END DO

   ! same for array B
   CALL MPI_TYPE_VECTOR( nn(3), nn(2), n(2), MPI_REAL,
                                             types(1), ierr)
   disp(2) = sizeofreal*nn(2)
   CALL MPI_TYPE_STRUCT(2, blen, disp, types, typeb, ierr)
   CALL MPI_TYPE_COMMIT(typeb, ierr)
   ALLOCATE (dispb(p(2)*p(3)), countb(p(2)*p(3)))
   DO i = 1, p(2)
      DO j = 1, p(3)
        dispb((i-1)*p(3)+j) = ((j-1)*p(2) + (i-1))*nn(3)
        countb((i-1)*p(3)+j) = 1
```

```
         END DO
      END DO

      ! same for array C
      CALL MPI_TYPE_VECTOR(nn(3), nn(1), n(1), MPI_REAL,
                                             types(1), ierr)
      disp(2) = sizeofreal*nn(1)
      CALL MPI_TYPE_STRUCT(2, blen, disp, types, typec, ierr)
      CALL MPI_TYPE_COMMIT(typec, ierr)
      ALLOCATE (dispc(p(1)*p(3)), countc(p(1)*p(3)))
      DO i = 1, p(1)
         DO j = 1, p(3)
            dispc((i-1)*p(3)+j) = ((j-1)*p(1) + (i-1))*nn(3)
            countc((i-1)*p(3)+j) = 1
         END DO
      END DO
END IF


! and now, the computation

! 1. scatter matrix A
IF (coords(3).EQ.0)
   CALL MPI_SCATTERV(A, counta, dispa, typea,
           AA, nn(1)*nn(2), MPI_REAL, 0, Comm_2D(3), ierr)
END IF


! 2. scatter matrix B
IF (coords(1).EQ.0) THEN
   CALL MPI_SCATTERV(B, countb, dispb, typeb,
           BB, nn(2)*nn(3), MPI_REAL, 0, Comm_2D(1), ierr)
END IF


! 3. broadcast matrix AA in z dimension
CALL MPI_BCAST(AA, nn(1)*nn(2), MPI_REAL, 0, comm_1D(3), ierr)


! 4. broadcast matrix BB in x dimension
 CALL MPI_BCAST(BB, nn(2)*nn(3), MPI_REAL, 0, comm_1D(1), ierr)
```

```
! 5. compute submatrix products
DO j = 1, nn(3)
   DO i = 1, nn(1)
      CC(i,j) = 0
      DO k = 1, nn(2)
         CC(i,j) = CC(i,j) + AA(i,k)*BB(k,j)
      END DO
   END DO
END DO


! 6. reduce subproducts in y dimension
! need additional matrix, since one cannot reduce "in place"
ALLOCATE (CC1(nn(1),nn(3)))
CALL MPI_REDUCE(CC, CC1, nn(1)*nn(3), MPI_REAL, MPI_SUM,
                                    0, comm_1D(2), ierr)


! 7. gather results from plane (x,0,z) to node 0
IF (coords(2).EQ.0) THEN
   CALL MPI_GATHERV(CC1, nn(1)*nn(3), MPI_REAL,
              C, countc, dispc, typec, 0, comm_2D(2), ierr)
END IF


! clean up
DEALLOCATE(AA, BB, CC)
DEALLOCATE (CC1)
IF (rank.EQ.0) THEN
   DEALLOCATE (counta, countb, countc, dispa, dispb, dispc)
   MPI_TYPE_FREE( typea, ierr)
   MPI_TYPE_FREE( typeb, ierr)
   MPI_TYPE_FREE( typec, ierr)
   MPI_TYPE_FREE( types(1), ierr)
END IF
MPI_COMM_FREE( pcomm, ierr)
MPI_COMM_FREE( comm_3D, ierr)
DO i = 1, 3
   MPI_COMM_FREE( comm_2D(i), ierr)
   MPI_COMM_FREE( comm_1D(i), ierr)
END DO
```

```
! returns matrix C at process 0
RETURN
END
```

7 Environmental Management

This chapter discusses routines for getting and, where appropriate, setting various parameters that relate to the MPI implementation and the execution environment. It discusses error handling in MPI and the procedures available for controlling MPI error handling. The procedures for entering and leaving the MPI execution environment are also described here. Finally, the chapter discusses the interaction between MPI and the general execution environment.

7.1 Implementation Information

7.1.1 Environmental Inquiries

A set of attributes that describe the execution environment are attached to the communicator MPI_COMM_WORLD when MPI is initialized. The value of these attributes can be inquired by using the function MPI_ATTR_GET described in Chapter 5. It is erroneous to delete these attributes, free their keys, or change their values.

The list of predefined attribute keys include

MPI_TAG_UB Upper bound for tag value.

MPI_HOST Host process rank, if such exists, MPI_PROC_NULL, otherwise.

MPI_IO rank of a node that has regular I/O facilities (possibly rank of calling process). Nodes in the same communicator may return different values for this parameter.

MPI_WTIME_IS_GLOBAL Boolean variable that indicates whether clocks are synchronized.

Vendors may add implementation specific parameters (such as node number, real memory size, virtual memory size, etc.)

These predefined attributes do not change value between MPI initialization (MPI_INIT) and MPI completion (MPI_FINALIZE).

Advice to users. Note that in the C binding, the value returned by these attributes is a *pointer* to an **int** containing the requested value. (*End of advice to users.*)

The required parameter values are discussed in more detail below:

Tag Values Tag values range from 0 to the value returned for MPI_TAG_UB, inclusive. These values are guaranteed to be unchanging during the execution of an MPI program. In addition, the tag upper bound value must be *at least* 32767. An

MPI implementation is free to make the value of MPI_TAG_UB larger than this; for example, the value $2^{30} - 1$ is also a legal value for MPI_TAG_UB (on a system where this value is a legal int or INTEGER value).

The attribute MPI_TAG_UB has the same value on all processes in the group of MPI_COMM_WORLD.

Host Rank   The value returned for MPI_HOST gets the rank of the HOST process in the group associated with communicator MPI_COMM_WORLD, if there is such. MPI_PROC_NULL is returned if there is no host. This attribute can be used on systems that have a distinguished *host* processor, in order to identify the process running on this processor. However, MPI does not specify what it means for a process to be a HOST, nor does it requires that a HOST exists.

The attribute MPI_HOST has the same value on all processes in the group of MPI_COMM_WORLD.

I/O Rank   The value returned for MPI_IO is the rank of a processor that can provide language-standard I/O facilities. For Fortran, this means that all of the Fortran I/O operations are supported (e.g., OPEN, REWIND, WRITE). For C, this means that all of the ANSI-C I/O operations are supported (e.g., fopen, fprintf, lseek).

If every process can provide language-standard I/O, then the value MPI_ANY-_SOURCE will be returned. Otherwise, if the calling process can provide language-standard I/O, then its rank will be returned. Otherwise, if some process can provide language-standard I/O then the rank of one such process will be returned. The same value need not be returned by all processes. If no process can provide language-standard I/O, then the value MPI_PROC_NULL will be returned.

Advice to users.   MPI does not require that all processes provide language-standard I/O, nor does it specify how the standard input or output of a process is linked to a particular file or device. In particular, there is no requirement, in an interactive environment, that keyboard input be broadcast to all processes which support language-standard I/O. (*End of advice to users.*)

Clock Synchronization   The value returned for MPI_WTIME_IS_GLOBAL is 1 if clocks at all processes in MPI_COMM_WORLD are synchronized, 0 otherwise. A collection of clocks is considered synchronized if explicit effort has been taken to synchronize them. The expectation is that the variation in time, as measured by calls to MPI_WTIME, will be less then one half the round-trip time for an MPI message of length zero. If time is measured at a process just before a send and at another process just after a matching receive, the second time should be always higher than the first one.

The attribute MPI_WTIME_IS_GLOBAL need not be present when the clocks are not synchronized (however, the attribute key MPI_WTIME_IS_GLOBAL is always valid). This attribute may be associated with communicators other then MPI-_COMM_WORLD.

The attribute MPI_WTIME_IS_GLOBAL has the same value on all processes in the group of MPI_COMM_WORLD.

MPI_GET_PROCESSOR_NAME(name, resultlen)

OUT	name	A unique specifier for the current physical node.
OUT	resultlen	Length (in printable characters) of the result returned in name

```
int MPI_Get_processor_name(char *name, int *resultlen)
```

```
MPI_GET_PROCESSOR_NAME( NAME, RESULTLEN, IERROR)
    CHARACTER*(*) NAME
    INTEGER RESULTLEN,IERROR
```

This routine returns the name of the processor on which it was called at the moment of the call. The name is a character string for maximum flexibility. From this value it must be possible to identify a specific piece of hardware; possible values include "processor 9 in rack 4 of mpp.cs.org" and "231" (where 231 is the actual processor number in the running homogeneous system). The argument name must represent storage that is at least MPI_MAX_PROCESSOR_NAME characters long. MPI_GET_PROCESSOR_NAME may write up to this many characters into name.

The number of characters actually written is returned in the output argument, resultlen.

Rationale. The definition of this function does not preclude MPI implementations that do process migration. In such a case, successive calls to MPI_GET-_PROCESSOR_NAME by the same process may return different values. Note that nothing in MPI requires or defines process migration; this definition of MPI_GET-_PROCESSOR_NAME simply allows such an implementation. (*End of rationale.*)

Advice to users. The user must provide at least MPI_MAX_PROCESSOR_NAME space to write the processor name — processor names can be this long. The user should examine the output argument, resultlen, to determine the actual length of the name. (*End of advice to users.*)

The constant MPI_BSEND_OVERHEAD provides an upper bound on the fixed overhead per message buffered by a call to MPI_BSEND.

7.2 Timers and Synchronization

MPI defines a timer. A timer is specified even though it is not "message-passing," because timing parallel programs is important in "performance debugging" and because existing timers (both in POSIX 1003.1-1988 and 1003.4D 14.1 and in Fortran 90) are either inconvenient or do not provide adequate access to high-resolution timers.

MPI_WTIME()

```
double MPI_Wtime(void)
```

```
DOUBLE PRECISION MPI_WTIME()
```

MPI_WTIME returns a floating-point number of seconds, representing elapsed wall-clock time since some time in the past.

The "time in the past" is guaranteed not to change during the life of the process. The user is responsible for converting large numbers of seconds to other units if they are preferred.

This function is portable (it returns seconds, not "ticks"), it allows high-resolution, and carries no unnecessary baggage. One would use it like this:

```
{
    double starttime, endtime;
    starttime = MPI_Wtime();
     ....  stuff to be timed  ...
    endtime   = MPI_Wtime();
    printf("That took %f seconds\n",endtime-starttime);
}
```

The times returned are local to the node that called them. There is no requirement that different nodes return "the same time." (But see also the discussion of MPI_WTIME_IS_GLOBAL in Section 7.1.1).

MPI_WTICK()

`double MPI_Wtick(void)`

`DOUBLE PRECISION MPI_WTICK()`

MPI_WTICK returns the resolution of MPI_WTIME in seconds. That is, it returns, as a double precision value, the number of seconds between successive clock ticks. For example, if the clock is implemented by the hardware as a counter that is incremented every millisecond, the value returned by MPI_WTICK should be 10^{-3}.

7.3   Initialization and Exit

One goal of MPI is to achieve *source code portability*. By this we mean that a program written using MPI and complying with the relevant language standards is portable as written, and must not require any source code changes when moved from one system to another. This explicitly does *not* say anything about how an MPI program is started or launched from the command line, nor what the user must do to set up the environment in which an MPI program will run. However, an implementation may require some setup to be performed before other MPI routines may be called. To provide for this, MPI includes an initialization routine MPI_INIT.

MPI_INIT()

`int MPI_Init(int *argc, char ***argv)`

`MPI_INIT(IERROR)`
    `INTEGER IERROR`

This routine must be called before any other MPI routine. It must be called at most once; subsequent calls are erroneous (see MPI_INITIALIZED).

All MPI programs must contain a call to MPI_INIT; this routine must be called before any other MPI routine (apart from MPI_INITIALIZED) is called. The version for ANSI C accepts the argc and argv that are provided by the arguments to main:

```
int main(argc, argv)
int argc;
char **argv;
{
    MPI_Init(&argc, &argv);
```

```
    /* parse arguments */
    /* main program    */

    MPI_Finalize();      /* see below */
}
```

The Fortran version takes only IERROR.

An MPI implementation is free to require that the arguments in the C binding must be the arguments to **main**.

Rationale. The command line arguments are provided *to* MPI_Init to allow an MPI implementation to use them in initializing the MPI environment. They are passed by reference to allow an MPI implementation to *provide* them in environments where the command-line arguments are not provided to **main**. (*End of rationale.*)

MPI_FINALIZE()

```
int MPI_Finalize(void)
```

```
MPI_FINALIZE(IERROR)
    INTEGER IERROR
```

This routines cleans up all MPI state. Once this routine is called, no MPI routine (even MPI_INIT) may be called. The user must ensure that all pending communications involving a process complete before the process calls MPI_FINALIZE.

MPI_INITIALIZED(flag)

OUT	flag	Flag is true if MPI_INIT has been called and false otherwise.

```
int MPI_Initialized(int *flag)
```

```
MPI_INITIALIZED(FLAG, IERROR)
    LOGICAL FLAG
    INTEGER IERROR
```

This routine may be used to determine whether MPI_INIT has been called. It is the *only* routine that may be called before MPI_INIT is called.

MPI_ABORT(comm, errorcode)

| IN | comm | communicator of tasks to abort |
| IN | errorcode | error code to return to invoking environment |

```
int MPI_Abort(MPI_Comm comm, int errorcode)
```

```
MPI_ABORT(COMM, ERRORCODE, IERROR)
    INTEGER COMM, ERRORCODE, IERROR
```

This routine makes a "best attempt" to abort all tasks in the group of comm. This function does not require that the invoking environment take any action with the error code. However, a Unix or POSIX environment should handle this as a `return errorcode` from the main program or an `abort(errorcode)`.

MPI implementations are required to define the behavior of MPI_ABORT at least for a comm of MPI_COMM_WORLD. MPI implementations may ignore the comm argument and act as if the comm was MPI_COMM_WORLD.

Advice to users. The behavior of MPI_ABORT(comm, errorcode), for comm other then MPI_COMM_WORLD, is implementation-dependent. One the other hand, a call to MPI_ABORT(MPI_COMM_WORLD, errorcode) should always cause all processes in the group of MPI_COMM_WORLD to abort. (*End of advice to users.*)

7.4 Error Handling

MPI provides the user with reliable message transmission. A message sent is always received correctly, and the user does not need to check for transmission errors, timeouts, or other error conditions. In other words, MPI does not provide mechanisms for dealing with failures in the communication system. If the MPI implementation is built on an unreliable underlying mechanism, then it is the job of the implementor of the MPI subsystem to insulate the user from this unreliability, or to reflect unrecoverable errors as exceptions.

Of course, errors can occur during MPI calls for a variety of reasons. A **program error** can occur when an MPI routine is called with an incorrect argument (nonexisting destination in a send operation, buffer too small in a receive operation, etc.) This type of error would occur in any implementation. In addition, a **resource error** may occur when a program exceeds the amount of available system resources (number of pending messages, system buffers, etc.). The occurrence of this type of error depends on the amount of available resources in the system and the resource allocation mechanism used; this may differ from system to system. A high-quality implementation will provide generous limits on the important resources so as to alleviate the portability problem this represents.

An MPI implementation cannot or may choose not to handle some errors that occur during MPI calls. These can include errors that generate exceptions or traps, such as floating point errors or access violations; errors that are too expensive to detect in normal execution mode; or "catastrophic" errors which may prevent MPI from returning control to the caller in a consistent state.

Another subtle issue arises because of the nature of asynchronous communications. MPI can only handle errors that can be attached to a specific MPI call. MPI calls (both blocking and nonblocking) may initiate operations that continue asynchronously after the call returned. Thus, the call may complete successfully, yet the operation may later cause an error. If there is a subsequent call that relates to the same operation (e.g., a wait or test call that completes a nonblocking call, or a receive that completes a communication initiated by a blocking send) then the error can be associated with this call. In some cases, the error may occur after all calls that relate to the operation have completed. (Consider the case of a blocking ready mode send operation, where the outgoing message is buffered, and it is subsequently found that no matching receive is posted.) Such errors will not be handled by MPI.

The set of errors in MPI calls that are handled by MPI is implementation-dependent. Each such error generates an MPI **exception**. A good quality implementation will attempt to handle as many errors as possible as MPI exceptions. Errors that are not handled by MPI will be handled by the error handling mechanisms of the language run-time or the operating system. Typically, errors that are not handled by MPI will cause the parallel program to abort.

The occurrence of an MPI exception has two effects:

- An MPI **error handler** will be invoked.

- If the error handler did not cause the process to halt, then a suitable error code will be returned by the MPI call.

Some MPI calls may cause more than one MPI exception (see Section 2.9). In such a case, the MPI error handler will be invoked once for each exception, and multiple error codes will be returned.

After an error is detected, the state of MPI is undefined. That is, the state of the computation after the error-handler executed does *not* necessarily allow the user to continue to use MPI. The purpose of these error handlers is to allow a user to issue user-defined error messages and to take actions unrelated to MPI (such as flushing I/O buffers) before a program exits. An MPI implementation is free to allow MPI to continue after an error but is not required to do so.

Advice to implementors. A good quality implementation will, to the greatest possible extent, circumscribe the impact of an error, so that normal processing can continue after an error handler was invoked. The implementation documentation will provide information on the possible effect of each class of errors. (*End of advice to implementors.*)

7.4.1 Error Handlers

A user can associate an error handler with a communicator. The specified error handling routine will be used for any MPI exception that occurs during a call to MPI for a communication with this communicator. MPI calls that are not related to any communicator are considered to be attached to the communicator MPI_COMM_WORLD. The attachment of error handlers to communicators is purely local: different processes may attach different error handlers to communicators for the same communication domain.

A newly created communicator inherits the error handler that is associated with the "parent" communicator. In particular, the user can specify a "global" error handler for all communicators by associating this handler with the communicator MPI_COMM_WORLD immediately after initialization.

Several predefined error handlers are available in MPI:

MPI_ERRORS_ARE_FATAL The handler, when called, causes the program to abort on all executing processes. This has the same effect as if MPI_ABORT was called by the process that invoked the handler (with communicator argument MPI_COMM_WORLD).

MPI_ERRORS_RETURN The handler has no effect (other than returning the error code to the user).

Implementations may provide additional predefined error handlers and programmers can code their own error handlers.

The error handler MPI_ERRORS_ARE_FATAL is associated by default with MPI-_COMM_WORLD after initialization. Thus, if the user chooses not to control error handling, every error that MPI handles is treated as fatal. Since (almost) all MPI calls return an error code, a user may choose to handle errors in his or her main code, by testing the return code of MPI calls and executing a suitable recovery code when the call was not successful. In this case, the error handler MPI_ERRORS_RETURN

will be used. Usually it is more convenient and more efficient not to test for errors
after each MPI call, and have such an error handled by a non-trivial MPI error
handler.

An MPI error handler is an opaque object, which is accessed by a handle. MPI
calls are provided to create new error handlers, to associate error handlers with
communicators, and to test which error handler is associated with a communicator.

MPI_ERRHANDLER_CREATE(function, errhandler)

IN	function	user defined error handling procedure
OUT	errhandler	MPI error handler

```
int MPI_Errhandler_create(MPI_Handler_function *function,
        MPI_Errhandler *errhandler)
```

```
MPI_ERRHANDLER_CREATE(FUNCTION, HANDLER, IERROR)
    EXTERNAL FUNCTION
    INTEGER ERRHANDLER, IERROR
```

Register the user routine function for use as an MPI exception handler. Returns
in errhandler a handle to the registered exception handler.

In the C language, the user routine should be a C function of type MPI_Handler-
_function, which is defined as:

```
typedef void (MPI_Handler_function)(MPI_Comm *, int *, ...);
```

The first argument is the communicator in use. The second is the error code to
be returned by the MPI routine that raised the error. If the routine would have
returned multiple error codes (see Section 2.9), it is the error code returned in the
status for the request that caused the error handler to be invoked. The remaining arguments are "stdargs" arguments whose number and meaning is implementation-
dependent. An implementation should clearly document these arguments. Addresses are used so that the handler may be written in Fortran.

Rationale. The variable argument list is provided because it provides an ANSI-
standard hook for providing additional information to the error handler; without
this hook, ANSI C prohibits additional arguments. (*End of rationale.*)

MPI_ERRHANDLER_SET(comm, errhandler)

IN	comm	communicator to set the error handler for
IN	errhandler	new MPI error handler for communicator

```
int MPI_Errhandler_set(MPI_Comm comm, MPI_Errhandler errhandler)
```

```
MPI_ERRHANDLER_SET(COMM, ERRHANDLER, IERROR)
    INTEGER COMM, ERRHANDLER, IERROR
```

Associates the new error handler errorhandler with communicator comm at the calling process. Note that an error handler is always associated with the communicator.

MPI_ERRHANDLER_GET(comm, errhandler)

IN	comm	communicator to get the error handler from
OUT	errhandler	MPI error handler currently associated with communicator

```
int MPI_Errhandler_get(MPI_Comm comm, MPI_Errhandler *errhandler)
```

```
MPI_ERRHANDLER_GET(COMM, ERRHANDLER, IERROR)
    INTEGER COMM, ERRHANDLER, IERROR
```

Returns in errhandler (a handle to) the error handler that is currently associated with communicator comm.

Example: A library function may register at its entry point the current error handler for a communicator, set its own private error handler for this communicator, and restore before exiting the previous error handler.

MPI_ERRHANDLER_FREE(errhandler)

IN	errhandler	MPI error handler

```
int MPI_Errhandler_free(MPI_Errhandler *errhandler)
```

```
MPI_ERRHANDLER_FREE(ERRHANDLER, IERROR)
```

```
INTEGER ERRHANDLER, IERROR
```

Marks the error handler associated with errhandler for deallocation and sets errhandler to MPI_ERRHANDLER_NULL. The error handler will be deallocated after all
communicators associated with it have been deallocated.

7.4.2 Error Codes

Most MPI functions return an error code indicating successful execution (MPI_SUC-
CESS), or providing information on the type of MPI exception that occurred. In
certain circumstances, when the MPI function may complete several distinct operations, and therefore may generate several independent errors, the MPI function
may return multiple error codes. This may occur with some of the calls described
in Section 2.9 that complete multiple nonblocking communications. As described
in that section, the call may return the code MPI_ERR_IN_STATUS, in which case a
detailed error code is returned with the status of each communication.

The error codes returned by MPI are left entirely to the implementation (with
the exception of MPI_SUCCESS, MPI_ERR_IN_STATUS and MPI_ERR_PENDING). This
is done to allow an implementation to provide as much information as possible in
the error code. Error codes can be translated into meaningful messages using the
function below.

MPI_ERROR_STRING(errorcode, string, resultlen)

IN	errorcode	Error code returned by an MPI routine
OUT	string	Text that corresponds to the errorcode
OUT	resultlen	Length (in printable characters) of the result returned in string

```
int MPI_Error_string(int errorcode, char *string, int *resultlen)
```

```
MPI_ERROR_STRING(ERRORCODE, STRING, RESULTLEN, IERROR)
    INTEGER ERRORCODE, RESULTLEN, IERROR
    CHARACTER*(*) STRING
```

Returns the error string associated with an error code or class. The argument
string must represent storage that is at least MPI_MAX_ERROR_STRING characters
long.

The number of characters actually written is returned in the output argument,
resultlen.

Rationale. The form of this function was chosen to make the Fortran and C bindings similar. A version that returns a pointer to a string has two difficulties. First, the return string must be statically allocated and different for each error message (allowing the pointers returned by successive calls to MPI_ERROR_STRING to point to the correct message). Second, in Fortran, a function declared as returning CHARACTER*(*) can not be referenced in, for example, a PRINT statement. (*End of rationale.*)

The use of implementation-dependent error codes allows implementers to provide more information, but prevents one from writing portable error-handling code. To solve this problem, MPI provides a standard set of specified error values, called **error classes**, and a function that maps each error code into a suitable error class.

Valid error classes are

MPI_SUCCESS	No error
MPI_ERR_BUFFER	Invalid buffer pointer
MPI_ERR_COUNT	Invalid count argument
MPI_ERR_TYPE	Invalid datatype argument
MPI_ERR_TAG	Invalid tag argument
MPI_ERR_COMM	Invalid communicator
MPI_ERR_RANK	Invalid rank
MPI_ERR_REQUEST	Invalid request
MPI_ERR_ROOT	Invalid root
MPI_ERR_GROUP	Invalid group
MPI_ERR_OP	Invalid operation
MPI_ERR_TOPOLOGY	Invalid topology
MPI_ERR_DIMS	Invalid dimension argument
MPI_ERR_ARG	Invalid argument of some other kind
MPI_ERR_UNKNOWN	Unknown error
MPI_ERR_TRUNCATE	Message truncated on receive
MPI_ERR_OTHER	Known error not in this list
MPI_ERR_INTERN	Internal MPI error
MPI_ERR_IN_STATUS	Error code is in status
MPI_ERR_PENDING	Pending request
MPI_ERR_LASTCODE	Last error code

Most of these classes are self explanatory. The use of MPI_ERR_IN_STATUS and MPI_ERR_PENDING is explained in Section 2.9. The list of standard classes may be extended in the future.

The function MPI_ERROR_STRING can be used to compute the error string associated with an error class.

The error codes satisfy,

$$0 = \text{MPI\_SUCCESS} < \text{MPI\_ERR}.... \leq \text{MPI\_ERR\_LASTCODE}.$$

MPI_ERROR_CLASS(errorcode, errorclass)

IN	errorcode	Error code returned by an MPI routine
OUT	errorclass	Error class associated with errorcode

```
int MPI_Error_class(int errorcode, int *errorclass)
```

```
MPI_ERROR_CLASS(ERRORCODE, ERRORCLASS, IERROR)
    INTEGER ERRORCODE, ERRORCLASS, IERROR
```

The function MPI_ERROR_CLASS maps each error code into a standard error code (error class). It maps each standard error code onto itself.

Rationale. The difference between MPI_ERR_UNKNOWN and MPI_ERR_OTHER is that MPI_ERROR_STRING can return useful information about MPI_ERR_OTHER.

Note that MPI_SUCCESS = 0 is necessary to be consistent with C practice.

The value of MPI_ERR_LASTCODE can be used for error-checking, or for selecting error codes for libraries that do not conflict with MPI error codes.

(*End of rationale.*)

Advice to implementors. An MPI implementation may use error classes as the error codes returned by some or all MPI functions. Another choice is to use error classes as "major error codes", extended with additional bits that provide "minor" error codes. Then, the MPI_ERROR_CLASS function merely needs to truncate the full error code.

Implementations may go beyond this document in supporting MPI calls that are defined here to be erroneous. For example, MPI specifies strict type matching rules between matching send and receive operations: it is erroneous to send a floating point variable and receive an integer. Implementations may go beyond these type matching rules, and provide automatic type conversion in such situations. It will be helpful to generate warnings for such nonconforming behavior. (*End of advice to implementors.*)

7.5   Interaction with Executing Environment

There are a number of areas where an MPI implementation may interact with the operating environment and system. While MPI does not mandate that any services (such as I/O or signal handling) be provided, it does strongly suggest the behavior to be provided if those services are available. This is an important point in achieving portability across platforms that provide the same set of services.

7.5.1   Independence of Basic Runtime Routines

MPI programs require that library routines that are part of the basic language environment (such as date and write in Fortran and printf and malloc in ANSI C) and are executed after MPI_INIT and before MPI_FINALIZE operate independently and that their *completion* is independent of the action of other processes in an MPI program.

Note that this in no way prevents the creation of library routines that provide parallel services whose operation is collective. However, the following program is expected to complete in an ANSI C environment regardless of the size of MPI_COMM_WORLD (assuming that I/O is available at the executing nodes).

```
int rank;
MPI_Init( argc, argv );
MPI_Comm_rank( MPI_COMM_WORLD, &rank );
if (rank == 0) printf( "Starting program\n" );
MPI_Finalize();
```

The corresponding Fortran 77 program is also expected to complete.

An example of what is *not* required is any particular ordering of the action of these routines when called by several tasks. For example, MPI makes neither requirements nor recommendations for the output from the following program (again assuming that I/O is available at the executing nodes).

```
MPI_Comm_rank( MPI_COMM_WORLD, &rank );
printf( "Output from task rank %d\n", rank );
```

In addition, calls that fail because of resource exhaustion or other error are not considered a violation of the requirements here (however, they are required to complete, just not to complete successfully).

7.5.2   Interaction with Signals in POSIX

MPI does not specify either the interaction of processes with signals, in a UNIX environment, or with other events that do not relate to MPI communication. That is, signals are not significant from the view point of MPI, and implementors should attempt to implement MPI so that signals are transparent: an MPI call suspended by a signal should resume and complete after the signal is handled. Generally, the state of a computation that is visible or significant from the view-point of MPI should only be affected by MPI calls.

The intent of MPI to be thread and signal safe has a number of subtle effects. For example, on Unix systems, a catchable signal such as SIGALRM (an alarm signal) must not cause an MPI routine to behave differently than it would have in the absence of the signal. Of course, if the signal handler issues MPI calls or changes the environment in which the MPI routine is operating (for example, consuming all available memory space), the MPI routine should behave as appropriate for that situation (in particular, in this case, the behavior should be the same as for a multithreaded MPI implementation).

A second effect is that a signal handler that performs MPI calls must not interfere with the operation of MPI. For example, an MPI receive of any type that occurs within a signal handler must not cause erroneous behavior by the MPI implementation. Note that an implementation is permitted to prohibit the use of MPI calls from within a signal handler, and is not required to detect such use.

It is highly desirable that MPI not use SIGALRM, SIGFPE, or SIGIO. An implementation is *required* to clearly document all of the signals that the MPI implementation uses; a good place for this information is a Unix 'man' page on MPI.

8 The MPI Profiling Interface

8.1 Requirements

To satisfy the requirements of the MPI profiling interface, an implementation of the MPI functions *must*

1. provide a mechanism through which all of the MPI defined functions may be accessed with a name shift. Thus all of the MPI functions (which normally start with the prefix "MPI_") should also be accessible with the prefix "PMPI_".

2. ensure that those MPI functions which are not replaced may still be linked into an executable image without causing name clashes.

3. document the implementation of different language bindings of the MPI interface if they are layered on top of each other, so that the profiler developer knows whether the profile interface must be implemented for each binding, or whether it needs to be implemented only for the lowest level routines.

4. ensure that where the implementation of different language bindings is done through a layered approach (e.g. the Fortran binding is a set of "wrapper" functions which call the C implementation), these wrapper functions are separable from the rest of the library. This is necessary to allow a separate profiling library to be correctly implemented, since (at least with Unix linker semantics) the profiling library must contain these wrapper functions if it is to perform as expected. This requirement allows the person who builds the profiling library to extract these functions from the original MPI library and add them into the profiling library without bringing along any other unnecessary code.

5. provide a no-op routine MPI_PCONTROL in the MPI library.

8.2 Discussion

The objective of the MPI profiling interface is to ensure that it is relatively easy for authors of profiling (and other similar) tools to interface their codes to MPI implementations on different machines.

Since MPI is a machine independent standard with many different implementations, it is unreasonable to expect that the authors of profiling tools for MPI will have access to the source code which implements MPI on any particular machine. It is therefore necessary to provide a mechanism by which the implementors of such tools can collect whatever performance information they wish *without* access to the underlying implementation.

The MPI Forum believed that having such an interface is important if MPI is to be attractive to end users, since the availability of many different tools will be a significant factor in attracting users to the MPI standard.

The profiling interface is just that, an interface. It says *nothing* about the way in which it is used. Therefore, there is no attempt to lay down what information is collected through the interface, or how the collected information is saved, filtered, or displayed.

While the initial impetus for the development of this interface arose from the desire to permit the implementation of profiling tools, it is clear that an interface like that specified may also prove useful for other purposes, such as "internetworking" multiple MPI implementations. Since all that is defined is an interface, there is no impediment to it being used wherever it is useful.

As the issues being addressed here are intimately tied up with the way in which executable images are built, which may differ greatly on different machines, the examples given below should be treated solely as one way of implementing the MPI profiling interface. The actual requirements made of an implementation are those detailed in Section 8.1, the whole of the rest of this chapter is only present as justification and discussion of the logic for those requirements.

The examples below show one way in which an implementation could be constructed to meet the requirements on a Unix system (there are doubtless others which would be equally valid).

8.3   Logic of the Design

Provided that an MPI implementation meets the requirements listed in Section 8.1, it is possible for the implementor of the profiling system to intercept all of the MPI calls which are made by the user program. Whatever information is required can then be collected before calling the underlying MPI implementation (through its name shifted entry points) to achieve the desired effects.

8.3.1   Miscellaneous Control of Profiling

There is a clear requirement for the user code to be able to control the profiler dynamically at run time. This is normally used for (at least) the purposes of

- Enabling and disabling profiling depending on the state of the calculation.
- Flushing trace buffers at non-critical points in the calculation
- Adding user events to a trace file.

These requirements are met by use of the **MPI_PCONTROL**.

MPI_PCONTROL(level, ...)

    IN   **level**   Profiling level

```
int MPI_Pcontrol(const int level, ...)
```

```
MPI_PCONTROL(level)
    INTEGER LEVEL
```

MPI libraries themselves make no use of this routine, and simply return immediately to the user code. However the presence of calls to this routine allows a profiling package to be explicitly called by the user.

Since MPI has no control of the implementation of the profiling code, The MPI Forum was unable to specify precisely the semantics which will be provided by calls to **MPI_PCONTROL**. This vagueness extends to the number of arguments to the function, and their datatypes.

However to provide some level of portability of user codes to different profiling libraries, the MPI Forum requested the following meanings for certain values of level.

- **level = 0**: Profiling is disabled.
- **level = 1**: Profiling is enabled at a normal default level of detail.
- **level = 2**: Profile buffers are flushed. (This may be a no-op in some profilers).
- All other values of **level** have profile library defined effects and additional arguments.

The MPI Forum also requested that the default state after MPI_INIT has been called is for profiling to be enabled at the normal default level. (i.e. as if MPI_PCONTROL had just been called with the argument 1). This allows users to link with a profiling library and obtain profile output without having to modify their source code at all.

The provision of **MPI_PCONTROL** as a no-op in the standard MPI library allows users to modify their source code to obtain more detailed profiling information, but still be able to link exactly the same code against the standard MPI library.

8.4   Examples

8.4.1   Profiler Implementation

Suppose that the profiler wishes to accumulate the total amount of data sent by
the MPI_Send() function, along with the total elapsed time spent in the function.
This could trivially be achieved thus

```
static int totalBytes;
static double totalTime;
int MPI_Send(void * buffer, const int count, MPI_Datatype datatype,
             int dest, int tag, MPI_comm comm)
{
   double tstart = MPI_Wtime();        /* Pass on all the arguments */
   int extent;
   int result   = PMPI_Send(buffer,count,datatype,dest,tag,comm);

   MPI_Type_size(datatype,&extent);  /* Compute size */
   totalBytes += count * extent;

   totalTime  += MPI_Wtime() - tstart;

   return result;
}
```

8.4.2   MPI Library Implementation

On a Unix system, in which the MPI library is implemented in C, then there are
various possible options, of which two of the most obvious are presented here. Which
is better depends on whether the linker and compiler support weak symbols.

Systems With Weak symbols   If the compiler and linker support weak external
symbols (e.g. Solaris 2.x, other system V.4 machines), then only a single library is
required through the use of #pragma weak thus

```
#pragma weak MPI_Send = PMPI_Send
int PMPI_Send(/* appropriate args */)
{
    /* Useful content */
}
```

Figure 8.1
Resolution of MPI calls on systems with weak links.

The effect of this #pragma is to define the external symbol MPI_Send as a weak definition. This means that the linker will not complain if there is another definition of the symbol (for instance in the profiling library), however if no other definition exists, then the linker will use the weak definition. This type of situation is illustrated in Fig. 8.1, in which a profiling library has been written that profiles calls to MPI_Send() but not calls to MPI_Bcast(). On systems with weak links the link step for an application would be something like

```
% cc ... -lprof -lmpi
```

References to MPI_Send() are resolved in the profiling library, where the routine then calls PMPI_Send() which is resolved in the MPI library. In this case the weak link to PMPI_Send() is ignored. However, since MPI_Bcast() is not included in the profiling library, references to it are resolved via a weak link to PMPI_Bcast() in the MPI library.

Systems without Weak Symbols In the absence of weak symbols then one possible solution would be to use the C macro pre-processor thus

```
#ifdef PROFILELIB
#      ifdef __STDC__
#          define FUNCTION(name) P##name
#      else
#          define FUNCTION(name) P/**/name
#      endif
#else
#      define FUNCTION(name) name
#endif
```

Figure 8.2
Resolution of MPI calls on systems without weak links.

Each of the user visible functions in the library would then be declared thus

```
int FUNCTION(MPI_Send)(/* appropriate args */)
{
    /* Useful content */
}
```

The same source file can then be compiled to produce the MPI and the PMPI versions of the library, depending on the state of the **PROFILELIB** macro symbol.

It is required that the standard MPI library be built in such a way that the inclusion of MPI functions can be achieved one at a time. This is a somewhat unpleasant requirement, since it may mean that each external function has to be compiled from a separate file. However this is necessary so that the author of the profiling library need only define those MPI functions that are to be intercepted, references to any others being fulfilled by the normal MPI library. Therefore the link step can look something like this

```
% cc ... -lprof -lpmpi -lmpi
```

Here `libprof.a` contains the profiler functions which intercept some of the MPI functions. `libpmpi.a` contains the "name shifted" MPI functions, and `libmpi.a` contains the normal definitions of the MPI functions. Thus, on systems without weak links the example shown in Fig. 8.1 would be resolved as shown in Fig. 8.2

8.4.3   Complications

Multiple Counting   Since parts of the MPI library may themselves be implemented using more basic MPI functions (e.g. a portable implementation of the collective operations implemented using point to point communications), there is potential for profiling functions to be called from within an MPI function which was called from a profiling function. This could lead to "double counting" of the time spent in the inner routine. Since this effect could actually be useful under some circumstances (e.g. it might allow one to answer the question "How much time is spent in the point to point routines when they're called from collective functions ?"), the MPI Forum decided not to enforce any restrictions on the author of the MPI library which would overcome this. Therefore, the author of the profiling library should be aware of this problem, and guard against it. In a single threaded world this is easily achieved through use of a static variable in the profiling code which remembers if you are already inside a profiling routine. It becomes more complex in a multi-threaded environment (as does the meaning of the times recorded!)

Linker Oddities   The Unix linker traditionally operates in one pass. The effect of this is that functions from libraries are only included in the image if they are needed at the time the library is scanned. When combined with weak symbols, or multiple definitions of the same function, this can cause odd (and unexpected) effects.

Consider, for instance, an implementation of MPI in which the Fortran binding is achieved by using wrapper functions on top of the C implementation. The author of the profile library then assumes that it is reasonable to provide profile functions only for the C binding, since Fortran will eventually call these, and the cost of the wrappers is assumed to be small. However, if the wrapper functions are not in the profiling library, then none of the profiled entry points will be undefined when the profiling library is called. Therefore none of the profiling code will be included in the image. When the standard MPI library is scanned, the Fortran wrappers will be resolved, and will also pull in the base versions of the MPI functions. The overall effect is that the code will link successfully, but will not be profiled.

To overcome this we must ensure that the Fortran wrapper functions are included in the profiling version of the library. We ensure that this is possible by requiring that these be separable from the rest of the base MPI library. This allows them to be extracted out of the base library and placed into the profiling library using the Unix **ar** command.

8.5   Multiple Levels of Interception

The scheme given here does not directly support the nesting of profiling functions, since it provides only a single alternative name for each MPI function. The MPI Forum gave consideration to an implementation which would allow multiple levels of call interception; however, it was unable to construct an implementation of this which did not have the following disadvantages

- assuming a particular implementation language.
- imposing a run time cost even when no profiling was taking place.

Since one of the objectives of MPI is to permit efficient, low latency implementations, and it is not the business of a standard to require a particular implementation language, the MPI Forum decided to accept the scheme outlined above.

Note, however, that it is possible to use the scheme above to implement a multi-level system, since the function called by the user may call many different profiling functions before calling the underlying MPI function.

Unfortunately such an implementation may require more cooperation between the different profiling libraries than is required for the single level implementation detailed above.

9 Conclusions

This book has attempted to give a complete description of the MPI specification, and includes code examples to illustrate aspects of the use of MPI. After reading the preceding chapters programmers should feel comfortable using MPI to develop message-passing applications. This final chapter addresses some important topics that either do not easily fit into the other chapters, or which are best dealt with after a good overall understanding of MPI has been gained. These topics are concerned more with the interpretation of the MPI specification, and the rationale behind some aspects of its design, rather than with semantics and syntax. Future extensions to MPI and the current status of MPI implementations will also be discussed.

9.1 Design Issues

9.1.1 Why is MPI so big?

One aspect of concern, particularly to novices, is the large number of routines comprising the MPI specification. In all there are 128 MPI routines, and further extensions (see Section 9.5) will probably increase their number. There are two fundamental reasons for the size of MPI. The first reason is that MPI was designed to be rich in functionality. This is reflected in MPI's support for derived datatypes, modular communication via the communicator abstraction, caching, application topologies, and the fully-featured set of collective communication routines. The second reason for the size of MPI reflects the diversity and complexity of today's high performance computers. This is particularly true with respect to the point-to-point communication routines where the different communication modes (see Sections 2.1 and 2.13) arise mainly as a means of providing a set of the most widely-used communication protocols. For example, the synchronous communication mode corresponds closely to a protocol that minimizes the copying and buffering of data through a rendezvous mechanism. A protocol that attempts to initiate delivery of messages as soon as possible would provide buffering for messages, and this corresponds closely to the buffered communication mode (or the standard mode if this is implemented with sufficient buffering). One could decrease the number of functions by increasing the number of parameters in each call. But such approach would increase the call overhead and would make the use of the most prevalent calls more complex. The availability of a large number of calls to deal with more esoteric features of MPI allows one to provide a simpler interface to the more frequently used functions.

9.1.2   Should we be concerned about the size of MPI?

There are two potential reasons why we might be concerned about the size of
MPI. The first is that potential users might equate size with complexity and decide
that MPI is too complicated to bother learning. The second is that vendors might
decide that MPI is too difficult to implement. The design of MPI addresses the first
of these concerns by adopting a layered approach. For example, novices can avoid
having to worry about groups and communicators by performing all communication
in the pre-defined communicator MPI_COMM_WORLD. In fact, most existing message-
passing applications can be ported to MPI simply by converting the communication
routines on a one-for-one basis (although the resulting MPI application may not
be optimally efficient). To allay the concerns of potential implementors the MPI
Forum at one stage considered defining a core subset of MPI known as the MPI
subset that would be substantially smaller than MPI and include just the point-
to-point communication routines and a few of the more commonly-used collective
communication routines. However, early work by Lusk, Gropp, Skjellum, Doss,
Franke and others on early implementations of MPI showed that it could be fully
implemented without a prohibitively large effort [12, 16]. Thus, the rationale for
the MPI subset was lost, and this idea was dropped.

9.1.3   Why does MPI not guarantee buffering?

MPI does not guarantee to buffer arbitrary messages because memory is a finite
resource on all computers. Thus, all computers will fail under sufficiently adverse
communication loads. Different computers at different times are capable of providing differing amounts of buffering, so if a program relies on buffering it may fail
under certain conditions, but work correctly under other conditions. This is clearly
undesirable.

Given that no message passing system can guarantee that messages will be
buffered as required under all circumstances, it might be asked why MPI does
not guarantee a minimum amount of memory available for buffering. One major
problem is that it is not obvious how to specify the amount of buffer space that
is available, nor is it easy to estimate how much buffer space is consumed by a
particular program.

Different buffering policies make sense in different environments. Messages can
be buffered at the sending node or at the receiving node, or both. In the former
case,

• buffers can be dedicated to one destination in one communication domain,

- or dedicated to one destination for all communication domains,
- or shared by all outgoing communications,
- or shared by all processes running at a processor node,
- or part of the buffer pool may be dedicated, and part shared.

Similar choices occur if messages are buffered at the destination. Communication buffers may be fixed in size, or they may be allocated dynamically out of the heap, in competition with the application. The buffer allocation policy may depend on the size of the messages (preferably buffering short messages), and may depend on communication history (preferably buffering on busy channels).

The choice of the right policy is strongly dependent on the hardware and software environment. For instance, in a dedicated environment, a processor with a process blocked on a send is idle and so computing resources are not wasted if this processor copies the outgoing message to a buffer. In a time shared environment, the computing resources may be used by another process. In a system where buffer space can be in paged memory, such space can be allocated from heap. If the buffer space cannot be paged, or has to be in kernel space, then a separate buffer is needed. Flow control may require that some amount of buffer space be dedicated to each pair of communicating processes.

The optimal strategy strongly depends on various performance parameters of the system: the bandwidth, the communication start-up time, scheduling and context switching overheads, the amount of potential overlap between communication and computation, etc. The choice of a buffering and scheduling policy may not be entirely under the control of the MPI implementor, as it is partially determined by the properties of the underlying communication layer. Also, experience in this arena is quite limited, and underlying technology can be expected to change rapidly: fast, user-space interprocessor communication mechanisms are an active research area [28, 20].

Attempts by the MPI Forum to design mechanisms for querying or setting the amount of buffer space available to standard communication led to the conclusion that such mechanisms will either restrict allowed implementations unacceptably, or provide bounds that will be extremely pessimistic on most implementations in most cases. Another problem is that parameters such as buffer sizes work against portability. Rather then restricting the implementation strategies for standard communication, the choice was taken to provide additional communication modes for those users that do not want to trust the implementation to make the right choice for them.

9.2   Portable Programming with MPI

The MPI specification was designed to make it possible to write portable message
passing programs while avoiding unacceptable performance degradation. Within
the context of MPI, "portable" is synonymous with "safe." Unsafe programs may
exhibit a different behavior on different systems because they are non-deterministic:
Several outcomes are consistent with the MPI specification, and the actual outcome
to occur depends on the precise timing of events. Unsafe programs may require
resources that are not always guaranteed by MPI, in order to complete successfully.
On systems where such resources are unavailable, the program will encounter a
resource error. Such an error will manifest itself as an actual program error, or will
result in deadlock.

There are three main issues relating to the portability of MPI programs (and,
indeed, message passing programs in general).

1. The program should not depend on the buffering of messages by MPI or lower levels
   of the communication system. A valid MPI implementation may, or may not, buffer
   messages of a given size (in standard mode).

2. The program should not depend upon whether collective communication routines,
   such as MPI_Bcast(), act as barrier synchronizations. In a valid MPI implementation collective communication routines may, or may not, have the side effect of
   performing a barrier synchronization.

3. The program should ensure that messages are matched by the intended receive
   call. Ambiguities in the specification of communication can lead to incorrect or
   non-deterministic programs since race conditions may arise. MPI provides message
   tags and communicators to help avoid these types of problem.

If proper attention is not paid to these factors a message passing code may fail
intermittently on a given computer, or may work correctly on one machine but not
on another. Clearly such a program is not portable. We shall now consider each of
the above factors in more detail.

9.2.1   Dependency on Buffering

A message passing program is dependent on the buffering of messages if its communication graph has a cycle. The communication graph is a directed graph in which
the nodes represent MPI communication calls and the edges represent dependencies
between these calls: a directed edge uv indicates that operation v might not be
able to complete before operation u is started. Calls may be dependent because

they have to be executed in succession by the same process, or because they are matching send and receive calls.

Example 9.1 Code for periodic shift in which the processes are arranged with a ring topology (i.e. a one-dimensional, periodic topology) where communicates data to its clockwise neighbor. A degenerate instance of this is when a process sends a message to itself. The following code uses a blocking send in standard mode to send a message to its clockwise neighbor, and a blocking receive to receive a message from its anti-clockwise neighbor.

```
...
MPI_Comm_size(comm, &size);
MPI_Comm_rank(comm, &rank);
clock = (rank+1)%size;
anticlock = (rank+size-1)%size;

MPI_Send (buf1, count, MPI_INT, clock, tag, comm);
MPI_Recv (buf2, count, MPI_INT, anticlock, tag, comm, &status);
```

The execution of the code results in the dependency graph illustrated in Figure 9.1, for the case of a three process group.

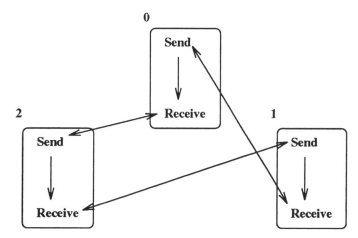

Figure 9.1
Cycle in communication graph for cyclic shift.

The arrow from each send to the following receive executed by the same process reflects the program dependency within each process: the receive call cannot be executed until the previous send call has completed. The double arrow between each send and the matching receive reflects their mutual dependency: Obviously, the receive cannot complete unless the matching send was invoked. Conversely, since a standard mode send is used, it may be the case that the send blocks until a matching receive occurs.

The dependency graph has a cycle. This code will only work if the system provides sufficient buffering, in which case the send operation will complete locally, the call to MPI_Send() will return, and the matching call to MPI_Recv() will be performed. In the absence of sufficient buffering MPI does not specify an outcome, but for most implementations deadlock will occur, i.e., the call to MPI_Send() will never return: each process will wait for the next process on the ring to execute a matching receive. Thus, the behavior of this code will differ from system to system, or on the same system, when message size (count) is changed.

There are a number of ways in which a shift operation can be performed portably using MPI. These are

1. alternate send and receive calls (only works if more than one process),

2. use a blocking send in buffered mode,

3. use a nonblocking send and/or receive,

4. use a call to MPI_Sendrecv(),

If at least one process in a shift operation calls the receive routine before the send routine, and at least one process calls the send routine before the receive routine, then at least one communication can proceed, and, eventually, the shift will complete successfully. One of the most efficient ways of doing this is to alternate the send and receive calls so that all processes with even rank send first and then receive, and all processes with odd rank receive first and then send. Thus, the following code is portable provided there is more than one process, i.e., clock and anticlock are different:

```
if (rank%2) {
   MPI_Recv (buf2, count, MPI_INT, anticlock, tag, comm, &status);
   MPI_Send (buf1, count, MPI_INT, clock, tag, comm);
   }
else {
   MPI_Send (buf1, count, MPI_INT, clock, tag, comm);
   MPI_Recv (buf2, count, MPI_INT, anticlock, tag, comm, &status);
   }
```

The resulting communication graph is illustrated in Figure 9.2. This graph is acyclic.

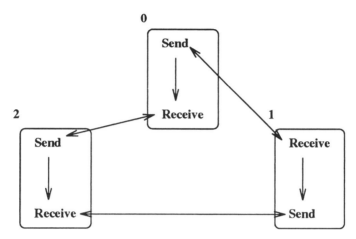

Figure 9.2
Cycle in communication graph is broken by reordering send and receive.

If there is only one process then clearly blocking send and receive routines cannot be used since the send must be called before the receive, and so cannot complete in the absence of buffering.

We now consider methods for performing shift operations that work even if there is only one process involved. A blocking send in buffered mode can be used to perform a shift operation. In this case the application program passes a buffer to the MPI communication system, and MPI can use this to buffer messages. If the buffer provided is large enough, then the shift will complete successfully. The following code shows how to use buffered mode to create a portable shift operation.

```
...
MPI_Pack_size (count, MPI_INT, comm, &buffsize)
buffsize += MPI_BSEND_OVERHEAD
userbuf = malloc (buffsize)
MPI_Buffer_attach (userbuf, buffsize);
MPI_Bsend (buf1, count, MPI_INT, clock, tag, comm);
MPI_Recv  (buf2, count, MPI_INT, anticlock, tag, comm, &status);
```

MPI guarantees that the buffer supplied by a call to **MPI_Buffer_attach()** will be used if it is needed to buffer the message. (In an implementation of MPI that pro-

vides sufficient buffering, the user-supplied buffer may be ignored.) Each buffered
send operations can complete locally, so that a deadlock will not occur. The acyclic
communication graph for this modified code is shown in Figure 9.3. Each receive
depends on the matching send, but the send does not depend anymore on the
matching receive.

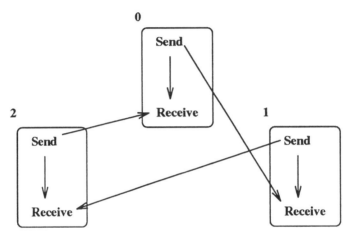

Figure 9.3
Cycle in communication graph is broken by using buffered sends.

Another approach is to use nonblocking communication. One can either use a
nonblocking send, a nonblocking receive, or both. If a nonblocking send is used,
the call to MPI_Isend() initiates the send operation and then returns. The call
to MPI_Recv() can then be made, and the communication completes successfully.
After the call to MPI_Isend(), the data in buf1 must not be changed until one is
certain that the data have been sent or copied by the system. MPI provides the
routines MPI_Wait() and MPI_Test() to check on this. Thus, the following code is
portable,

```
...
MPI_Isend (buf1, count, MPI_INT, clock, tag, comm, &request);
MPI_Recv (buf2, count, MPI_INT, anticlock, tag, comm, &status);
MPI_Wait (&request, &status);
```

The corresponding acyclic communication graph is shown in Figure 9.4. Each

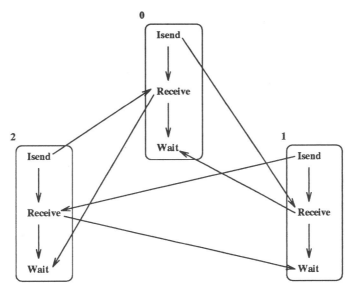

Figure 9.4
Cycle in communication graph is broken by using nonblocking sends.

receive operation depends on the matching send, and each wait depends on the matching communication; the send does not depend on the matching receive, as a nonblocking send call will return even if no matching receive is posted.

(Posted nonblocking communications do consume resources: MPI has to keep track of such posted communications. But the amount of resources consumed is proportional to the number of posted communications, not to the total size of the pending messages. Good MPI implementations will support a large number of pending nonblocking communications, so that this will not cause portability problems.)

An alternative approach is to perform a nonblocking receive first to initiate (or "post") the receive, and then to perform a blocking send in standard mode.

```
...
MPI_Irecv (buf2, count, MPI_INT, anticlock, tag, comm, &request);
MPI_Send (buf1, count, MPI_INT, clock, tag, comm):
MPI_Wait (&request, &status);
```

The call to MPI_Irecv() indicates to MPI that incoming data should be stored in
buf2; thus, no buffering is required. The call to MPI_Wait() is needed to block until
the data has actually been received into buf2. This alternative code will often result
in improved performance, since sends complete faster in many implementations
when the matching receive is already posted.

Finally, a portable shift operation can be implemented using the routine MPI-
_Sendrecv(), which was explicitly designed to send to one process while receiving
from another in a safe and portable way. In this case only a single call is required;

```
. . .
MPI_Sendrecv (buf1, count, MPI_INT, clock, tag,
              buf2, count, MPI_INT, anticlock, tag, comm, &status);
```

9.2.2 Collective Communication and Synchronization

The MPI specification purposefully does not mandate whether or not collective
communication operations have the side effect of synchronizing the processes over
which they operate. Thus, in one valid implementation collective communication
operations may synchronize processes, while in another equally valid implementation they do not. Portable MPI programs, therefore, must not rely on whether or
not collective communication operations synchronize processes. Thus, the following
assumptions must be avoided.

1. We assume MPI_Bcast() acts as a barrier synchronization and it doesn't.

```
MPI_Irecv (buf2, count, MPI_INT, anticlock, tag, comm, &status);
MPI_Bcast (buf3, 1, MPI_CHAR, 0, comm);
MPI_Rsend (buf1, count, MPI_INT, clock, tag, comm);
```

Here if we want to perform the send in ready mode we must be certain that the
receive has already been initiated at the destination. The above code is nonportable
because if the broadcast does not act as a barrier synchronization we cannot be sure
this is the case.

2. We assume that MPI_Bcast() does not act as a barrier synchronization and it
does. Examples of this case are given in Examples 4.24, 4.25, and 4.26 starting on
page 196.

9.2.3 Ambiguous Communications and Portability

MPI employs the communicator abstraction to promote software modularity by allowing the construction of independent communication streams between processes,

thereby ensuring that messages sent in one phase of an application are not incorrectly intercepted by another phase. Communicators are particularly important in allowing libraries that make message passing calls to be used safely within an application. The point here is that the application developer has no way of knowing if the tag, group, and rank completely disambiguate the message traffic of different libraries and the rest of the application. Communicators, in effect, provide an additional criterion for message selection, and hence permits the construction of independent tag spaces.

We discussed in Section 5.5 possible hazards when a library uses the same communicator as the calling code. The incorrect matching of sends executed by the caller code with receives executed by the library occurred because the library code used wildcarded receives. Conversely, incorrect matches may occur when the caller code uses wildcarded receives, even if the library code by itself is deterministic.

Consider the example in Figure 9.5. If the program behaves correctly processes 0 and 1 each receive a message from process 2, using a wildcarded selection criterion to indicate that they are prepared to receive a message from any process. The three processes then pass data around in a ring within the library routine. If separate communicators are not used for the communication inside and outside of the library routine this program may intermittently fail. Suppose we delay the sending of the second message sent by process 2, for example, by inserting some computation, as shown in Figure 9.6. In this case the wildcarded receive in process 0 is satisfied by a message sent from process 1, rather than from process 2, and deadlock results.

Even if neither caller nor callee use wildcarded receives, incorrect matches may still occur if a send initiated before the collective library invocation is to be matched by a receive posted after the invocation (Ex. 5.10, page 226). By using a different communicator in the library routine we can ensure that the program is executed correctly, regardless of when the processes enter the library routine.

9.3   Heterogeneous Computing with MPI

Heterogeneous computing uses different computers connected by a network to solve a problem in parallel. With heterogeneous computing a number of issues arise that are not applicable when using a homogeneous parallel computer. For example, the computers may be of differing computational power, so care must be taken to distribute the work between them to avoid load imbalance. Other problems may arise because of the different behavior of floating point arithmetic on different machines. However, the two most fundamental issues that must be faced in heterogeneous

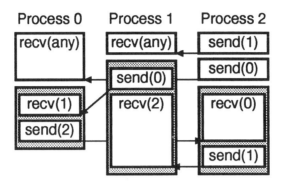

Figure 9.5
Use of communicators. Numbers in parentheses indicate the process to which data are being sent or received. The gray shaded area represents the library routine call. In this case the program behaves as intended. Note that the second message sent by process 2 is received by process 0, and that the message sent by process 0 is received by process 2.

computing are,

- incompatible data representation,
- interoperability of differing implementations of the message passing layer.

Incompatible data representations arise when computers use different binary representations for the same number. In MPI all communication routines have a datatype argument so implementations can use this information to perform the appropriate representation conversion when communicating data between computers.

Interoperability refers to the ability of different implementations of a given piece of software to work together as if they were a single homogeneous implementation. A prerequisite of interoperability for MPI would be the standardization of the MPI's internal data structures, of the communication protocols, of the initialization, termination and error handling procedures, of the implementation of collective operations, and so on. Since this has not been done, there is no support for interoperability in MPI. In general, hardware-specific implementations of MPI will not be interoperable. However it is still possible for different architectures to work together if they both use the same portable MPI implementation.

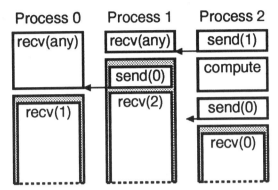

Figure 9.6
Unintended behavior of program. In this case the message from process 2 to process 0 is never received, and deadlock results.

9.4 MPI Implementations

At the time of writing several portable implementations of MPI exist,

- the MPICH implementation from Argonne National Laboratory and Mississippi State University [12], available by anonymous ftp at info.mcs.anl.gov/pub/mpi. This version is layered on PVM or P4 and can be run on many systems.

- The CHIMP implementation from Edinburgh Parallel Computing Center, available by anonymous ftp at ftp.epcc.ed.ac.uk/pub/chimp/release/chimp.tar.Z.

- the LAM implementation from the Ohio Supercomputing Center, a full MPI standard implementation using LAM, a UNIX cluster computing environment. Available by anonymous ftp at tbag.osc.edu/pub/lam.

- The UNIFY system provides a subset of MPI within the PVM environment, without sacrificing the PVM calls already available. Available by anonymous ftp at ftp.erc.msstate.edu/unify.

In addition, hardware-specific MPI implementations exist for the Cray T3D, the IBM SP-2, The NEC Cinju, and the Fujitsu AP1000.

Information on MPI implementations and other useful information on MPI can be found on the MPI web pages at Argonne National Laboratory (http://www.mcs.anl.gov/mpi), and at Mississippi State Univ (http://www.erc.msstate.edu/mpi). Additional information can be found on the MPI newsgroup comp.parallel.mpi and on netlib.

9.5   Extensions to MPI

When the MPI Forum reconvened in March 1995, the main reason was to produce
a new version of MPI that would have significant new features. The original MPI
is being referred to as MPI-1 and the new effort is being called MPI-2. The need
and desire to extend MPI-1 arose from several factors. One consideration was that
the MPI-1 effort had a constrained scope. This was done to avoid introducing a
standard that was seen as too large and burdensome for implementors. It was also
done to complete MPI-1 in the Forum-imposed deadline of one year. A second
consideration for limiting MPI-1 was the feeling by many Forum members that
some proposed areas were still under investigation. As a result, the MPI Forum
decided not to propose a standard in these areas for fear of discouraging useful
investigations into improved methods.

The MPI Forum is now actively meeting and discussing extensions to MPI-1 that
will become MPI-2. The areas that are currently under discussion are:

External Interfaces: This will define interfaces to allow easy extension of MPI
with libraries, and facilitate the implementation of packages such as debuggers and
profilers. Among the issues considered are mechanisms for defining new nonblocking
operations and mechanisms for accessing internal MPI information.

One-Sided Communications: This will extend MPI to allow communication
that does not require execution of matching calls at both communicating processes.
Examples of such operations are put/get operations that allow a process to access
data in another process' memory, messages with interrupts (e.g., active messages),
and Read-Modify-Write operations (e.g., fetch and add).

Dynamic Resource Management: This will extend MPI to allow the acquisition
of computational resources and the spawning and destruction of processes after
MPI_INIT.

Extended Collective: This will extend the collective calls to be non-blocking and
apply to inter-communicators.

Bindings: This will produce bindings for Fortran 90 and C++.

Real Time: This will provide some support for real time processing.

Since the MPI-2 effort is ongoing, the topics and areas covered are still subject to
change.

The MPI Forum set a timetable at its first meeting in March 1995. The goal
is release of a preliminary version of certain parts of MPI-2 in December 1995 at
Supercomputing '95. This is to include dynamic processes. The goal of this early

release is to allow testing of the ideas and to receive extended public comments. The complete version of MPI-2 will be released at Supercomputing '96 for final public comment. The final version of MPI-2 is scheduled for release in the spring of 1997.

Bibliography

[1] V. Bala and S. Kipnis. Process groups: a mechanism for the coordination of and communication among processes in the Venus collective communication library. Technical report, IBM T. J. Watson Research Center, October 1992. Preprint.

[2] V. Bala, S. Kipnis, L. Rudolph, and Marc Snir. Designing efficient, scalable, and portable collective communication libraries. In *SIAM 1993 Conference on Parallel Processing for Scientific Computing*, pages 862–872, March 1993.

[3] Luc Bomans and Rolf Hempel. The Argonne/GMD macros in FORTRAN for portable parallel programming and their implementation on the Intel iPSC/2. *Parallel Computing*, 15:119–132, 1990.

[4] J. Bruck, R. Cypher, P. Elustond, A. Ho, C-T. Ho, V. Bala, S. Kipnis, , and M. Snir. Ccl: A portable and tunable collective communicationlibrary for scalable parallel computers. *IEEE Trans. on Parallel and Distributed Systems*, 6(2):154–164, 1995.

[5] R. Butler and E. Lusk. User's guide to the p4 programming system. Technical Report TM-ANL–92/17, Argonne National Laboratory, 1992.

[6] Ralph Butler and Ewing Lusk. Monitors, messages, and clusters: the p4 parallel programming system. *Journal of Parallel Computing*, 20(4):547–564, April 1994.

[7] Robin Calkin, Rolf Hempel, Hans-Christian Hoppe, and Peter Wypior. Portable programming with the parmacs message–passing library. *Parallel Computing*, 20(4):615–632, April 1994.

[8] S. Chittor and R. J. Enbody. Performance evaluation of mesh–connected wormhole–routed networks for interprocessor communication in multicomputers. In *Proceedings of the 1990 Supercomputing Conference*, pages 647–656, 1990.

[9] S. Chittor and R. J. Enbody. Predicting the effect of mapping on the communication performance of large multicomputers. In *Proceedings of the 1991 International Conference on Parallel Processing, vol. II (Software)*, pages II–1 – II–4, 1991.

[10] R. Cypher and E. Leu. The semantics of blocking and nonblocking send and receive primitives. In *8th International Parallel Processing Symposium*, pages 729–735, April 1994.

[11] J. J. Dongarra, R. Hempel, A. J. G. Hey, and D. W. Walker. A proposal for a user-level, message passing interface in a distributed memory environment. Technical Report TM-12231, Oak Ridge National Laboratory, February 1993.

[12] Nathan Doss, William Gropp, Ewing Lusk, and Anthony Skjellum. A model implementation of MPI. Technical report, Argonne National Laboratory, 1993.

[13] Edinburgh Parallel Computing Centre, University of Edinburgh. *CHIMP Concepts*, June 1991.

[14] Edinburgh Parallel Computing Centre, University of Edinburgh. *CHIMP Version 1.0 Interface*, May 1992.

[15] Message Passing Interface Forum. MPI: A message-passing interface standard. *International Journal of Supercomputer Applications*, 8(3/4), 1994. Special issue on MPI.

[16] H. Franke, H. Wu, C.E. Riviere, P.Pattnaik, and M. Snir. MPI programming environment for IBM SP1/SP2. In *15th International Conference on Distributed Computing Systems*, pages 127–135, June 1995.

[17] A. Geist, A. Beguelin, J. Dongarra, W. Jiang, R. Manchek, and V. Sunderam. *PVM: A Users' Guide and Tutorial for Networked Parallel Computing*. MIT Press, 1994. The book is available electronically, the url is ftp://www.netlib.org/pvm3/book/pvm-book.ps.

[18] G. A. Geist, M. T. Heath, B. W. Peyton, and P. H. Worley. A user's guide to PICL: a portable instrumented communication library. Technical Report TM-11616, Oak Ridge National Laboratory, October 1990.

[19] William D. Gropp and Barry Smith. Chameleon parallel programming tools users manual. Technical Report ANL-93/23, Argonne National Laboratory, March 1993.

[20] V. Karamcheti and A.A. Chien. Software overheads in messaging layers: Where does the time go? In *6th International Conference on Architectural Support for Programming Languages and Operating Systems (ASPLOS VI)*, pages 51–60, October 1994.

[21] O. Krämer and H. Mühlenbein. Mapping strategies in message–based multiprocessor systems. *Parallel Computing*, 9:213–225, 1989.

[22] nCUBE Corporation. *nCUBE 2 Programmers Guide, r2.0*, December 1990.

[23] Parasoft Corporation, Pasadena, CA. *Express User's Guide*, version 3.2.5 edition, 1992.

[24] Paul Pierce. The NX/2 operating system. In *Proceedings of the Third Conference on Hypercube Concurrent Computers and Applications*, pages 384–390. ACM Press, 1988.

[25] A. Skjellum and A. Leung. Zipcode: a portable multicomputer communication library atop the reactive kernel. In D. W. Walker and Q. F. Stout, editors, *Proceedings of the Fifth Distributed Memory Concurrent Computing Conference*, pages 767–776. IEEE Press, 1990.

[26] A. Skjellum, S. Smith, C. Still, A. Leung, and M. Morari. The Zipcode message passing system. Technical report, Lawrence Livermore National Laboratory, September 1992.

[27] V.S. Sunderam, G.A. Geist, J. Dongarra, and R. Manchek. The PVM concurrent computing system: Evolution, experiences, and trends. *Parallel Computing*, 20(4):531–545, April 1994.

[28] T. von Eicken, D.E. Culler, S.C. Goldstein, and K.E. Shauser. Active messages: a mechanism for integrated communication and computation. In *19th Annual International Symposium on Computer Architecture*, pages 256–266, May 1992.

[29] D. Walker. Standards for message passing in a distributed memory environment. Technical Report TM-12147, Oak Ridge National Laboratory, August 1992.

Index

Constants Index

Function Index